Between Depression and Disarmament

The International Armaments Business, 1919–1939

This business history analyzes the connections between private business, disarmament, and rearmament as they affected arms procurement and military technology transfers in Eastern Europe from 1919 to 1939. Rather than focusing on the negotiations or the political problems involved with the Disarmament Conferences, this study concerns itself with the business effects of the disarmament discussions. Accordingly, Schneider-Creusot, Škoda, Vickers, and their respective business activities in Eastern European markets serve as the chief subjects for this book, and the core primary sources relied upon include their unpublished corporate archival documents. Shifting the scope of analysis to consider the business dimension allows for a fresh appraisal of the linkages between the arms trade, disarmament, and rearmament. The business approach also explodes the myth of the 'merchants of death' from the inside. It concludes by tracing the armaments business between 1939 and 1941 as it transitioned from peacetime to war.

JONATHAN A. GRANT is Professor of Modern Russian History at Florida State University. His previous publications include *Rulers, Guns and Money* (2007) and *Big Business in Russia* (1999).

Between Depression and Disarmament

The International Armaments Business, 1919–1939

Jonathan A. Grant

Florida State University

CAMBRIDGE
UNIVERSITY PRESS

CAMBRIDGE
UNIVERSITY PRESS

University Printing House, Cambridge CB2 8BS, United Kingdom

One Liberty Plaza, 20th Floor, New York, NY 10006, USA

477 Williamstown Road, Port Melbourne, VIC 3207, Australia

314–321, 3rd Floor, Plot 3, Splendor Forum, Jasola District Centre, New Delhi - 110025, India

79 Anson Road, #06-04/06, Singapore 079906

Cambridge University Press is part of the University of Cambridge.

It furthers the University's mission by disseminating knowledge in the pursuit of education, learning, and research at the highest international levels of excellence.

www.cambridge.org
Information on this title: www.cambridge.org/9781108428354
DOI: 10.1017/9781108552721

© Jonathan A. Grant 2018

First published 2018

Printed in the United Kingdom by Clays, St Ives plc

A catalogue record for this publication is available from the British Library

ISBN 978-1-108-42835-4 Hardback

Dedicated with love to Laila Susana Beth Grant,
who grew up with this book

Contents

Tables

Acknowledgments

This book would not have been possible without the support of many people. First, I would like to thank Professor Katsuhiko Yokoi of Meiji University, Tokyo, for inviting me in 2008 to join his research group devoted to the arms trade in the interwar era. Professor Yokoi's encouragement, along with the support of a Grant-in-Aid for Scientific Research from the Japanese Ministry of Education for the four-year research project from 2008 to 2011, enabled me to embark on writing this book. Among archivists, I owe special thanks to Eric Van Slander and Martin A. Gedra at the US National Archives II (College Park, Maryland) for cracking the seemingly indecipherable reference codes of the US military attaché reports that proved invaluable for this study. Additional thanks are due to Xavier Breuil at the Historical Archives Department of the Société Générale for graciously allowing me access to the banking records and to Stephen Walton, the Senior Curator at the Imperial War Museum (Duxford), for arranging for me to view the Krupp Archives Essen files while I was in London. The staffs at the British National Archives (Kew), the French Foreign Ministry Archives (Paris), the Académie François Bourdon (Schneider Archive, Le Creusot), and the Manuscripts Division of Cambridge University Library (Vickers Archive) deserve much praise and appreciation as well. For funding support, I also thank the Council on Research and Creativity at Florida State University for awarding me a Planning Grant to conduct much of the research in 2010–2011 and Blair Ruble at the Woodrow Wilson Center for providing a Kennan Short-Term Grant, which enabled me to conduct archival research at College Park in 2012. Most important of all, I wish to express my gratitude to my wife, Lynn, and my daughter, Laila, for their patience and loving support while accompanying me on the long research trips abroad. They both were there every step of the way.

Abbreviations

IWM	Imperial War Museum, London
MAE	French Foreign Ministry Archive, Paris
SA	Schneider Archive, Académie François Bourdon, Le Creusot, France
SG	Société Générale Archive, Paris
VA	Vickers Archive, Manuscripts Division, Cambridge University Library, Cambridge, UK

British National Archives, Kew

ADM	Admiralty
AIR	Air Ministry
BT	Board of Trade
CAB	Cabinet Papers
FO	Foreign Office
GFM	German Foreign Ministry, Captured German Documents microfilm
T	Treasury
WO	War Office

US National Archives II, College Park, Maryland

RG	Record Group
USDS	US Department of State

Introduction

In a statement of corporate strategy for the British armaments firm Vickers in late October 1918, Sir Basil Zaharoff, the rather notorious arms salesman, noted the business prospects for the coming postwar order in Eastern Europe that would emerge following the peace settlement to end the Great War. Zaharoff wrote,

The first thing these new states will do will be to arm...both for land and sea. We should be prepared, in conjunction with Banks and financiers, to send representatives to their countries the moment they are free, and to offer them their first public loan, out of which we will of course be paid for the armament they will order from us. Although the Big Powers may insist upon these states not arming, nothing can prevent their arming, as they will claim it is for policing their own nation.[1]

Even before the conclusion of the Armistice, Zaharoff presciently had identified the issues of concerns about the private armaments trade, disarmament, and rearmament that would occupy a central place in the history of interwar Europe.

Merchants of Death

Private enterprise had stood at the center of the international arms trade in the pre-1914 world. For private armaments producers in the nineteenth century, Russia, the Ottoman Empire, and the Balkan states served as vital markets. As an engine of growth contracts from these East European customers proved crucial for the sustainability of the supplier firms from west and Central Europe. Overall the region became the most important defense market in the world 1860–1914. Krupp, Vickers, Schneider, and Škoda had all emerged as major armaments

---

[1] VA, File 450, Sir Basil Zaharoff to John T. Coffin, October 31, 1918, also quoted in R. P. T. Davenport-Hines, "Vickers' Balkan Conscience Aspects of Anglo-Romanian Armaments 1918–39," *Business History*, vol. 25, no. 3 (1983), 288.

1

producers and exporters by 1904.[2] These four firms anchored the tremendous expansion of military-industrial production within their respective countries during the Great War.

For the Central Powers, Krupp and, to a lesser extent, Škoda provided the backbone of wartime industrial mobilization. By 1914, Krupp of Essen already held pride of place as the largest German company and the largest armaments firm in the world. Krupp employed 20,000 workers by 1887 and that figure increased to 25,000 by 1899. In the financial year preceding the war, 1913–1914, 54 percent of Krupp's output consisted of war materiel. During the war, Krupp added 40,000 additional workers, and the military share of Krupp's output ranged from 70 to 90 percent. German monthly output of field guns was 100 in December 1914, 270 in summer 1915, and 480 by December 1915. Krupp's actual output of new guns reached 2,481 August 1915–July 1916 compared to 1,264 in first year of the war. All told, Krupp by itself turned out 10,843 complete artillery pieces and 9,439 gun barrels over the course of the war. Although not nearly as impressive as Krupp, Škoda too, expanded dramatically. The Austrian firm had a workforce of 9,600 in 1913, but increased to 14,000 workers in 1914, and ultimately reached 30,000 by 1916. Škoda produced 3,554 gun barrels in 1916 up from 240 in 1914.[3]

Among the Allies, French war production achieved phenomenal levels by ultimately out producing Britain and equipping the American Expeditionary Force. On the eve of the Great War, French government arsenals employed 38,000 workers compared to 12,500 in private armaments factories. By 1918, roughly 80 percent of France's 1.675 million armament workers labored in private plants. Because German occupation deprived the French of key elements in their coal and steel sectors, Schneider-Creusot enhanced its position as France's largest metallurgical complex during the war. Starting the war with some 12,000 workers, Schneider employed 20,000 workers in 1917. In addition, Creusot functioned as the main clearing center for domestic and imported metals. In September 1914, Schneider received an order for eighty artillery pieces. By May 1915, the firm received additional orders for 512 75mm pieces. When France launched its major heavy artillery program (155mm guns and 220mm howitzers) in 1916, again the French government looked to Schneider to manufacture over half of them (390 guns). By the end of the war, France was churning out 971 artillery pieces a month and 261,200

[2] J. A. Grant, *Rulers, Guns, and Money, The Global Arms Trade in the Age of Imperialism* (Cambridge, MA: Harvard University Press, 2007).

[3] H. James, *Krupp: A History of a Legendary German Firm* (Princeton, NJ: Princeton University Press, 2012), 2, 39, 97, 115, 135, 140; H. Strachan, *The First World War, Volume I: To Arms* (Oxford: Oxford University Press, 2003), 1030, 1036–1037, 1047–1048.

shells daily compared to Britain's 689 artillery pieces per month and 229,400 shells a day.[4] In terms of aircraft engine production, France produced roughly 90,000 aircraft engines during the war, more than double that of Britain or Germany, and the firm Gnôme et Rhône turned out more engines than any other firm in the world.[5] For Britain, Vickers in Barrow had produced only nineteen eighteen-pounder artillery pieces in 1914, but dramatically increased its output to 1,191 pieces in 1915. Even though the firm fell behind its production schedule for machine guns, delivering 1,022 out of 1,792 weapons due by July 1915, ultimately Vickers by itself supplied 30 percent of all machine gun for the British Army during the war, and the Vickers machine gun became the preferred weapon of British army. In terms of naval construction, Vickers built total displacement tonnage of 200,000 including submarines.[6]

Criticism of the armaments business and legendarily nefarious arms traders, especially Zaharoff, emerged already during the war and immediately after. In 1915, Jane Addams's Women's International League for Peace and Freedom meeting at The Hague found "in the private profits accruing from the great arms factories a powerful hindrance to the abolition of war."[7] Upon the entry of the US into the conflict in 1917, President Woodrow Wilson in Point IV of his Fourteen Points called for "Adequate guarantees given and taken that national armaments will be reduced to the lowest point consistent with domestic safety." After the war, the League of Nations in Article 8 of its Covenant expanded on Addams's and Wilson's points by asserting, "The Members of the League recognise that the maintenance of peace requires the reduction of national armaments to the lowest point consistent with national safety and the enforcement by common action of international obligations... The Members of the League agree that the manufacture by private enterprise of munitions and implements of war is open to grave objections. The Council shall advise how the evil effects attendant upon such manufacture can be prevented, due regard being had to the

---

[4] J. F. Godfrey, *Capitalism at War: Industrial Policy and Bureaucracy in France, 1914–1918* (New York: Berg, 1987), 221–222, 257; G. Hardach, "Industrial Mobilization in 1914–1918: Production, Planning, and Ideology," in Patrick Fridenson (ed.), *The French Home Front 1914–1918* (Providence, RI: Berg, 1992), 60, 63, 74; A. Bostrom, "Supplying the Front, French Artillery Production during the First World War," *French Historical Studies*, vol. 39, no. 2 (2016), 261, 282; Strachan, 1052.

[5] J. M. Laux, "Gnôme et Rhône – An Aviation Engine Firm in the First World War," in Fridenson, *The French Home Front 1914–1918*, 149–150.

[6] J. D. Scott, *Vickers: A History* (London: Weidenfeld and Nicolson, 1962), 104–105, 112; Strachan, 1068.

[7] Quoted in R. H. Ferrell, "The Merchants of Death, Then and Now," *Journal of International Affairs*, vol. 26, no. 1 (1972), 29.

necessities of those Members of the League which are not able to manufacture the munitions and implements of war necessary for their safety." By 1921, a League Commission compiled a list of complaints against the private arms trade including that arms firms (1) caused wars, (2) employed political influence to win orders, (3) formed "rings" to exploit home government, (4) and employed bribery to secure foreign orders.

After receding into the background by the mid 1920s, the "Merchants of Death" critique reemerged full force in Britain and the US in the period 1933–1937. In part, such a turn in public perception stemmed from the changing international context from the mid 1920s to the mid 1930s. The image of the legendary arms trader faded away in the mid 1920s as the Locarno Treaty ushered in an era of rising hopes for peaceful solutions to international conflicts, especially between France and Germany. Such optimism lasted until 1933 when Germany withdrew from the Disarmament Conference in Geneva.[8] Subsequently, German rearmament came out openly under Hitler, and rearmament turned into arms race. By that time, many politicians had come to agree with Sir Edward Grey, British Foreign Secretary in 1914, who subsequently wrote, "The moral is obvious: it is that great armaments lead inevitably to war ... The enormous growth of armaments in Europe, the sense of insecurity and fear caused by them – it was these that made war inevitable."[9] As rearmament accelerated, the accepted causal connection between armaments and war heightened popular anxiety and fostered an environment conducive to exposing the culprits responsible for the whole unsavory business, namely the private arms manufacturers. As David Anderson has shown, "Between 1933 and 1936 especially, Britain witnessed a feverish revival of the 'Merchants of Death' controversy which ended unresolved under the treads of a rearmament campaign that had to be shielded from public criticism."[10]

The mid 1930s witnessed the publication of the most popularly famous treatments of the subject. Fenner Brockway precipitated the deluge with his pamphlet *The Bloody Traffic* (1933), in which he rehashed the Zaharoff stories from before 1914 and added contemporary indictments of the French firm Schneider-Creusot with its powerful subsidiary Škoda as the most important private armaments concern in Europe. He also laid out the process by which the armament salesman induced small

---

[8] D. G. Anderson, "British Rearmament and the 'Merchants of Death': The 1935–36 Royal Commission on the Manufacture of and Trade in Armaments," *Journal of Contemporary History*, vol. 29, no. 1 (1994), 8.

[9] Quoted in C. Kitching, *Britain and the Problem of International Disarmament, 1919–1934* (London: Routledge, 1999), 9.

[10] Anderson, 5–6.

countries to buy arms that they could not afford by taking loans from foreign banks. Those banks then turned to their home governments to guarantee the payments, and in exchange the home governments gained political and economic influence over the small buyer states.[11] Other works soon followed Brockway including a journalistic investigation published in *Fortune* magazine in spring 1934 entitled "Arms and the Men," H. C. Engelbracht and F. C. Hanighen's work *Merchants of Death: A Study of the International Armament Industry* (1934), and Philip Noel-Baker's *The Private Manufacture of Armaments* (1937). *Merchants of Death*'s popularity even earned it a place as a Book-of-the Month Club selection.[12] The evils of the armaments business purportedly included causing wars, using political influence to gain orders, colluding in armorers' rings and interlocking directorates to exploit their home governments, and employing bribery to secure foreign orders.[13] These accounts spurred government munitions inquiries in the US (Senate Munitions Inquiry or Nye Committee) and Britain (Royal Commission on the Manufacture of and Trade in Armaments).[14] In France, too, attacks on the Merchants of Death only began in 1933. The first article calling out French war profiteers appeared in October 1933, Jean Gaultier-Boissière's "Les marchands de canons contre la Nation." Gaston Gros's *La République des coquins* followed in 1934. Based on the largely inconclusive findings of parliamentary commissions from the 1920s that looked into war profits, these attacks harshly condemned the wartime industrialists.[15] Concealment of war profits was common practice in France. For example, a parliamentary investigation calculated Gnôme et Rhône's net profit at ₣33.6 million in 1916 as opposed to ₣14.3 million reported by the firm.[16]

As journalistic and political exposés rather than scholarly studies, much of the Merchants of Death accounts have lacked concrete evidence from within the firms themselves. Clive Trebilcock, writing in

---

[11] F. Brockway, *The Bloody Traffic* (London: Victor Gollancz Ltd., 1933), 22–23, 38–50, 202–203, 205, 262.

[12] Ferrell, 31.

[13] H. C. Engelbrecht and F. C. Hanighen, *Merchants of Death: A Study of the International Armaments Industry* (New York: Dodd, Mead, 1934), 4; C. Trebilcock, "Legends of the British Armaments Industry, 1890–1914; A Revision," *Journal of Contemporary History*, vol. 5, no. 4 (1970), 4.

[14] For Nye Committee, see M. R. Wilson, *Destructive Creation: American Business and the Winning of World War II* (Philadelphia: University of Pennsylvania Press, 2016), 32–47; M. W. Coulter, *The Senate Munitions Inquiry of the 1930s: Beyond the Merchants of Death* (Westport, CT: Greenwood Press, 1997); J. E. Wiltz, *In Search of Peace: The Senate Munitions Inquiry, 1934–1936* (Baton Rouge: Louisiana State University Press, 1963). For the Royal Commission, see Anderson, 5–37.

[15] Godfrey, 219–220.   [16] Hardach, 77; Laux, 147.

1970 about the pre-1914 period generally and Zaharoff specifically, dismissed much of the interwar period criticism as overly "obsessed with the 'arms traffic' and neglecting the industry behind it. It was out of this preoccupation that many of the legends of the armourers grew." In particular, Trebilcock observed that bribery constituted more of a problem of the given country as market rather than armaments as a product.[17] Although there are a number of very good business histories covering individual armaments firms such as Vickers, Krupp. Škoda, or Schneider-Creusot, by and large that scholarship has not devoted much attention to the role of arms exports or the interwar era.[18] While the gist of the complaints about the Merchants of Death (bribery, corruption, and the desire to keep factories working) may be generally on target, the specifics have been inaccurate or lacking entirely. Consequently, much of the issues remain unaddressed and not seriously investigated.

One such issue is the question of ownership versus corporate control. Many contemporaries and scholars have assumed that Eugene Schneider played a key role as a merchant of death because Schneider-Creusot purchased the majority of Škoda stock in 1919. As Brockway put it, "Through the Škoda works, Schneider-Creusot extends its connections wide over Eastern Europe."[19] Engelbrecht described "Schneider's empire" over Central and Eastern Europe and Škoda as, "another octopus with many tentacles."[20] He also accused Schneider and Škoda of selling hundreds of tanks to Hitler.[21] In *Merchants of Death*, the authors further claimed financial connections from Eugene Schneider to fund Hitler through the agency of two Germans who were allegedly directors of Škoda.[22] Although these unsubstantiated allegations have not been borne out, historians have tended to accept Škoda as simply an extension of the French firm throughout the interwar period. In this way,

---

[17] Trebilcock, 3–19, quote 19. For a more recent survey of the literary image of Zaharoff, see J. Moine, "Basil Zaharoff (1849–1936), le 'marchand de canons,'" *Ethnologie française*, nouvelle série, t. 36, no. 1, De la censure à l'autocensure (2006), 139–152.

[18] Scott, *Vickers*; V. Karlický, *Svét Okřídleného Šípu Koncern Škoda Plzeň 1918–1945* (Plzeň: Škoda, 1999); James, *Krupp*. Some journal articles do take up the arms business. See C. Beaud, "Une multinationale française au lendemain de la Première Guerre mondiale: Schneider et l'Union Européenne Industrielle et Financière," *Histoire, économie et société*, 2e année, vol. 4 (1983), 625–645; K. Tenfelde, "Disarmament and Big Business: The Case of Krupp, 1918–1925," *Diplomacy & Statecraft*, vol. 16, no. 3 (2005), 531–549; C. M. Leitz, "Arms Exports from the Third Reich, 1933–1939: The Example of Krupp," *The Economic History Review*, New Series, vol. 51, no. 1 (1998), 133–154.

[19] Brockway, 259.

[20] H. C. Engelbrecht, "The International Armament Industry," *Annals of the American Academy of Political and Social Science*, vol. 175 (1934), 76.

[21] H. C. Engelbrecht, "The Problem of the Munitions Industry," *The Annals of the American Academy of Political and Social Science*, vol. 174 (1934), 121.

[22] Engelbrecht and Hanighen, 3.

Škoda serves as a proxy for Schneider, and in turn Schneider serves as a proxy for French government influence. Thus, as Mogens Pelt describes it, "Schneider-Creusot served as France's industrial spearhead in the area. The French firm controlled Škoda, the leading Czechoslovak company within steel and armament production: by this means, France also controlled the industry in both Romania and Yugoslavia."[23] Insights for International Business studies offer a more comprehensive understanding of the actions taken within the Schneider–Škoda relationship. As Anoop Madhok observed, overemphasis on the level of equity ownership predominated in the older literature, but "ownership in any case need not equate with control...minority ownership does not mean sacrificing control and one can have control without ownership. Equity ownership may provide only an illusion of control, whereas actual control can come through other avenues."[24] As we shall see, in pointing the finger at Eugene Schneider the literature has been misdirected.

Disarmament and Arms Traffic Control

The first efforts to control arms trafficking were rooted in European concerns about maintaining colonial control in the late nineteenth century. Although England had enabled the King to prohibit the transport of gunpowder, arms, and ammunition under the Tonnage and Poundage Act of 1660, and The Customs Act of July 5, 1825, listed arms and ammunition as goods that could be prohibited from export by proclamation or Order in Council, the British only created a temporary licensing system for arms trafficking during the Crimean War as a means to prevent the delivery of weapons to Russia. The system consisted of a series of instructions to British customs officials that allowed them to prevent the export of prohibited items to Russia or specific areas in Europe and the Mediterranean from which they could potentially have been transshipped to Russia. Otherwise, customs officers could not impede the export of arms.[25] The 1890 Brussels Convention was the first major international agreement that attempted to limit arms trafficking as a method to suppress

---

[23] M. Pelt, *Tobacco, Arms and Politics; Greece and Germany from World Crisis to World War, 1929–41* (Copenhagen: University of Copenhagen Press, 1998), 159. A similar view is expressed by Steiner. See Z. Steiner, *The Triumph of the Dark: European International History, 1933–1939* (Oxford: Oxford University Press, 2011), 378.

[24] A. Madhok, "How Much Does Ownership Really Matter? Equity and Trust Relations in Joint Venture Relationships," *Journal of International Business Studies*, vol. 37, no. 1 (2006), 7.

[25] E. Atwater, "British Control over the Export of War Materials," *The American Journal of International Law*, vol. 33 (1939): 292–296.

the slave trade in Africa, but arms control had not been the primary goal of the convention.[26]

Colonial security continued to drive British concerns for controlling the arms traffic after 1919. Specifically, the possibilities of colonials or anti-imperialist subversive communist groups getting their hands on weapons motivated British authorities to prevent the large stocks of world war surplus weapons from pouring into the British Empire. The British government extended the licensing system imposed during the First World War, but transferred oversight of the arms traffic to the Board of Trade. On March 24, 1921, the new order specified a prohibition against the export of most arms and ammunition unless a license was obtained from the Board of Trade. The 1921 order thus established standing controls over armament exports from the UK in peacetime. Under British law, with a general license one could ship anywhere except to Germany, Austria, Hungary, Bulgaria, Russia, China, and colonial Africa. The Ethiopian Arms Traffic Treaty of August 21, 1931, expanded the British licensing system for arms export to include Ethiopia. The new licensing regime did not severely restrict the flow of weapons as the vast majority of requests for export licenses received approval. Indeed, between 1931 and 1937 British licenses granted for the export of war materiel averaged over 400 annually. On the other hand, the British government only denied twenty-seven licenses over the whole period. In practice the British Foreign Office, in consultation with the armed forces, determined whether or not to issue an export license based on those ministries' interpretation of national policy. The Board of Trade then executed the decision.[27]

The attempts to control arms exports gained their greatest momentum during the two decades following the First World War. Moved by the public disgust with the private arms trade as a cause of the Great War, the League of Nations considered control of the arms traffic as fitting under the broad umbrella of general disarmament because limiting arms exports would generally promote peace and avoid war. The European colonial powers actually found common ground in the desire to regulate the arms traffic based on their mutual fears that the arms trade threatened to undermine their hold over their empires. The smaller states opposed arms traffic controls as an infringement of their sovereignty and a threat to their security. In this instance, the Great Powers concurred on

---

[26] D. R. Stone, "Imperialism and Sovereignty: The League of Nations' Drive to Control the Global Arms Trade," *Journal of Contemporary History*, vol. 35, no. 2 (2000), 213–215.

[27] Atwater, 297–302, 314–315.

the need to control arms trafficking, but the smaller states led by delegates from the East European states of Greece, Turkey, and Romania, worked diligently to ensure that no Geneva agreement would impede their ability to acquire arms as they pleased. Although the attempt at Geneva to exercise effective international control over the arms trade through an official Arms Traffic Convention failed, the interwar period efforts did bear some fruit in establishing the licensing of arms exports, publicity, and publication of export figures as principles for a future arms control regime. For example, by the end of the 1930s, the licensing of arms exports had become normative for Belgium, Sweden, France, Britain, and the US.[28]

The interwar era also witnessed the development of the arms embargo as a tool of arms trade control. In particular, the arms embargo on warlord China 1919–1929 was the most sustained effort of this kind. The US, Britain, France, and Italy agreed not to allow the sale of arms and war materiel to China in the hope that denying all parties the means to equip their forces would end the internal fighting and prevent any further disintegration of the country. However, many other countries, most notably Czechoslovakia, did not join the embargo and private firms from those countries enjoyed very profitable returns. In fairness, French and Italian officials also violated the embargo in pursuit of the China arms trade. Even though it failed, the China arms embargo did mark the first international embargo against a single country.[29]

Studies of general disarmament in the interwar era tend to focus on explaining the movement's failure. International approaches to disarmament have concentrated on the role of the League of Nations and the international Disarmament Conferences since the League's Covenant set disarmament as a fundamental task in 1919. This process culminated with the failure of the World Disarmament Conference in Geneva between February 1932 and June 1934.[30] Many works have approached the problem from the perspective of an individual major power and why

---

[28] Stone, 214, 222–224, 226–229.

[29] G. Xu, "American-British Aircraft Competition in South China, 1926–1936," *Modern Asian Studies*, vol. 35, no. 1 (2001), 158; A. Skřivan Jr., "Czechoslovak Arms Exports to China in the Interwar Period," *ÖT KONTINENS, az Új- és Jelenkori Egyetemes Történeti Tanszék közleményei*, no. 2010 (2011), 233–244.

[30] A. Webster, "The Transnational Dream: Politicians, Diplomats and Soldiers in the League of Nations' Pursuit of International Disarmament, 1920–1938," *Contemporary European History*, vol. 14, no. 4 (2005), 494–495; A. Webster, "Piecing Together the Interwar Disarmament Puzzle: Trends and Possibilities," *International Journal*, vol. 59, no. 1 (2003/2004), 198; Z. Steiner, *The Lights That Failed: European International History, 1919–1933* (Oxford: Oxford University Press, 2005), 755–796, 812–815.

that power opposed disarmament.[31] Although one study of French policy emphasized that the goal of French policy was how not to disarm,[32] more recent works emphasize that France sought security guarantees as the precondition for disarmament as expressed in French minister Edourd Herriot's 1924 formula of arbitration-security-disarmament. France demanded security guarantees applying to Eastern Europe, and French representatives called for the consideration of land, naval, and air armaments limitations in connection with limits on the size of conscript armies and industrial capacity.[33] David Edgerton and others have painted a picture of Britain paying only half-hearted lip service to disarmament while maintaining high levels of military expenditure during the 1920s.[34] Carolyn Kitching has argued that overall, Britain lacked a real strategy for international disarmament other than reacting to the motions of other powers. While British ministers might have talked about arms reductions for economic reasons as a manifestation of Britain's unilateral disarmament, they paid no attention to international obligations for multilateral disarmament as required by the Treaty of Versailles and the Covenant of the League of Nations. She concludes that when Britain could no longer avoid the disarmament issue the policy became trying "to ensure that the blame for failure to meet international obligations was placed firmly on the shoulders of others."[35] Contrary to the myth that Britain tried to foster "disarmament by example," British defense expenditures increased 1924–1929, and in per capita terms British figures exceeded the levels of any other power.[36]

In contrast to Kitching, others argue that Britain actively sought disarmament. Thomas Davies argues that the British government advocated a direct approach to disarmament whereby countries should disarm first,

[31] E. Bennett, *German Rearmament and the West, 1932–1933* (Princeton, NJ: Princeton University Press, 1979); M. Vaïsse, *Sécurité d'abord: la politique française en matière de désarmement, 9 decembre 1930–17 avril 1934* (Paris: Publications de la Sorbonne, 1981); C. Hall, *Britain, America and Arms Control, 1921–1937* (London: Macmillan, 1987); D. Richardson, *The Evolution of British Disarmament Policy in the 1920s* (London: Printer, 1989); P. Jackson, "France and the Problems of Security and International Disarmament after the First World War," *Journal of Strategic Studies*, vol. 29, no. 2 (2006), 247–280.

[32] Vaïsse, 25.

[33] P. Jackson, *Beyond the Balance of Power: France and the Politics of National Security in the Era of the First World War* (Cambridge: Cambridge University Press, 2013), 374–375, 429; A. Adamthwaite, *Grandeur and Misery: France's Bid for Power in Europe, 1919–1940* (London: Arnold, 1995), 127, 190–191.

[34] K. Narizny, "Both Guns and Butter, or Neither: Class Interests in the Political Economy of Rearmament," *The American Political Science Review*, vol. 97, no. 2 (2003), 209–210; D. Edgerton, *Warfare State, Britain, 1920–1970* (Cambridge: Cambridge University Press, 2006), 5, 18, 23.

[35] Kitching, 5.   [36] Ibid., 21.

and then security would follow. This British position collided with the French indirect approach seeking security as the necessary precondition before disarmament could proceed. According to Davies, "The need to bridge the divide between the British and French approaches to disarmament was the principal challenge for the disarmament movement for the next dozen years."[37] David Kearn sees the central difference in the British "disarmament first" position versus the "security first" French view arising from the new concept of qualitative disarmament that emerged in the mid 1920s. Britain, the US, and Germany accepted the qualitative approach, which identified certain types of armaments as aggressive. According to Kearn, "Britain was a consistent supporter of qualitative disarmament throughout the period, supporting the prohibition of tanks and heavy caliber artillery, as well as bomber aircraft."[38] B. J. C. McKercher argues that the British government actively pursued an international disarmament regime under the League of Nations 1925–1933, and that British policy shifted "from one working toward disarmament to one embarking on rearmament" between October 1933 and March 1936.[39]

While the general disarmament literature has not taken up the question of the arms trade in a sustained way, specific literature on the naval disarmament does speak to the issue. Donald Stoker, Jr., has convincingly argued that even though Britain, the US, and France interpreted the agreements differently, an unintended consequence of the Washington Agreements stemming from the Washington Naval Conference 1921–1922 was restricted naval purchases for the smaller states of the Baltic. For example, in 1924 the British refused the sale of destroyers and submarines to Poland on the grounds that the transactions would violate their understanding of the Washington Agreements. While less strict in their views than the British, American officials used the treaties to discourage sales they opposed. Meanwhile, the French would allow exceptions to the agreements in pursuit of French interests.[40] Serhat Güvenç noted in his study of Turkish naval purchases that the "pro-disarmament producers" (Britain and the US) cut off state guarantees or subventions for foreign sales. As a result, Turkey found its options for naval suppliers severely restricted because Turkey could not afford

---

[37] T. R. Davies, *Possibilities of Transnational Activism: The Campaign for Disarmament between the Two World Wars* (Boston: Brill Academic, 2006), 64.

[38] D. W. Kearn Jr., *Great Power Security Cooperation: Arms Control and the Challenge of Technological Change* (Lanham, MD: Lexington Books, 2015), 99–100, quote 103.

[39] B. J. C. McKercher,"From Disarmament to Rearmament: British Civil-Military Relations and Policy Making, 1933–1934," *Defence Studies*, vol. 1, no. 1 (2001), 22.

[40] D. J. Stoker Jr., *Britain, France and the Naval Arms Trade in the Baltic 1919–1939: Grand Strategy and Failure* (London: Frank Cass, 2003), 52, 58–59, 61–62.

to purchase warships without the aid of foreign credits and government guarantees.[41] Even though naval disarmament did not figure so prominently in Eastern Europe since most countries primarily operated as land powers, Güvenç's point about Turkish naval difficulties should be applied more broadly throughout the region and extended beyond the naval trade to encompass military and aircraft sales as well.

Rearmament

Because of rearmament and the coming of World War II, studies of the arms trade have generally neglected the 1920s and paid more attention to the 1930s. Most approaches treat the arms trade as a political phenomenon and adopt a state-centered approach without much regard for the private business dimensions. In the seminal scholarly examination of the interwar arms trade using supplier and buyer countries as the units of analysis, the political scientist Robert Harkavy established a very good composite of the contours of the global armaments business for the years 1930 to 1940. He showed that Britain and France were the biggest arms exporters overall if one took into account all the categories of armaments for land, sea, and air.[42] More recently, Joseph Maiolo examined rearmament and the arms race as a central feature of the international system during the interwar era starting with Soviet rearmament in 1929. He takes the arms race as an independent and overriding force rather than a simple choice of whether to arm or not. He shows how the arms race wave buffeted all the Major Powers (the Soviet Union, Japan, Germany, Great Britain, France, Italy, and the US) as it rolled through the sea of international relations.[43]

Scholarship dedicated to the study of the arms trade for individual East European countries remains sparse. Usually these works only

[41] S. Güvenç, "Building a Republican Navy in Turkey: 1924–1939," *International Journal of Naval History*, vol. 1, no. 1 (April 2002), 4.

[42] R. E. Harkavy, *The Arms Trade and International Systems* (Cambridge, MA: Ballinger, 1975), 68.

[43] J. Maiolo, *Cry Havoc: How the Arms Race Drove the World to War, 1931–1941* (New York: Basic Books, 2010); R. Frankenstein, *Le Prix du Réarmement Français, 1935–1939* (Paris: Publications de la Sorbonne, 1982). Examples of Britain and Rearmament include R. P. Shay Jr., *British Rearmament in the Thirties: Politics and Profits* (Princeton, NJ: Princeton University Press, 1977); G. C. Peden, *British Rearmament and the Treasury, 1932–1939* (Edinburgh: Scottish Academic Press, 1979); G. A. H. Gordon, *British Seapower and Procurement between the wars: A Reappraisal of Rearmament* (Annapolis, MD: Naval Institute Press, 1988); J. Ruggiero, *Neville Chamberlain and British Rearmament: Pride, Prejudice, and Politics* (Westport, CT: Greenwood Press, 1999); E. W. Bennett, *German Rearmament and the West, 1932–1933* (Princeton, NJ: Princeton University Press, 1979).

employ a bilateral approach examining the role of the arms trade with one Great Power and one small state. For example, Mogens Pelt focuses on Greece and Germany, Christian Leitz considers Romania and Germany, while Martin Thomas addresses France and Romania, and Glyn Stone considers Britain and Finland.[44] The place of the armaments business in Turco-Italian relations and German-Soviet relations has also received some attention.[45] More broadly, Donald J. Stoker, Jr. does treat the Baltic region as a whole in a multilateral way for the entire interwar period, but he only examines the naval trade.[46] In terms of armaments production within Eastern Europe, M. Hauner dedicates a chapter to the armaments business throughout the region and Aleš Skřivan Jr. has recently detailed the arms industry in Czechoslovakia in an article.[47]

Scholars are divided on the role of the British Treasury in either inhibiting or promoting rearmament. Treasury emerged from the Great War with increased influence and power as in addition to controlling public spending it now also monitored external finance and controlled exchange policy.[48] G. C. Peden has argued that through its economic orthodoxy of reduced taxation and balanced budgets to prevent inflation the Treasury did more to limit British sea power than the Washington Naval Treaty or the London Conference of 1936. The British government found itself under intense popular pressure to reduce the armed forces, and Treasury used the adoption in 1919 of the Ten-Year Rule (the projection that no major war was expected for the next ten years) to

---

[44] Pelt, *Tobacco*; C. Leitz, "Arms as Levers: 'Matériel' and Raw Materials in Germany's Trade with Romania in the 1930s," *The International History Review*, vol. 19, no. 2 (1997), 312–332; M. Thomas, "To Arm an Ally: French Arms Sales to Romania, 1926–1940," *The Journal of Strategic Studies*, vol. 19, no. 2 (1996), 231–259; G. Stone, "Britain and the Provision of Arms to Finland, 1936–1940," in K. Hamilton and E. Johnson (eds.), *Arms and Disarmament in Diplomacy* (London: Vallentine Mitchell, 2008), 151–172.

[45] B. Millman, "Essay and Reflection: Credit and Supply in Turkish Foreign Policy and the Tripartite Alliance of October 1939: A Note," *The International History Review*, vol. 16, no. 1 (1994), 70–80; D. Barlas and S. Güvenç, "To Build a Navy with the Help of an Adversary: Italian-Turkish Naval Arms Trade, 1929–1932," *Middle Eastern Studies*, vol. 38, no. 4 (2002), 143–168; H. W. Gatzke, "Russo-German Military Collaboration during the Weimar Republic," *The American Historical Review*, vol. 63, no. 3 (1958), 565–597.

[46] Stoker, *Britain, France*.

[47] M. Hauner, "Military Budgets and the Armaments Industry," in M. C. Kaser and E. A. Radice (eds.), *The Economic History of Eastern Europe 1919–1939* (Oxford: Clarendon Press, 1986), 49–116; A. Skřivan Jr., "On the Nature and Role of Arms Production in Interwar Czechoslovakia," *The Journal of Slavic Military Studies*, vol. 23, no. 4 (2010), 630–640.

[48] K. Burk, "The Treasury: From Impotence to Power," in K. Burk (ed.), *War and State, the Transformation of British Government, 1914–1919* (London: George Allen & Unwin, 1982), 84–107.

persuade defense departments to accept lower estimates down from £604 million in 1919 to £111 million in 1922 to a low of £103 in 1932. In this way, Treasury's position acted as the determining force in restricting defense expenditures and inhibiting rearmament. According to Peden, the fiscal tightfistedness of both Conservative and Labour governments and the constraints of the annual estimates meant that the Admiralty could not lay down all the ships it wished even within the Naval Treaty restrictions.[49] Indeed, several historians see Treasury's role as crucial in restricting defense spending by 1926, if not earlier, and in wanting to limit rearmament because of opposition to anything that would disrupt business as usual.[50] Richard S. Grayson argues that the British commitment to disarmament flowed from Treasury's financial reasons. McKercher goes further in suggesting that Treasury support for reductions in defense spending motivated British disarmament policy and in a corresponding way Treasury took a leading role in changing the policy for rearmament.[51] John Robert Ferris offers a more nuanced appraisal. While acknowledging Treasury's hostility toward excessive expenditure on armaments and the leading role of Treasury and the Foreign Office in pushing for arms limitation 1925–1929, he generally dismisses Treasury's role in controlling the services. In his view, Treasury control and the Ten-Year Rule only affected strategic policy for a very limited time 1926–1928. More significantly, the period 1921–1927 should be seen as a peak of British peacetime military preparation rather than a low point. Thus, interpreting the 1920s as an era of disarmament and the 1930s as one of rearmament misses the consistent willingness for rearmament in British strategic policy.[52] R. A. C. Parker argues that historians have been too harsh in holding Treasury responsible for restricting British rearmament because it held onto outdated financial policies. Indeed, Parker notes that Treasury was less concerned about finance than balance of trade, and by the end of 1936 Treasury had resolved to borrow to pay for rearmament. Starting in 1937 one-quarter of total

---

[49] Peden, 8–11.
[50] B. McKercher, "Old Diplomacy and New: The Foreign Office and Foreign Policy, 1919–1939," in M. Dockrill and B. McKercher (eds.), *Diplomacy and World Power: Studies in British Foreign Policy, 1890–1950* (Cambridge: Cambridge University Press, 1996), 106; Shay, 282–283; Gordon, 96–100; B. Coombs, *British Tank Production and the War Economy, 1934–1945* (London: Bloomsbury Academic, 2015), 25; T. C. Imlay, *Facing the Second World War: Strategy, Politics, and Economics in Britain and France 1938–1940* (Oxford: Oxford University Press, 2003), 320–321.
[51] R. S. Grayson, *Austen Chamberlain and the Commitment to Europe: British Foreign Policy, 1924–29* (London: Frank Cass, 1997), 150, 164; McKercher, "From Disarmament to Rearmament," 22.
[52] J. R. Ferris, *Men, Money, and Diplomacy: The Evolution of British Strategic Policy, 1919–26* (Ithaca, NY: Cornell University Press, 1989), 29, 33–34, 172, 179–182.

defense spending derived from loans, and that figure increased to one-third in 1938.[53] Finally, Robert Self gives Treasury most of the credit for managing British rearmament successfully through strict rationing of finances within a phased expansion program that avoided overheating the economy.[54]

Turning to the topic of French and British foreign policy toward Eastern Europe through the interwar era a consensus has broadly appeared that highlights French attempts to create an exclusive sphere of influence in the East Central and southeastern (Balkan) states out of security concerns. These efforts derived from a traditional balance of power for French eastern policy, which had previously relied on tsarist Russia. With the Russian Empire gone, French policy sought to use the new, smaller states of Czechoslovakia, Romania, and most importantly Poland as replacements to counter Germany. However, despite French attempts to promote Czech-Polish cooperation, mutual suspicion between Poland and Czechoslovakia prevented the conversion of these states into firm anti-German, potential French wartime allies. France only secured a military assistance treaty with Poland, whereas Czechoslovakia, Romania, and Yugoslavia remained minimally committed. French interest in Eastern Europe also waxed and waned in relation to French-German relations, and France considered such eastern ties burdensome when relations with Germany improved following the Locarno Treaty in 1925. Starting in 1937 the French diplomatically tried to transform the Little Entente Alliance of Czechoslovakia, Romania, and Yugoslavia into an anti-German collective security alliance, but ultimately French efforts proved unsuccessful.[55] If French policy failed, British policy toward Eastern Europe reflected neglect. British policy makers considered Eastern Europe unstable, British trade links with the region were weak, and the role of Czechoslovakia specifically or Eastern Europe

---

[53] R. A. C. Parker, "British Rearmament 1936–9: Treasury, Trade Unions and Skilled Labour," *The English Historical Review*, vol. 96, no. 379 (1981), 306, 311, 314.

[54] R. Self, "Neville Chamberlain and Rearmament: Did the Treasury win the Battle of Britain?," *20th Century History Review*, vol. 3, no. 1 (2007), 13.

[55] The standard works on French policy toward Eastern Europe remain P. S. Wandcyz, *France and Her Eastern Allies 1919–1925, French-Czechoslovak-Polish Relations from the Paris Peace Conference to Locarno* (Minneapolis: University of Minnesota Press, 1962), and the same author's *The Twilight of French Eastern Alliances 1926–1936, French-Czechoslovak-Polish Relations from Locarno to the Remilitarization of the Rhineland* (Princeton, NJ: Princeton University Press, 1988). See also P. Jackson, *Beyond the Balance of Power*, 235, 238–239, 364–369; R. J. Young, *In Command of France, French Foreign Policy and Military Planning, 1933–1940* (Cambridge, MA: Harvard University Press, 1978), 8–10, 66, 145; Steiner, *The Lights That Failed*, 602, 610, 629; M. Thomas, *Britain, France and Appeasement, Anglo-French Relations in the Popular Front Era* (Oxford: Berg, 1996), 183–184, 232.

generally did not factor into British military calculations through 1938.[56] Indeed, according to Talbot Imlay, only after Germany took over rump Czechoslovakia in the Prague coup of March 15, 1939, did Britain take up the idea of an Eastern Front with focus on Romania and Poland.[57] Paul Hehn's work appears as a major outlier in that he views the 1930s as an overt political contest between Britain and Germany for control of Eastern Europe in which Germany used the armaments trade as the means to secure the region's strategic raw materials.[58]

While the role of the Great Powers looms large in the literature, it would be mistaken to overlook the agency of the Eastern European states in the period. As Anita J. Prażmowska cautions, the Eastern European states played a more active role than mere pawns in the game of Great Power rivalries, and "in each of the many crises which affected the region, the states of eastern Europe were active, though not always willing, participants."[59] Most obviously, Czechoslovakia, Yugoslavia, and Romania initiated the creation of the Little Entente alliance through a series of treaties and military conventions signed 1920–1921. Those three countries had gained territory from the dismemberment of Austria-Hungary as a result of the Paris Peace settlements ending the Great War. In August 1920, Czechoslovakia and Yugoslavia signed an alliance aimed against Hungary. Following an attempt at Habsburg restoration on the Hungarian throne in 1921 the states made further arrangements. Czechoslovakia and Romania formed a treaty agreement in April 1921, followed soon after by an agreement between Romania and Yugoslavia in June. This collection of pacts constituted the Little Entente. After initially opposing the Little Entente, France came around to supporting this alliance through a series of bilateral treaties with Czechoslovakia (1924), Romania (1926), and Yugoslavia (1927). The French had earlier signed a pact with Poland in 1921.[60]

The agency of Eastern European states meant that the Eastern Europe market did not operate as a simple microcosm of the global armaments market. An abbreviated summary of Harkavy's findings are listed in

[56] E. Goldstein, "The Evolution of British Diplomatic Strategy for the Locarno Pact, 1924–1925," in M. Dockrill and B. McKercher (eds.), *Diplomacy and World Power, Studies in British Foreign Policy, 1890–1950* (Cambridge: Cambridge University Press, 1996), 125–126; Grayson, 260; Imlay, 79.

[57] Imlay, 95.

[58] P. N. Hehn, *A Low Dishonest Decade: The Great Powers, Eastern Europe, and the Economic Origins of World War II, 1930–1941* (New York: Continuum, 2002).

[59] A. J. Prażmowska, *Eastern Europe and the Origins of the Second World War* (New York: St. Martin's Press, 2000), ix.

[60] Jackson, *Beyond the Balance of Power*, 369, 376; B. Jelavich, *History of the Balkans, Twentieth Century*, vol. 2 (Cambridge: Cambridge University Press, 1983), 141; M. Ádám, *The Versailles System and Central Europe* (Aldershot, UK: Ashgate, 2004), 85–87.

Table I.1 *Global Exports of Combat Aircraft, Tanks, Submarines, and Warships, 1930–1940*

Country	Combat aircraft		Tanks		Submarines		Warships	
	Number	Percentage	Number	Percentage	Number	Percentage	Number	Percentage
US	3,218	22.8	574	14.7	4	8.0	3	2.3
Britain	2,435	17.3	1,017	26.1	18	36.0	76	58.9
France	2,204	15.6	1,091	27.9	10	5.0	13	10.1
Italy	1,786	12.7	424	10.9	24	12.0	23	17.8
Germany	1,336	9.5	160	4.1	4	8.0	–	–

Source: Robert E. Harkavy, *The Arms Trade and International Systems* (Cambridge, MA: Ballinger, 1975), 61–68, 73–74.

Table I.1, but Harkavy's global trade figures need to be put in context for Eastern Europe. For example, although the US ranked first for combat aircraft exports globally, American sales went overwhelmingly to Latin America and China rather than Eastern Europe. In considering the relatively strong showing for Italy and the seemingly weak showing for German exports it should be noted that Germany did not reenter the armaments trade officially until 1935, whereas Italy occupied its strongest position in the naval trade which peaked in Greece and Turkey in 1932. Thus, Germany proved more important and Italy less important in the armaments business in Eastern Europe in the second half of the 1930s. More significantly, the global picture fails to capture the crucial Czechoslovakian market dominance in Eastern Europe where Škoda served as the principal supplier to the Little Entente states (Table I.2). In summation, Harkavy concluded that "It is clear that both British and French arms manufacturers declined as the 1930s progressed, corresponding to the erosion of their nations' joint influence and

Table I.2 *Naval Deliveries by East European Buyer, 1930–1940*

Country	Destroyers	Submarines
Turkey	4 (Italian)	10 (4 British, 3 German, 2 Italian, 1 Spanish)
Poland	2 (British)	5 (3 French, 2 Dutch)
Greece	6 (4 Italian, 2 British)	–
	2 (1 British, 1 French)	–
Yugoslavia		
Estonia	–	2 (British)

Source: Conway's All the World's Fighting Ships, 1922–1946 (London: Conway Maritime Press, 1980), 349–354, 357–360, 366, 405–408.

power throughout the world, a trend clearly manifested in any number of ways."[61]

A closer examination of the Eastern European armaments business yields a significant modification of Harkavy's analysis. British and French arms manufacturers did not decline in the region as evidenced by the ever-increasing demands and requests from the Eastern European states to purchase British and French armaments. Rather, what occurred was a refusal to export armaments at the expense of British and French domestic rearmament. The Eastern European states were clamoring for British and French war materiel. The hindrance came from London and Paris. Understood from the vantage point of the Eastern Europe arms market, British and French defense firms did not decline. Quite the contrary, they were booming thanks to dramatic increases in home orders. It would be more accurate to say that British and French firms had their hands full with their own rearmaments. They could not also take on the rearmament of Eastern Europe without much more financial support than they were allowed by the French and British governments. Analysis of the reasons why sales negotiations fell through deepens our understanding of the armaments business and helps prevent a misreading of the political meaning of arms sales. Moreover, a Business history approach reveals the contingent nature of contract negotiations and financing as well as the many failures and false starts that in the end did not yield a profitable result. The sales that got away tell much about the armaments business, and not considering them leaves an incomplete picture of the armaments dynamic.

This Study

Since the end of the Cold War, scholars have shown a renewed interest in the interwar era. Trends in the contemporary multipolar international system since the 1990s seem to evidence similar patterns to those of the interwar years. Scholars have noted similarities in terms of arms supplier-recipient relations, supplier markets, levels of arms dependency by buyers, and the rapid turnover of generations of weapons due to dramatic technological change.[62] Among historians the past decade has witnessed

---

[61] Harkavy, *Arms Trade*, 80.

[62] R. E. Harkavy, "The Changing International System and the Arms Trade," *Annals of the American Academy of Political and Social Science*, vol. 535 (1994), 11–28; E. Sköns and H. Wulf, "The Internationalization of the Arms Industry," *Annals of the American Academy of Political and Social Science*, vol. 535 (1994), 43–57; M. Brzoska and F. S. Pearson, "Developments in the Global Supply of Arms: Opportunity and Motivation," *Annals of the American Academy of Political and Social Science*, vol. 535 (1994), 58–72;

major treatments in the international history of the 1920s including traditional state-centered studies of international politics, but also extending to examinations of transnational movements and organizations, such as the League of Nations.[63] However, private businesses generally have not figured in these analyses.

This study elucidates the existing discussions of the international history of the interwar era by putting the armaments business front and center. Through the lens of Business history, it analyzes the connections between private business, disarmament, and rearmament as they affected arms procurement and military technology transfers in the countries of Eastern Europe during the interwar era 1919–1939. Accordingly, Schneider-Creusot, Škoda, Vickers, and their respective business activities in Eastern European markets serve as the chief subjects for this book. As a means to investigate the view from the board room, the core primary sources relied upon include the unpublished corporate archival documents. For Schneider, the company records are available in the Académie François Bourdon in Le Creusot. These records along with correspondence from the French bank Société Générale in Paris include much about the Škoda Company as well. The Vickers archive is housed at the Cambridge University Library in Cambridge. In London, the Imperial War Museum holds microfilm copies of the Krupp Archives for the interwar period. The Eastern European arms market played a pivotal role in the business strategies of the armaments firms for their survival and prosperity. The arms sales to Eastern Europe beckoned to the business leaders as the best means to save their firms from the potentially lean times and to increase profits.

Among the buyer countries, the states of southeastern Europe (Romania, Yugoslavia, Greece, and Turkey) receive the most consistent attention due to their prominence in the arms export market, but the

---

J. L. Johnson, "Financing the Arms Trade," *Annals of the American Academy of Political and Social Science*, vol. 535 (1994), 110–121; Webster, "Piecing Together," 187–198; E. O. Goldman, *Sunken Treaties, Naval Arms Control between the Wars* (University Park: Pennsylvania State University Press, 1994), 4–8, 31–31, 239–272.

[63] R. Boyce, *The Great Interwar Crisis and the Collapse of Globalization* (London, 2009); P. O. Cohrs, *The Unfinished Peace after World War I: America, Britain and the Stabilisation of Europe, 1919–1932* (Cambridge: Cambridge University Press, 2006); M. C. Pugh, *Liberal Internationalism: The Interwar Movement for Peace in Britain* (Basingstoke, UK: Palgrave Macmillan, 2012); D. Laqua (ed.), *Internationalism Reconfigured: Transnational Ideas and Movements between the World Wars* (New York: I. B. Tauris, 2011); H. McCarthy, *The British People and the League of Nations: Democracy, Citizenship and Internationalism, 1918–1945* (Manchester, UK: Manchester University Press, 2011); P. Clavin, *Securing the World Economy: The Reinvention of the League of Nations, 1920–1946* (Oxford: Oxford University Press, 2013); and S. Pedersen, "Back to the League of Nations," *American Historical Review*, vol. 112 (2007), 1091–1117.

armaments business in northeastern Europe (Poland, the Soviet Union, Baltic States, and Finland) also get its due when appropriate. All these countries faced similar developmental problems linked to their late industrialization and the rivalries over contested borders brought about by the peace treaties ending World War I. These states gave high priority to establishing their armed forces to safeguard their newly found national independence, and consequently they all proved eager customers for the armaments business. In order to follow the various Eastern European governments, I have used the British, French, German, and American diplomatic files with special attention to the intelligence reports. No arms deal remained secret for long. The military attachés proved very adept at uncovering and verifying information. They compared notes with their colleagues in other embassies and had the ears of company representatives. Therefore, British intelligence reports from the British National Archives, French attaché reports from the French Foreign Ministry Archives in Paris, American military intelligence reports housed in National Archives II in College Park, Maryland, and the captured German diplomatic and attaché documents available on microfilm in London and College Park often provide intimate details of contracts and ongoing arms sale negotiations. I have also used the published Soviet archival materials made available in Yuri Dyakov & Tatyana Bushuyeva (eds.), *The Red Army and the Wehrmacht, How the Soviets Militarized Germany, 1922–33, and Paved the Way for Fascism* (New York: Prometheus Books, 1995).

Rather than focusing on the negotiations or the political problems involved with the Disarmament Conferences, this study concerns itself with the business effects of the disarmament discussions. Shifting the scope of analysis to consider the business dimension allows for a fresh appraisal of the linkages between the arms trade, disarmament, and rearmament. An examination of the armaments business in Eastern Europe during the 1920s offers a chance to explore how pressures for disarmament collided with the desire of the East European states to procure arms to secure their newly won independence. The consequences of disarmament for the foreign arms trade must not be overlooked. The British Treasury's fiscal policies indirectly promoted disarmament, even though the motivation stemmed from preoccupation with financial soundness rather than forthright support of disarmament. Despite the vicissitudes of British Cabinets from Conservative to Labour over the interwar period, Treasury and Overseas Trade consistently remained in opposition to any financial support for arms exports. On this score, British actions, especially by Treasury, had a significant effect on the shape of the armaments business. Treasury's role as a hindrance for rearmament should be reframed as a force for disarmament, even if Treasury fostered disarmament by default. Had France followed a similar course, it is conceivable that the vital funding for the armaments business in Eastern Europe would have dried up entirely in the 1920s.

British and American discomfort with the armaments business as contrary to the goal of disarmament in the 1920s inhibited sales from firms in those countries, effectively giving the French and Czechs a huge advantage. The Trade Facilities Act of 1921 served in practice as the single most important action taken by the British government in efforts to promote disarmament and inhibit the arms business. This Parliamentary Act barred the state from providing credits or guarantees for armaments sales. Specifically, the 1921 Act prohibited financial guarantees by the British Treasury for loans used for the manufacture of munitions of war. This situation accentuated the supplier vacuum and restricted the choice of arms suppliers. Given the poor state of their economies, the governments in Eastern Europe depended on foreign credits and government guarantees for purchasing armaments.

This book tells the story of the armaments business in Eastern Europe by giving due attention to the 1920s through the first four chapters. The Anglo-French competition operated as the central tension in the arms trade in Eastern Europe during the 1920s. With the removal of Germany and Austria from the arms trade due to the peace treaty restrictions on those countries following the First World War, French firms gained much of the markets that formerly went to Austrian and German firms. Chapter 1 follows the French firm Schneider-Creusot as it purchased the controlling shares in the Škoda Works in Plzeň, Czechoslovakia in 1919. Škoda proved a powerful junior partner for Schneider's armaments business, and by the end of the twenties Škoda had surpassed Schneider as the primary armaments exporter to the countries of Eastern Europe. Also important, the Schneider–Škoda corporate alliance operated behind the scenes. This corporate alliance has been overlooked by contemporaries and scholars alike. Contrary to the conventional position, this work argues that Schneider did not serve as a tool of the French government, and Škoda exercised a good deal of autonomy from Schneider. In practice Škoda behaved as an ally rather than an acquisition, and, like many an ally, Škoda pursued its own interests at times crossing Schneider. Chapter 2 turns to Vickers and the other British armaments firms. At roughly the same time as Schneider's moves in Czechoslovakia, British war industrialists looked to supersede German industry in export markets with special attention to Eastern Europe. As part of that strategy the Vickers firm focused attention on Romania as the best place for British industry to establish itself while also pursuing armaments orders across Eastern Europe. British firms' sales suffered directly from the British government's support for disarmament. Chapter 3 focuses on Romania and analyzes the major Škoda scandal of 1933. The large Romanian artillery order with Škoda in 1930 and the subsequent publicity around the Škoda scandal in 1933 lay at the intersection of several lines of conflict: between the French government and Czechs over control of Škoda within Czechoslovakia, between Schneider and Škoda in competition for orders, and within Romania between Cabinet and Opposition as a domestic political conflict. A background of bribery and corruption in arms orders as a way of doing business also informed the Škoda scandal. This case, the most flagrant example of the "Merchants of Death" in action, shows that Schneider did not pull the strings and Škoda very much operated on its own. Chapter 4 takes up the aircraft business in the 1920s from the Baltic to the Black Sea with special attention to the Junkers Company's dealings in establishing joint venture military aircraft facilities in the Soviet Union and Turkey as a form of surreptitious rearmament to circumvent restrictions imposed by the Treaty of Versailles. The efforts of other firms (French, British, American) to gain control of the aircraft market in Eastern Europe as well as East European countries' efforts to develop their own domestic capacity also receive attention. Ultimately, Czechoslovakia and Poland emerged as military aircraft exporters in their own right.

The armaments business in the 1930s forms the subject of the remaining chapters. Chapter 5 analyzes the armaments business in Eastern Europe between the two forces of depression and disarmament 1930–1934. The opening of the Soviet Union as a buyer for Western defense products proved the most significant development for the tank market. In 1930, Vickers was saved from unemployment only by large tank orders from the Soviet Union. Yet, the British ambivalence about the arms trade and its conflict with the goals of disarmament combined with increasing popular hostility against the armaments business as the "Merchants of Death" directly affected the arms trade in Eastern Europe. Popular disapproval of the private arms trade in France also dampened Schneider's business.

Chapter 6 covers the Rearmament period 1934–1938. This period saw the end of laissez faire in the arms business as supplier governments increasingly became involved directly after 1934. As Germany openly launched rearmament, Britain and France responded in kind. British and French rearmament increased pressure on the armaments firms to give priority to domestic orders over exports, and this added to the frenzy of demand for arms purchases by the East European states, especially for aircraft, tanks, and artillery. The widespread use of clearing agreements and barter deals by Eastern European states as means to pay for armaments during the 1930s presented ways to surmount the financial difficulties and demonstrated the survivability of the armaments business. Škoda successfully beat back challenges to its market dominance from German challengers Krupp and Rheinmetall by matching the German government's clearing agreements with its own import-export company Omnipol. However, the Munich Agreement in September 1938 stripped the Sudetenland from Czechoslovakia and exposed Škoda and other Czech firms in Bohemia to direct physical threat by Nazi Germany. Faced with the deteriorating situation, Schneider finally sold out its stake in Škoda, and in the process brought to a close the most important business alliance for the armaments business of the interwar period.

Chapter 6 concludes by tracing the armaments business in transition from peacetime to war 1939–1941. In effect both sides tried to turn the arms trade into a tool of economic warfare and forging alliances for the coming struggle. The Nazi-Soviet Non-Aggression Pact was but the most prominent example of the German policy of securing agricultural products and raw materials from the countries of southeastern Europe in exchange for German arms and other industrial goods. The German annexation of rump Czechoslovakia on March 15, 1939, ultimately placed Škoda under German control as part of the Nazi state-owned Reichswerke Hermann Göring. Although the German invasion of Poland and the subsequent Soviet moves into eastern Poland, the Baltic States, and Finland brought the start of World War II to northeastern Europe in 1939, the interwar era continued a little longer for southeastern Europe. After the fall of France in the summer of 1940, Schneider and Škoda found themselves once again brought together, but this time under the control of the Göring Works, which now became the dominant armaments enterprise in wartime Europe. Škoda had come full circle bouncing from acquisition to ally and back to acquisition.

1   The Schneider–Škoda Alliance, 1919–1930

The Škoda Company found itself in a calamitous position at the end of the Great War. The defeat and collapse of Austria-Hungary meant that the firm would never collect the millions owed by the Habsburg military administration. In addition to that loss, roughly K 500 million, Škoda had incurred total liabilities of almost K 400 million brought on by the huge expansion in wartime armaments manufacturing capacity for which, seemingly, there would be little postwar demand. As a consequence, the company suffered from a critical lack of operating capital.[1]

In the first half of 1919, a complicated process unfolded to rescue the Škoda factory from bankruptcy. Initially, the new president of the board at Škoda, Joseph Šimonek, looked to Czech domestic financial institutions, especially Živnostenská Bank (Živnobanka), for financial support. That bank already showed an interest in January 1919 to provide Škoda Works with operating loans worth $588,235 (CZK 25 million), which, though not sufficient, would have helped the factory. Negotiations began for the redemption of shares of Škoda Works held by Baron Karl Škoda in an Austrian bank, under the control of Živnobanka. The discussions included offering the post chair of the Škoda Board of Trustees to the head of Živnobanka, Dr. Jaroslav Preiss. However, Živnobanka alone possessed insufficient resources for the Škoda acquisition, even with a syndicate of Czech banks under its leadership.[2] Lacking the capital to purchase the Škoda shares on its own, the bank turned to the Schneider group, headed by Eugene Schneider and consisting of Schneider et Cie and its financial partner, the Banque de l'Union Parisienne (BUP).

Historians have tended to view the French purchase of majority ownership in the Czech enterprise and the subsequent evolution of Škoda's business strategy as a major defense firm from the perspective of one

---

[1] V. Karlický, *Svét Okřídleného Šípu Koncern Škoda Plzeň 1918–1945* (Plzeň: Škoda, 1999), 633.

[2] R. Diestler, *Příbeh zapomenutého průmyslníka: život a doba Karla Loevensteina, generálního ředitele Škodových závodů* (Praha: Grada, 2010), 17.

of the two national sides. In a seminal work, Alice Teichova analyzed the Schneider–Škoda relationship primarily from the vantage point of French banking and corporate control. In her assessment, the French influence proved paramount in directing Škoda throughout the period 1919–1938. While acknowledging a Czech desire for greater autonomy from French control and disagreements between French shareholders and Czech domestic interests, she concludes that "the main policy decisions on production, commerce, trade, and finance were taken in the central offices of the French concern in Paris."[3] More recently, Aleš Skřivan Jr. has examined Škoda's strategy from the perspective of domestic business interests and Czechoslovak state interests. In his analysis, the Czechoslovak Army was Škoda's most important customer during the interwar period, and therefore its demands largely influenced both the arms production program and the general economic strategy of the company.[4] As these and other historians have shown, domestic and external factors undoubtedly shaped Škoda's armaments strategy in that French corporate control/management interacted with the market demands of Škoda's largest customer, i.e., the Czechoslovak government.[5]

Nevertheless, an explanation of the ups and downs in the Schneider–Škoda relationship in the decade following the Schneider acquisition of 1919 requires recognition that the relations involved more than simply two monolithic national sides. The Schneider industrial and financial group pursued its own course that at times placed it at odds with the policy of the French government. Among the Czechs, the Czechoslovak government, Živnobanka's industrial and financial group led by Preiss, and, finally, Škoda management itself participated in multilateral relations among themselves and with French partners. The Czechoslovak government envisioned plans for domestic defense industries that would make the country self-sufficient in armaments and included the manufacture of arms for export. To that end, the Czechoslovak government took a majority stake in the rifle and machine gun enterprise Československó Zbrojovka Brno (ČZB) in partnership with Škoda. Živnobanka and Preiss worked as a guiding interest in building the national Czechoslovak defense sector and actively participated in the key enterprises of Škoda, Českomoravská Kolben-Daněk (ČKD), and Czechoslovak Explosives.

---

[3] A. Teichova, *An Economic Background to Munich: International Business and Czechoslovakia 1918–1938* (Cambridge: Cambridge University Press, 1974), 198.

[4] A. Skřivan Jr., "On the Nature and Role of Arms Production in Interwar Czechoslovakia," *Journal of Slavic Military Studies*, vol. 23, no. 4 (2010), 632.

[5] P. H. Segal, *The French State and French Private Investment in Czechoslovakia, 1918–1938* (New York: Garland, 1987), 107, 140–141; Karlický, 33; Diestler, 21–22.

Rather than as a straightforward merger or acquisition, it is more useful to conceive of Schneider and Škoda as two firms in a corporate alliance akin to a joint venture environment. The tensions in the alliance fostered "opportunistic behavior" typically found within a joint venture, i.e., "self-interest seeking with guile" whereby one or more of the participants employ "the incomplete or distorted disclosure of information, especially to calculated efforts to mislead, distort, disguise, obfuscate, or otherwise confuse."[6] As Yadong Luo has expressed it, "In a joint venture setting opportunistic acts or behavior may be performed by a party to seek its own unilateral gains at the substantial expense of another party and/or the joint venture entity by breaching the contract or agreement, exercising private control, withholding or distorting information, withdrawing commitment, shirking obligation, or grafting joint earnings."[7] According to Luo, environmental volatility increases the tendency toward opportunism by reducing a party's anticipated returns or the stability of its income stream. When a party anticipates sustained or prolonged uncertainty of gains or income, it tends to behave more opportunistically.[8] Just such an environmental instability occurred in 1926–1927, when a steep decline in domestic armaments purchases by the Czechoslovak government spurred Škoda's management to seek compensation in exports. The ensuing French-Czechoslovak export competition sparked a rivalry between Schneider and Škoda in Eastern European markets that grew especially heated in Yugoslavia. Tensions emerged within the Schneider–Škoda alliance among three constituent groups: (1) the core of domestic Škoda management represented by Škoda's president Joseph Šimonek and general director Karl Loevenstein, (2) Schneider and his colleagues, and (3) Dr. Jaroslav Preiss with Živnobanka. These conflicts played out in tussles between the French and Czech financial groups for decisive leverage over the affairs of Škoda, while Škoda management sought autonomy for their firm. Besides being the flashpoint in the rivalry between Schneider and Škoda over exports, arms sales to Yugoslavia also served as the precipitant for a domestic showdown between Preiss/Živnobanka/ČKD and Škoda over ČZB and which group would win the primary backing of the Czechoslovak state.

Confronted by the prospect of nationalization by the newly independent Czechoslovak state after the war, Baron Karl Škoda put out feelers to

---

[6] O. E. Williamson, *The Economic Institutions of Capitalism* (New York: Free Press, 1985), 47.

[7] Y. Luo, "Are Joint Venture Partners More Opportunistic in a More Volatile Environment?," *Strategic Management Journal*, vol. 28 (2007), 41.

[8] Ibid.

French capital to purchase his shares. Late in January 1919, Baron Škoda approached the French armaments minister about selling the Austrian-held concern to a French metallurgical group. In January 1919, public opinion in Czechoslovakia and the Czechoslovak government were demanding that Škoda capital should be taken out of Austro-German hands and passed to Czechoslovak control. Noting that, prior to the war, Škoda had collaborated with Schneider in the Russian Putilov enterprise, the Czechs preferred the collaboration of French capital. A former Škoda representative in Italy, Walser, of Swiss nationality, approached Baron Škoda to enter into relations with a group of foreign interests. Walser conveyed the baron's desire to negotiate with the allied group and expressed a preference for French capital in the amount of roughly $2.35 million (CZK 100 million). Walser affirmed that the Czechoslovak government still viewed the operation favorably.[9] Šimonek, president of Škoda Works, was well known to Schneider from the prewar period, when both companies were interested in the construction of the Putilov shipyard in St. Petersburg. Already in February 1919, Gaston de Saint-Paul, the old Škoda representative in France, contacted Šimonek and proposed the idea of joining with Schneider. In April to May 1919, Šimonek appointed Saint-Paul to sound out a possible loan for the Škoda factories in the west. In early July 1919, the first Czech press report noted the arrival of French financing, specifically the participation of the arms company Schneider et Cie at the Škoda factory.[10]

Starting from the Peace Conference in 1919, French policy placed Czechoslovakia at the center of a new pro-French East Central European order. The French Army favorably viewed close ties with Czechoslovakia as a means to threaten the German underbelly while the French Foreign Ministry pursued Romania and Czechoslovakia as part of an anti-German coalition to offset the loss of tsarist Russia. To counter German resurgence, the French used the 1920s to recruit future wartime allies. Through the Quai d'Orsay, French policy worked out a political-military accord with Poland, including a mutual pledge to lend immediate assistance in the event of a German attack. The Treaty of Alliance and Friendship with Czechoslovakia, signed January 1924, involved joint consultation over defense and future collaboration of general staffs. Romania moved more firmly into the French orbit with the French-Romanian Treaty of June 1926, which allowed consultation in the event either became victim of unprovoked aggression. Lastly,

[9] MAE, Europe 1918–1929, Tchecoslovaquie, 84, Capt. Pagiot (Berne) to Ministère Reconstitution industrielle pour Produits métalurgiques, January 29, 1919; Lacroix (Berne) to MAE, February 1, 1919.
[10] Karlický, 19.

France and Yugoslavia signed a security guarantee in November 1927. The French government also wished to replace Germany as the region's dominant economic power, and such a vision included a French takeover of Škoda.[11]

The French government held the position that French capital must bring with it a guarantee of French control. The French Foreign Ministry subsequently contacted Schneider's agent Devies about Škoda. Dr. Edvard Beneš, the Czechoslovak foreign minister who was in Paris as part of the peace negotiations, entered into discussions with French government officials in the Ministries of Finance and Foreign Affairs and also with company representatives of Schneider to encourage French investment in Škoda.[12] By late August 1919, Victor Champigneul, an engineer of the Schneider concern, was negotiating an agreement through the Živnobanka to acquire a number of shares held by Baron Škoda, and preparations were in progress to convene a general assembly of shareholders.[13] The friendship between Šimonek and Champigneul played an important role in overcoming the mutual wariness between the two firms because the two men had known each other since the end of the last century. Champigneul steered Škoda to Schneider et Cie in negotiations regarding the company's entry into the enterprise. Živnobanka took over the baron's shares on September 15, 1919. Meanwhile, the Czechoslovak government discussed the issue of French entry into Škoda. Ten days after the aforementioned governmental meeting, the general meeting of the Škoda factory convened. It confirmed Schneider et Cie's entry in Škoda, increased the share capital, and changed Škoda into a corporation with majority ownership in the hands of Schneider. On the same day, there was also a meeting of the newly created nine-member board of directors, where one-third of French representatives participated. The French group bought Karl Škoda's 40,000 shares and then 9,725 more on the Vienna exchange. The cost of Škoda shares totaled more than $2.03 million (₣22 million). Schneider's corporate takeover was completed at the general meeting on September 25, 1919, with the Schneider Company owning 325,000 of 450,000 Škoda shares (73 percent).[14] The French Foreign Ministry learned that representatives from Schneider-Creusot had signed a contract that

---

[11] P. Jackson, *Beyond the Balance of Power: France and the Politics of National Security in the Era of the First World War* (Cambridge: Cambridge University Press, 2013), 235, 238, 368–369; R. J. Young, *In Command of France: French Foreign Policy and Military Planning, 1933–1940* (Cambridge, MA: Harvard University Press, 1978), 8–10.

[12] Segal, 100–103; Teichova, 195–196.

[13] SA, 187AQ072–07, Šimonek to Schneider et Cie, August 26, 1919.

[14] Diestler, 19; Segal, 105–111; Teichova, 195–196.

assured them control of Škoda on September 29, 1919.[15] Beneš told the general management of Škoda in a letter dated October 22, 1919, "Now Škoda-Works, by their fusion and by increasing their Czech and French capital, have completely freed themselves of any influence which the company could call foreign."[16]

The combination of French and Czech control required a balancing of respective interests, and consequently, Schneider simply could not take over all administrative positions as part of its corporate acquisition. At the birth of the Czechoslovak Republic, an influential group of economic nationalists played a key role in shaping the policy for the new Czechoslovak economy. This group included Finance Minister Alois Rašín, Prime Minister Karel Kramář, and Dr. Jaroslav Preiss, head of the Živnobanka, which was the biggest and most important financial institution in the country. These men had been imprisoned by Austro-Hungarian authorities for their nationalist opposition during the war, but with Czechoslovak independence, they could now pursue their goals of eliminating Austrian economic dominance and asserting Czechoslovak economic and business control of the domestic economy. According to Ilona Bažantová, Preiss played a decisive role in drafting the Nostrification Act, which required that joint-stock corporations create a headquarters in Czechoslovakia or relinquish their shares in Czechoslovak enterprises. Consequently, Preiss's Živnostenská Bank "became an industry flagship" and "pulled strings in almost all the country's biggest industrial companies."[17] On December 11, 1919, the Czechoslovak Chamber of Deputies passed the Nostrification Act, which also required that every board of directors have a majority of Czechoslovak citizens. Nonetheless, Schneider-Creusot's majority holdings entitled the French to important administrative positions. Eugene Schneider became the first vice president of the board of directors of Škoda in Plzeň in 1919. Colonel Ernest Weyl, an officer in the French Army, represented Schneider's corporate interests on the Škoda Board, and he oversaw Creusot's delegation stationed in Czechoslovakia. Simultaneously, Dr. Jaroslav Preiss, director general of Živnostenská Bank, served as second vice president. Preiss played a role as an advocate of Czech rather than French interests and sought to exercise a larger share in the capital and management of Škoda on behalf of his bank. Preiss

[15] MAE, Europe 1918–1929, Tchecoslovaquie. 84, Clément Simon (Prague) to MAE, September 29, 1919.
[16] Quoted in Teichova, 197.
[17] C. Johnstone, "Jaroslav Preiss: Banking and Business Colossus of Inter-war Czechoslovakia," September 8, 2011, www.radio.cz/en/section/czech-history/jaroslav-preiss-banking-and-business-colossus-of-inter-war-czechoslovakia.

favored creating a Czech national monopoly in the armaments sector as a means of diluting French influence within Czechoslovakia. Schneider sought to command the strategic development of Škoda through Škoda's Executive Committee while directing the main policy from Paris.[18]

In order to ensure permanent control and their representation in Škoda, the Schneider Company, and the Banque de l'Union Parisienne created a new holding company, the Union Européenne Industrielle et Financière (UEIF), and transferred much of their Škoda stock to the UEIF. The holding company preserved in its portfolio the "portion of the necessary shares to maintain control of the affairs through the group."[19] When the Škoda shares were ceded to UEIF in May 1920, the bloc's value had appreciated to roughly $2.22 million (₣24 million), and the holding company obtained 51 percent of Škoda's capital.[20] The UEIF Board of Directors was headed by Eugene Schneider and included Achille Fournier (Schneider's chief operating officer), Colonel Ernest Weyl, and Victor Champigneul. Armand de Saint-Sauveur oversaw the Schneider group's relations with the French Foreign Ministry. Achille Fournier reported to the Quai d'Orsay that "a category of privileged shares with plural votes, whose blockage would render impossible the transfer into foreign hands, assures our Group the permanent control of the foreign enterprises."[21]

Škoda Works still faced dire financial straits and needed capital just to continue operating. At a critical moment for the firm's finances in May 1920, the Škoda managers complained several times about Preiss's requirements in order to secure loans from Živnobanka that would have yielded complete control of all trade finance activity to his group. Simultaneously, in spring 1920, Preiss discomforted Schneider et Cie when he deflected the French efforts to gain shares in Živnobanka.[22] Ultimately, UEIF came to Škoda's rescue with an advance of $3.36 million (CZK 143 million) in 1920–1921 just to keep the enterprise going. At the same time, UEIF transferred to Schneider et Cie 229,567 shares of Škoda stock for approximately $1.88 million (₣24,017,541.09). Almost immediately, French capital provided an extremely important cash infusion, as Škoda's share capital increased to $3.38 million (144 million crowns) by 1921, up from $1.69 million. In May 1922, Škoda's general situation again required an augmentation of capital, and so UEIF offered a subscription to augment Škoda stock with 40,000 more shares

---

[18] Teichova, 98, 100, 103, 196, 210.
[19] SA, 187AQ072–07, Service des Finances Union Européenne Industrielle et Financière, October 25, 1921.
[20] Segal, 105–111.   [21] Ibid., 114–117.   [22] Diestler, 21–22.

totaling $0.375 million (F5,190,655.49). Schneider's 235,442 shares of Škoda stock increased in value by 6.48 percent.[23]

The French government strongly supported the acquisition of Škoda by French business interests. As acknowledged in the founding of the UEIF, "the French Government, for its part, encouraged the French industrial and financial groups to establish entrenched positions and protect new ventures in the regions where a prolonged occupation opened up new opportunities."[24] For the French War Ministry, having Schneider, France's largest and most important armaments firm, gain control of the largest armaments plant in East Central Europe would strengthen French military production and correspondingly weaken potential enemy military-industrial strength in a future conflict. Similarly, the French Foreign Ministry viewed the Škoda takeover as an economic reinforcement of French political influence in Czechoslovakia. According to the French Foreign Ministry in 1925, "if the Schneider Establishment interested itself in Škoda and has acquired the majority of shares, it is at the demand of the French Government which judged it indispensable to prevent the great arms factory of the Austro-Hungarian Empire from falling into enemy or even doubtful hands. It is beyond doubt that the French Government continues to be interested in the manner in which the business is conducted and that it will not let it escape from our control."[25]

Despite the intentions of the French government, Czechoslovakia did not obediently and passively serve as a tool of French influence. The Czechoslovak-Yugoslav-Romanian alliance system, dubbed the "Little Entente," began with the Czechoslovak-Yugoslav alliance in August 1920. The Czechoslovak-Romania alliance followed on April 24, 1921, and it contained a secret protocol for Czechoslovakia to provide armaments to Romania. The creation of the Little Entente caught France off guard, and it frustrated French efforts to include Hungary in a Danubian sphere. Indeed, Czech opposition to French foreign minister Maurice Paleologue's overtures to Hungary in 1920 had prompted the Little Entente as a response to potential Hungarian revisionism of the territorial losses through the Trianon Treaty. Although Beneš certainly valued bilateral relations with France, he sought to keep the Little Entente free from the encumbrance of any bloc, and

---

[23] SA, 187AQ072–07, Service des Finances L'Union Européenne Industrielle et Financière, October 25, 1921, Annexe I: Škoda; L'Union Européenne Industrielle et Financière Exercice 1920/1921, Bilan et Comptes, Meeting, May 1, 1922.

[24] SA, 187AQ072–07, note on creation of a company of control of industrial shares of Central Europe, March 1920.

[25] Segal, 113.

he rebuffed French pressure to join a military convention aimed at Germany.[26]

The Czechs placed due emphasis on the economic mission of the Little Entente, and insisted on the importance of fostering economic ties between Prague, Belgrade, and Bucharest. The role of the Škoda Works in providing armaments for the Little Entente countries was one way to promote economic unity within the alliance.[27] The Czechoslovak state thus actively encouraged Škoda to become the "Arsenal of the Little Entente." For the Czechoslovak government, supplying arms to the Little Entente made up part of its military strategy, and as a result the Czech Defense Ministry (MNO) played the leading role rather than the Foreign Ministry. With diplomatic and military motives to arm Yugoslavia and Romania as a means to tie them to the Czechoslovak alliance, the Czech state actively fronted the weapons and funding to make this happen. The Czech state could take a loss where a private firm would not, or could not afford such a course of action.

It would be mistaken, however, to consider that Schneider and Škoda merely served as an instrument of the policy of the French or Czechoslovak governments. Schneider and Škoda had their own reasons for a business alliance quite apart from their governments' motivations. In the pre-1914 era, both firms had pursued expansion strategies in the Balkans and Russia. Schneider had won the competition in Bulgaria, Serbia, and Greece while Škoda had achieved some limited success in Romania and the Ottoman Empire. Each firm had had to contend with the German firm Krupp. Even though they competed, the two firms also had collaborated in some significant business ventures. Schneider and Škoda had established a contractual relationship in 1904 when the French firm had enlisted the technical aid of Škoda in forging artillery pieces larger than 150mm. Then, in 1910 the two companies had collaborated in creating an artillery factory in Hungary. Of greatest import, in 1912 the two firms had worked together in Russia as investors and through technical agreements in the Nevskii Shipbuilding Factory and the Putilov Company, which was tsarist Russia's largest private armaments firm. Rather than seeking a quick profit by chance at the insistence of the French government, Schneider's acquisition of Škoda in 1919 fit into an overall expansion strategy developed by Schneider early in the twentieth century. Aware of the limitations of development within France,

---

[26] P. S. Wandcyz, *France and Her Eastern Allies 1919–1925: French-Czechoslovak-Polish Relations from the Paris Peace Conference to Locarno* (Minneapolis: University of Minnesota Press, 1962), 195–197, 241, 257, 300–303; Jackson, 365, 368, 417.

[27] P. Wandycz, "The Little Entente: Sixty Years Later," *The Slavonic and East European Review*, vol. 59, no. 4 (1981), 551–555.

Schneider-Creusot based future expansion on two objectives: financial direction of the company and international expansion of business.[28]

The UEIF functioned as an extension of Schneider's prewar Russian adventure, for which Fournier, director of financial affairs, had been the main architect. Already in 1919, E. Schneider and Fournier played a major role in the Czech venture. The unfortunate loss of the Russian ventures at the hands of the Bolsheviks could be recouped through Škoda. At least until 1921, the French business community believed that the Bolshevik regime was on the brink of collapse, and consequently in March 1920 Schneider planned to carry out from bases in Czechoslovakia its programs for expansion in central and southern Russia that had been drafted from the prewar era but that military events and the Bolshevik revolution had disrupted. As late as October 1921 Schneider considered Škoda as the best means of industrial reconstruction in Russia and thus a launching pad for Schneider back into Russia as well as facilitating the opening of markets in Eastern Europe.[29] Through Škoda, Schneider pursued a two-prong strategy for growth of its armaments sales. The first prong of Schneider's strategy was to secure a major portion of the Czechoslovak domestic market. The second prong involved establishing and defining artillery markets for itself and Škoda throughout Eastern Europe by directly coordinating the artillery departments of the two firms technically and commercially.

As would be reasonably expected, arms production for Škoda had decreased immediately after the war. In 1917–1918, armaments represented by far the most important items in the company's billing invoices (73.6 and 71 percent), then came down from 46.5 percent in 1920 to 22.2 percent in 1921 and 15.9 percent in 1922. However, the following year the armaments share increased to 43.6 percent including ammunition sales representing 19.4 percent. In 1920, Škoda employed 14,000 workers and had the capacity to produce 500,000 small arms rounds and 1,000 artillery shells per day. The Czechoslovak government consumed 33 percent of the output. The armaments section employed just over 29 percent of the total workforce. For members of the Czechoslovak Parliament as well as the Czechoslovak Ministry of Defense, Škoda

---

[28] J. A. Grant, *Rulers, Guns, and Money: The Global Arms Trade in the Age of Imperialism* (Cambridge, MA: Harvard University Press, 2007), 192–214, 217, 223–224; A. D'Angio, *Schneider et Cie et la naissance de l'ingénerie* (Paris: CNRS Editions, 2000), 173; J. A. Grant, *Big Business in Russia: The Putilov Company in late Imperial Russia, 1868–1917* (Pittsburgh, PA: Pittsburgh University Press, 1999), 92–112; C. Beaud, "Une multinationale française au lendemain de la Première Guerre mondiale: Schneider et l'Union Européenne Industrielle et Financière," *Histoire, économie et société*, 2e année, vol. 4 (1983), 627.

[29] Beaud, 627.

needed to be retained as a matter of state security because it was the only complete arsenal in the country. By that time Škoda manufactured field artillery (37mm); 75mm howitzers, and three models of 75mm mountain guns that had been designed and built by the Škoda plant for various governments. In addition, the plant was now manufacturing a new field gun caliber 83.5mm, and a range of antiaircraft guns. The full range of artillery models impressed the American military attaché so favorably that he arranged to have photographs sent back to the American Ordnance Department. By 1922, Škoda had grown such that it was second only to Krupp in size in Europe.[30]

Schneider's strategy for managing artillery markets functioned more as an old-fashioned cartel agreement between separate firms than the direction of a home office over a subsidiary, and in that way it revealed the nature of the relationship between Schneider and Škoda as more of a corporate alliance than a simple acquisition. The collaboration commenced already in 1920 when it was determined through UEIF that Schneider-Creusot would "retrocede to Škoda a notable part of the furnished artillery."[31] Upon visiting the Škoda plant in 1921, one of Schneider's directors remarked that, "It is uncontestable that the steelworks at Škoda are superior to ours."[32] By 1921, Škoda held $6.25 million (CZK 250 million) worth of artillery and munitions orders out of $23.58 million (CZK 955 million) worth of total orders, and Schneider hoped to use Škoda as a jumping off point "to export to the countries of the old Austro-Hungary, the Balkans, the Orient, and into Poland."[33] In late May 1922, Schneider and Škoda signed an artillery market-sharing agreement. The Artillery Convention covered all the artillery materiel, including ammunition and components equal to or greater than 1.5cm, vehicles and equipment to deploy or adjust artillery, and materiel to set up arms and munitions factories in other countries. The agreement established four categories of potential customer states:

---

[30] A. Marès, "Mission militaire et relations internationales: L'exemple franco-tchécoslovaque, 1918–1925," *Revue d'histoire moderne et contemporaine*, t. 30e, no. 4 (1983), 574–575; M. Hauner, "Military Budgets and the Armaments Industry," in M. C. Kaser and E. A. Radice (eds.), *The Economic History of Eastern Europe 1919–1939* (Oxford: Clarendon Press, 1986), 70–73; Karlický, 33, 53; RG 165, #2331-II-13 (4) Mil attaché Harry Cootes (Austria) to G-2, May 14, 1926; #2331-II-4 MID 367, Military attaché to MID, February 14, 1921; #2331-II-6, Major G. M. Barnes to Chief of Ordnance, DC, October 30, 1922; #2331-II-12, Col. Wm. N. Taylor to Assistant Chief of Staff, G-2, November 16, 1922.

[31] SA, 187AQ072–07, Note on Creation of a company of control of industrial shares of Central Europe, March 1920.

[32] SA, 1G0001–02, Instructions de Direction Usine du Creusot pour M. Lefevre en vue d'une Mission a Škoda, January 22, 1921.

[33] SA, 187AQ072–07, Annexe I; Škoda, October 25, 1921.

prohibited, reserved for Schneider, reserved for Škoda, and unreserved. Both Schneider and Škoda were prohibited from selling to the Soviet Union. Schneider claimed France, Belgium, Spain, and Latin America south of Mexico for itself. States reserved for Škoda included Austria, Czechoslovakia, Mexico, and Romania. In the category of unreserved countries Škoda had great power when negotiating contracts, although normally they were to be divided with 75 percent of the price to be realized by Schneider, and 25 percent Škoda. Significantly, Yugoslavia was originally designated in the "unreserved" category along with Bulgaria, Latvia, Lithuania, Switzerland, and Sweden.[34]

Working together, Schneider and Škoda gained markets in the Baltic. Poland seemed an especially promising market in the 1920s. French foreign policy promoted Czech-Polish cooperation throughout the interwar period, and as the largest country in France's eastern coalition, Poland was extremely important to France. The French-Polish Alliance of June 1922 included a secret military convention, and article 8 made the convention dependent on signing the Franco-Polish commercial treaties. On Polish insistence an annex to the commercial treaties stipulated that France would make a loan to Poland of almost $28.9 million (F400 million) for arming Polish forces. The French rejected the Polish request to borrow even more money, but did require that Poland purchase war materiel exclusively from France. Poland began placing orders for armaments in France in early 1923.[35] The Polish War Ministry's budget in 1924 amounted to 38.6 percent of the total national budget, and unlike virtually all the other European states, there were no vast stocks of war materiel left over on Polish territory after 1918. As a result, much of Polish expenditure would be devoted to the purchase of new material. French firms did well in Poland. Schneider field guns and Hotchkiss heavy machine guns had already been adopted. Creusot took an Estonian order for twenty artillery pieces in 1923, and a Polish order for twelve artillery pieces in December 1925. In 1927 the French government passed to Schneider a Polish request for fifty 155mm artillery pieces which resulted in another contract on August 12, and Schneider subsequently delivered the first pieces in October 1928. For its part, Škoda procured a licensing agreement to introduce production of 100mm howitzers with the largest manufacturer of heavy guns and shells in Poland, the Polish state-owned Starachowice Works, in 1928. Poland also ordered howitzers from Škoda for $9.09 million (CZK 300 million) to be paid for by loans over a nine-year

---

[34] Karlický, 29; D'Angio, 176.
[35] Wandycz, *Eastern Allies*, 217–219; Jackson, 239, 366, 415.

term.[36] Škoda scored a victory over the British firm Vickers when the Lithuanian government ordered 1,500 automatic rifles from the Czechs. The British Representative in Riga lamented that, "I left no stone unturned in my endeavors to secure the contract for Vickers . . . I am told that the real reason why the whole order was given to the Škoda Works was that they were able to effect immediate delivery."[37] Furthermore, Schneider honored its commitment to pass a share of its armaments orders to Škoda. For example in 1927–1928 Schneider acquired armaments orders amounting to $14.6 million (F365 million), of which $2.4 million worth of orders were retro-ceded to Škoda and the French firm Saint-Chamond. Included in these orders were $770,000 for Polish and Yugoslav torpedoes and Škoda model antiaircraft guns.[38] Again in 1931, this kind of collaboration between the two companies also resulted in gains for Škoda. In this instance, Škoda gained Polish orders for 220 artillery pieces (155mm) as part of a Schneider order totaling $20 million (F500 million) because according to Schneider part of the materials "were reserved for Škoda in compensation for the Romanian order."[39]

Yet, from the inception of the Artillery Convention, the Škoda managers expressed their displeasure over the proposal from Schneider to set cartel arrangements over Škoda, and they engaged in opportunistic practices to mislead the French about their flouting of the terms of the agreement. Šimonek and Loevenstein therefore tried to obviate the restrictions, which Šimonek considered "intolerable" and Loevenstein found "unreasonable."[40] An overview of Škoda's most important customers in 1921–1923 reveals the prominence of the Czechoslovak government (Table 1.1). However, these official figures are somewhat distorted by underreporting sales to Yugoslavia and Romania while increasing the share of supplies to the Czechoslovak government. Several arms deals with the Little Entente allies in fact were declared as a domestic delivery for the Czechoslovak Ministry of National Defense. To avoid the appearance of violating the Artillery Convention with Schneider, a significant portion of this material for Yugoslavia was supplied immediately by the Czech War Ministry from its warehouses, and then the War Ministry placed new orders with Škoda to replace the material. Such transactions thus appeared as state-to-state trading between the Czechoslovak government and the Little Entente countries

---

[36] FO 371/11005, Poland Annual Report, 1924, Muller to Austen Chamberlain, October 16, 1925.; SA, 0064Z0756, June 6, 1923; 01F0284, December 30, 1925; 187AQ548–16, March 10, 1937; Hauner, 107; Karlický, 76.

[37] FO 371/13271, Vaughn (Riga) to Austen Chamberlain, January 23, 1928.

[38] SA, 187AQ027–02, Marche des Industries pendant l'exercice 1927–1928, 22.

[39] SA,187AQ029–02, 45.   [40] Diestler, 21–22, 37.

Table 1.1 *Main Customer States of Škoda, 1921–1923, Converted into Millions of Dollars*

	1921			1922			1923	
State	Amount	%	State	Amount	%	State	Amount	%
Czech	11.275	45.48		7.58	75.19		10.40	62.19
France	8.36	33.72	Belgium	0.45	04.49		0.37	02.24
Romania	2.04	08.21	Italy	0.34	03.36	Italy	1.73	10.33
Greece	0.9	03.78	Spain	0.33	03.27	Britain	0.56	03.36
Yugoslavia	0.5	02.19		0.29	02.89		1.46	08.73
Austria	0.3	01.26	Poland	0.29	02.54	Germany	0.50	02.97

Source: Vladimír Karlický, *Svět Okřídleného Šípu Koncern Škoda Plzeň 1918–1945* (Plzeň: Škoda a.s., 1999), 52.

rather than a private contract with Škoda. For example, the Czech Ministry charged orders to Yugoslavia worth almost $1 million (CZK 41,887,714) in 1923, and in turn this was translated to the Škoda Works as a comparable order for ammunition to supply the Czechoslovak Army. The contract for the supply of arms and war materiel to Yugoslavia, signed on February 28, 1923, covered older deliveries from November 1921, which had been ordered by the Czech War Ministry on behalf of Yugoslavia.[41]

Working on its own, Schneider secured major defense orders from Greece. Schneider concluded its first significant Greek artillery contract in September 1924 to supply twenty-four batteries (4 guns per battery) of 75mm guns with 200,000 shells; eighteen batteries of 105mm guns with 50,000 shells; and eight batteries of 155mm pieces with 15,000 shells. The following year Schneider gained two additional artillery contracts in June to sell Greece a total of twelve batteries of 85mm howitzers and twelve batteries of 105mm with 80,000 shells, twelve batteries 75mm Model 1919 with 70,000 shells; six batteries 105mm mountain guns with 30,000 shells, and three batteries 155mm along with 10,000 shells. Schneider had also secured a contract with the Greek Navy in May 1924 for two submarines of 605 tons displacement. During 1926, total Greek artillery orders placed with Schneider amounted to seventy-two batteries (288 pieces) 75mm mountain guns, forty-eight batteries (192 guns) 105mm mountain howitzers, and twenty-five batteries (100 guns) 150mm howitzers. The Greeks had already taken delivery of forty

[41] Karlický, 52, 95; Diestler, 43.

batteries of the 75mm mountain pieces, twenty-five batteries 105mm field guns, and fifteen batteries of the 150mm howitzers.[42]

Schneider–Škoda relations entered a critical phase in the years 1926–1927. As previous customers and major sales were suddenly in doubt, each firm tried to take advantage of the other for its own benefit. Given the large size of its Greek orders, Schneider suffered a major blow when a new Greek government cancelled the previous government's order for field guns in April 1926.[43] To avoid holding onto this liability, Schneider responded by dumping its Greek problem on Škoda. When the American military attaché visited Škoda in January 1927, he observed the Plzeň plant completing forty-eight guns (twelve batteries) of 105mm for the Greeks. When he noticed the Schneider name plate on the trail and inquired about it, Loevenstein told him that it was an order that had been turned over to them by Schneider. He also stated that the order was originally made by Pangalos, the since deposed dictator of Greece, "which made it very bad, since, if the present Greek government did not pay Schneider, they couldn't hope for their money. I gathered from the tone of his conversation that he did not like the situation of the Schneider control."[44] Meanwhile, the Škoda management had to contend with a dramatic slump in its own armaments business. Škoda had only two main customers at the time, the Czechoslovak government and Yugoslavia, but unfortunately the domestic orders had plummeted. Škoda's arms sales to the Czechoslovak state (its biggest customer) had amounted to roughly $3.64 million (CZK 120 million) in 1925. In 1926 sales dropped by roughly a third, and by 1927 domestic sales totaled only about $0.88 million (CZK 29 million). The 1926 sales represented merely 25 percent of the value of sales from the previous year.[45] The Cannon Department was operating at only 20 percent capacity as of May 31, 1927, and that department's output of artillery as a portion of Škoda's total output had dropped from 10.7 percent in 1926 to 4.3 percent in 1927. As the Škoda Board put it, "In sum, the state of the munitions industry is precarious enough at the moment."[46] The Škoda management sought salvation in expanding exports, and

---

[42] SA, 0064Z0763–03, Schneider contract with Greece, September 12, 1924; SA 0064Z0763–03, Greek contract, June 18, 1925; SA, 0064Z0763–03, Schneider contract with Greece, June 17, 1925; SA, 0064Z0763–05, Schneider contract with Greece, May 17, 1924; FO 371/11345, Mil attaché Col. Giles (Athens), June 12, 1926.

[43] FO 371/11345 Cheetham to Austen Chamberlain, June 16, 1926.

[44] RG 165, #2331-II-17 (2) Mil att H. W. T. Eglin to G-2, January 14, 1927.

[45] Karlický, 598–599.

[46] SA, 01G0015-A-03, Situation des Industries des A. K. Škoda, January 1, 1928, 18–19, 39.

therefore pursued an end run around Schneider in Yugoslavia with clandestine support from the Czechoslovak government.

With both firms reeling from the sudden drop in their respective artillery revenues, the stage was now set for head to head competition between Schneider and Škoda for the Yugoslav business as each partner in the alliance looked out for its own interests. Within Škoda's management, Loevenstein started implementing his own ideas for industrial participation in the countries of the Little Entente. As the first step he looked to Yugoslavia. Subverting the Artillery Convention with Schneider, Loevenstein played a central role in the negotiation of trade, contract implementation, and subsequent distribution of profits that were ostensibly prohibited by Schneider. His obvious solution involved having the contracts entered into either by the Czechoslovak state or through a "consortium of Czechoslovak firms" including ČZB which was de facto the Czech government and Škoda. The first such Yugoslav agreement involved arms materiel in the amount of $9.09 million arranged through the respective governments in December 1925. Later, at the Prague Sokol festival in the summer of 1926, Loevenstein negotiated a proposal with Yugoslav General Nedić and Defense Minister Trifunovic to establish a metallurgical complex in Yugoslavia consisting of blast furnaces and foundries, rolling mills, coal mines, ore mines, and factories for aircraft and engines. The operations were to culminate with the creation of a public limited company in which Škoda would hold a 50 percent share and the Yugoslav government the remaining half.[47]

Over the course of 1927, the mutual opportunism of Creusot and Škoda came to a head in Yugoslavia. By now Škoda had been engaging in its Yugoslav business surreptitiously for several years, and it was Schneider's turn to violate the Artillery Convention for its own self-interest. In April, Schneider concluded a series of armament contracts with Yugoslavia. Starting relatively small, sixteen howitzers 120mm Model 1910 and some repair work on other howitzers, by the end of the month Schneider's total Yugoslav orders amounted to $143,000 (F3,652,000) with further Yugoslav orders valued at $51,221 spilling over into 1928.[48] Not to be outdone, the Czechoslovak government secretly placed and financed a large artillery order with Škoda on behalf of Yugoslavia. Saint-Sauveur lamented to the French Foreign Ministry in December 1927 that, "The Schneider Firm very much regrets the decision of our Allies (Škoda)... the Serbian Government just passed to the Škoda Works

[47] Diestler, 35.
[48] SA, 0064Z0756, Schneider contract with Yugoslavia, April 30, 1927; SA, 0064Z0756, Schneider contract with Yugoslavia, April 27, 1927; SA 187AQ027–02, Marche des Industries pendant l'Exercice 1927–28, October 1928.

orders that very probably would have gone, in other circumstances, to French industry."[49] With effective backing from its home government Škoda's management demonstrated far greater autonomy to pursue its own strategy than the French government or Schneider wished.

In 1928, the strains between Schneider and Škoda eased greatly as each firm's armaments business boomed. Schneider's profits from April 30 to November 10, 1928, reached $0.941 million (F24,084,722), and the company paid dividends worth $22.50 per share.[50] At the annual shareholders meeting in November 1928, Schneider's Board reported that, "The important orders from foreign governments given for artillery manufacture will allow us to sustain our special workshops and mechanical shops for a long time."[51] Likewise, Škoda's sales and profits reached their highest levels to date, and in fact exceeded Schneider's. Škoda's domestic arms sales in 1928 hit $3.37 million (CZK 111,119,513), arms exports totaled $3.45 million (CZK 114,010,567), and profits amounted to $1.62 million (CZK 53,362,000).[52] Although both Creusot and Škoda had violated the Artillery Convention with regards to Yugoslavia, the rising tide of the armaments business helped mitigate the need for opportunistic, self-interested behavior, and generally the two firms did make the agreement work going forward. In 1928 military sales to Argentina, Bulgaria, and Turkey they honored their accord, giving compensation to one another if the client insisted on dealing with the excluded firm.[53] The improvement in relations within the Schneider–Škoda alliance came just in time because a significant domestic challenge to Škoda lay over the horizon.

Building upon the industrial base bequeathed by the Austro-Hungarian Empire, the Czechoslovak government energetically pursued a path toward national self-sufficiency in the full array of armaments production. For example, the Nobel Dynamite Co. at Bratislava was the most important powder, dynamite, and fuse factory. Before the war most of the Balkan countries obtained the majority of their supplies from this factory, and it remained one of the most important military powder and explosive factories on the continent. The Czechoslovak government created a monopoly for manufacture of explosives given to a new company formed in 1920 as Czechoslovak Explosives Ltd. with Živnostenská Bank holding 42 percent of the shares. The British Explosives Ltd., the

---

[49] Segal, 139.
[50] SA, 187AQ027–02, Schneider et Cir Shareholders Meeting, November 15, 1928.
[51] SA, 187AQ027–02, Schneider Report to the General Shareholders Meeting, November 29, 1928.
[52] Karlický, 598–599; SG, Box 7526 Škoda piece 01597.   [53] Segal, 140–141.

The Schneider–Škoda Alliance 41

Table 1.2 *ČZB's Net Profit, 1920–1928, Converted into Millions of Dollars*

	1920	1921	1922	1923	1924	1925	1926	1927	1928
Profit	0.06	0.08	0.14	0.145	0.15	0.19	0.17	0.25	0.29

Source: Aleš Skřivan Jr., "On the Nature and Role of Arms Production in Interwar Czechoslovakia," *The Journal of Slavic Military Studies*, vol. 23, no. 4 (2010), 635.

Societe Centrale de Dynamites (French), and the factory's director, E. Phillip, each held 16 percent as well. In July 1925, Czechoslovak Explosives was slated to take over all the powder and dynamite machinery from the Nobel factory at Bratislava and exercise a monopoly. Their plans called for a very large factory capable of supplying the Carpathian and the Balkans, Austria, and Hungary. Meanwhile, the Roth Cartridge factory in Bratislava had no orders for rifles or cartridges at all. Roth's general manager expressed the view that the German firm was being deliberately killed by Czechs because it was not suitably national.[54]

The transformation of Czechoslovakia from arms importer to self-sufficient defense producer happened astoundingly quickly. Czech foreign purchases of arms and ammunition in the period 1919–1922 had consisted overwhelmingly of obsolete French equipment sold on terms determined by the French government through its exercise of military loans and military missions. With an eye toward developing domestic capacity, Czechoslovak factories turned to Austrian and German firms to provide a ready supply of machine tools for the manufacture of arms. Mauser, DWMF, and Wurttemburg Metal Works in Geislingen were all looking to unload their equipment as part of the imposed disarmament following the peace treaties. Škoda itself purchased 2,000 Mauser machines.[55]

An equally dramatic case of an ascendant arms manufacturer involved Československó Zbrojovka Brno (ČZB) (Table 1.2). The plant had started out as a branch of Vienna Arsenal in the city of Brno but was taken over by the Czechoslovak state in 1919. Imported German manufacturing equipment sufficient for daily output of 300 rifles (300,000 per year) not only met Czechoslovak domestic needs, but also enabled huge exports. Subsequently, the ČZB quickly emerged as one of world's leading exporters of small arms by the end of 1922. In 1924, the enterprise was founded as a joint-stock company with capital stock of $0.9 million

---

[54] RG 165, #2331-II-12 Col. Wm. N. Taylor to Assistant Chief of Staff, G-2, November 16, 1922; RG 165, #2331-II-7 E. R. W. McCabe to G-2, September 13, 1922.
[55] Mareš, 574–575; Hauner, 70–73.

(CZK 30 million) and the Czechoslovak government holding 75 percent of the shares. Škoda became partners with the Czechoslovak state in ČZB acquiring 20.5 percent participation. With Škoda's participation in ČZB in 1924, two directors from Škoda joined the board of ČZB and one director from Brno became a member of Škoda's Executive Committee. In 1924, Škoda held 15,098 shares out of 75,000. As of 1929 ČZB also had purchased the Roth Ammunition Works. The Brno-based company had 566 employees upon its establishment and the number had increased fourfold by 1922 (to approximately 2,400). By 1930, the factory in Brno employed 3,500 workers and produced rifles, automatic rifles, and light machine guns. The rifle production at ČZB reached its first culmination point in 1929, when 143,555 rifles were dispatched from the Brno plant.[56]

Within the first two years of its founding, ČZB was developing new weapons and exporting them in abundance. China proved a highly profitable market. In March 1924, a large contract for delivery of rifles, machine guns, trench mortars and field guns and ammunition was placed with Škoda Works of Plzeň from China through Škoda's agent Rosenthal in Beijing. In October 1927, Chinese authorities in Canton placed an order with Škoda for light field guns and Mauser rifles. At roughly the same time, ČZB sent 40,000 rifles to China after the Czechoslovak Ministry of National Defense had conducted the negotiations. Although the Czechoslovak government was not unsympathetic to British policy of preventing war materiel from reaching China, they were not prepared to deprive themselves of this lucrative trade so long as other countries were indulging in it. Škoda's intelligence service had definite information that Belgian, French, and Italian factories were busy exporting war materiel to China, and in fact Italian firms had recently made a definite proposal to the Škoda Works that they should combine in this trade and set up joint machinery in Trieste for the shipment of Italian and Czechoslovak war materiel from that port. Under these conditions, Škoda would not stand aside and allow the profitable China trade to fall into the hands of its foreign competitors.[57]

By 1926, ČZB had moved beyond the manufacture of old Mauser models and had engineered its own original, improved models such as

---

[56] Hauner, 70–73; Teichova, 199; FO 371/14329 Czechoslovakia, Annual Report, 1929, Macleay to Henderson, February 18, 1930, 32; Skřivan, "On the Nature," 634–635; FO 371/14329 W. Huxley (mil attaché Prague) to Legation, March 6, 1930.

[57] FO 371/ 10240 Sir George Clerk (Prague) to FO, October 9, 1924; FO 371/12425 Ronald Macleay (Prague) to George Mounsy, October 20, 1927; FO 371/12890 J. V. Perowne, Germany, Czechoslovakia and the Trade in Arms to China, June 5, 1928; FO 371/ 13180 FO Minute, Orme Sargent, May 17, 1928.

its light machine guns, Model 1924 and Model 1926, which exhibited significant technical superiority over comparable foreign makes. Turkey in November 1925 ordered 200 Brno machine guns. By 1926, ČZB had sold 32,000 Mauser rifles to Turkey, and the factory also had large orders for Yugoslavia. Mass production of new type Praga light machine gun Model No. 1 would begin shortly. The promising Yugoslav business brought disappointment for ČZB. In 1925, Yugoslavia had signed a contract with ČZB for 60,000 rifles worth $12.12 million (CZK 400 million) to be paid through Yugoslav state bonds. The following year the Brno works landed its first contract for 2,000 of its new light machine gun Model 1926 and during 1927 the firm delivered $3.03 million (CZK 100 million) worth of arms to its Yugoslav customer. The Yugoslavs wanted another credit amounting to $7–10 million and asked for technical assistance for developing their domestic arms industry at the Kragujevaç plant. In response ČZB offered a loan of $0.06 million (CZK 2 million) and to invest in one-third of the shares to develop a small rifle workshop in Kranj if Yugoslavia guaranteed to buy more arms. Unfortunately for ČZB, the Yugoslav government failed to honor its pledge to buy rifles. Although payment had been guaranteed by its state bonds, Yugoslavia lacked the funds to make good on its payments but could only pay with tobacco. Consequently, the payment renegotiations dramatically slashed the previous agreement for 150,000 rifles, 8,000 light machine guns, and 200 million cartridges worth $7.27–7.88 million down to only 3,000 light machine guns to be delivered by the end of 1930. ČZB would accept Yugoslav payment in tobacco to be supplied over eight years. With its profits going up in smoke, ČZB decided to halt further sales to Yugoslavia for the time being.[58]

In 1929, a rift opened up between Škoda Works and ČZB. Škoda had been serving as the main representative of Czechoslovak arms companies during negotiations in 1928 for arms supplies to Yugoslavia to be paid for with a hidden state credit. The Yugoslavs were initialing planning huge purchases totaling $45.5 million, but then reduced the figures by about a third. ČZB asked Yugoslavia to purchase at the least $3.03 million worth of weapons, especially rifles that had already been produced but for which they had no other buyers. However, in November 1928 Yugoslavia ordered the lion's share of war materiel from Škoda for about $26.12 million (plus another $9.24 million in interest) while ČZB received Yugoslav orders for only $1.5 million, or roughly half of what ČZB

[58] Skřivan, "On the Nature," 635; Hauner, 65, 70–73; FO 371/10856 WO to Rendel, November 17, 1925; RG 165, #2331-II-13 (4) Mil attaché Harry Cootes (Austria) to G-2, May 14, 1926.

had sought. ČZB claimed that it had been betrayed by the Škoda Works. By early spring 1929, ČZB denounced the cartel agreement under which, inter alia, Škoda had represented ČZB abroad. Brno's complaint received a sympathetic hearing within the Czechoslovak government, as the state was still the majority shareholder and influential generals sat on ČZB's Board. It appeared that Defense Ministry and the Czechoslovak Ministry of Finance were preparing to mobilize against Škoda.[59]

Into this dispute between Škoda and ČZB entered Jaroslav Preiss. As head of the Živnobanka and Director of ČKD, Preiss saw an opportunity to disrupt relations between ČZB and Škoda for the benefit of ČKD. ČKD (Českomoravská Kolben-Daněk a.s.) had been founded in 1927 from the merger of two smaller companies, Českomoravská-Kolben and Breitfeld-Daněk. On October 8, 1929, the Administrative Board of Brno met and quickly approved a cooperative agreement between ČZB and ČKD. Far more ominously for the Škoda company, the Management Board of ČZB reported that there was agreement on cooperation with the leadership of ČKD, which was so broad that ČKD's director general, Preiss, was pushing directly for merger of the two companies. From Brno, Škoda learned that this plan had the support of the Prime Minister and the Defense Ministry.[60]

In parallel with this plan ČKD unleashed a greater threat against Škoda. Within the framework of the government's plan for a new location for arms industry away from the vulnerable western border, in 1928 Škoda had signed an agreement with Defense Ministry. At the time of peak rupture between Škoda and ČZB during the fall of 1929 came word from the Czechoslovak General Staff that the understanding through which Škoda artillery had enjoyed a monopoly as the supplier for the Czechoslovak Army was under threat from ČKD. ČKD announced that it was proceeding into the artillery business and had acquired some patents from abroad, for example from Vickers. Indeed, back in 1924, Vickers had granted an exclusive license to Českomoravská to make and sell to the Czechoslovak Army 44mm and 60mm infantry equipment excluding ammunition. In April 1928, ČKD already had a Vickers license to make infantry guns, but now requested permission to supply guns to Yugoslavia. In the opinion of the Army Assessment Committee of Vickers, there was no chance for the British firm to get the order, but the Czechs were in a good position, and Vickers would receive royalty payments of 10–12.5 percent. Vickers's Committee agreed to let ČKD proceed. Simultaneously, ČZB proposed an agreement with Vickers. Under the Brno proposal, each company would inform the other of any

[59] Karlický, 102.   [60] Ibid., 103.

enquiries for machine rifles, the two companies would determine which company would submit a competitive price with a view to securing the order, and the prices which each company would quote. As compensation, the company that secured the order would pay the other firm a commission. Since Škoda was connected to Brno, and Škoda wanted to enter into the Vickers Romanian project at Copsa-Mica (see Chapter 2), Vickers's decision was put on hold.[61] Nonetheless, ČKD's foray into the artillery trade signified an attack on the very heart of Škoda's business.

Karl Loevenstein, the director general of Škoda, fought back, arguing to the Czechoslovak premiere on November 20, 1929, that Škoda's quality artillery work had required decades of experience, and his firm's weapons were immensely appreciated abroad. He noted specifically that Poland, Romania, and Yugoslavia were all asking Škoda to introduce them into the manufacture of its type, and the Little Entente allies almost exclusively used Škoda artillery. Why then would the Czechoslovak government suddenly seek to block the unification of armaments among its allies, and worse yet begin to support a rival works? Loevenstein also criticized Preiss of ČKD for wanting to get a seat at the table, which Škoda had built through longtime efforts as an armaments firm. Loevenstein also expressed skepticism that Preiss even wanted to come to an agreement with Škoda. When Škoda first began to talk with Českomorakska-Kolben in 1927, Českomoravská had acquired the Danek works behind Škoda's back and Loevenstein feared that Preiss was going to convert the Brno armaments factory in a similar fusion with ČKD. To forestall such a move, Loevenstein refused Preiss's proposal for a tripartite meeting with the Minister of National Defense to conclude the compromise agreement between Škoda on the one hand and ČKD and ČZB on the other.[62]

In the spring of 1930, the Czechoslovak state expanded the capital of Zbrojovka Brno from $0.9 million to $6.06 million. While preserving the government's majority shareholding, Škoda took over the rest of the new shares. Thus Škoda obtained 26 percent of ČZB (up from 20.5 percent). The result of the dispute found Škoda retaining its business monopoly by preventing the fusion of ČKD and Zbrojovka Brno, while renewing the previously strong cooperation between Zbrojovka and Škoda.[63]

Having come up short in his attempt to reorganize the Czech defense sector around his industrial-financial group, Preiss set his sights on weakening the French ownership in Škoda. He and his Živnobanka

[61] Karlický, 104; VA, File 1367, Board Minutes, Vickers Ltd., May 30, 1924; VA, Microfilm R286, Minutes of Army Sales Committee, April 2–3, 1928.
[62] Karlický, 104, 106.   [63] Ibid., 107–108.

launched a press campaign in Prague against French control of Škoda in spring 1930.[64] The French Foreign Ministry felt confident that Škoda remained firmly under French control financially and administratively. After all, as of January 1930, Schneider still held 55 percent of Škoda's shares. The Head of the Artillery Department was a French former artillery officer, and the French Foreign Ministry believed that the representative of Schneider and the UEIF in Prague, the mining engineer Aimé Leperq, energetically preserved for the group effective control of Škoda, while giving the Czechs "the appearance of management."[65] However, in spring 1930 financial difficulties arose which afforded an opportunity for Preiss to lead a Czech nationalist challenge. Škoda suffered chronic undercapitalization because its management preferred to use debt instruments and short-term loans to cover operating expenses for its armaments sales to Little Entente customers. Buyers such as Romania and Yugoslavia could only purchase Škoda weapons with long-term credits, and Schneider often preferred to arrange the financing for East European countries through BUP, or if the French banks were unavailable, British banks. With Schneider's approval, the management of Škoda in 1922 had negotiated a loan in London specifically to finance Romanian armament orders. The Bank of England and the National Provincial Bank issued Škoda a loan of $4.58 million (£1 million) in 1923 at with interest of 8 percent. After its conversion in 1926, the loan amount increased to $12.15 million, the bulk of which was devoted to funding new Yugoslav orders at Škoda. Through the 1920s, armaments deliveries to Little Entente buyers had required $15.2 million of Škoda's funds, but UEIF had long delayed increasing Škoda's capital because it was unable to subscribe at least half of such an issue itself. In 1930, Škoda received further Romanian orders of $30.3 million and had to try to negotiate an increase of the British loan to $24.3 million to meet the demands. When British creditors refused to lend more than half that amount, a French financial group formed to provide the other half. The French banks participating included Banque de l'Union Parisienne (30 percent), Banque des Pays du Nord (10 percent), Comptoir National D'Escampte de Paris (8.5 percent), Crédit Lyonnais (25.75 percent), Société Générale (25.75 percent), and Banque Nationale de Credit. Škoda found itself thus burdened with large foreign loans and each conversion was almost fully swallowed up by paying off old debts, commission, amortization, and interest payments.[66]

[64] Segal, 251.
[65] MAE, Europe 1930–1940, Tchecoslovaquie. 167, Note sur les relations Schneider–Škoda, January 18, 1930.
[66] Segal, 265, 270; SG, Box 7526 Škoda piece 01597; Teichova, 215.

Back in 1926, Škoda had taken a loan from the Anglo-Czech Bank, but now in need of capital expansion that loan was to be converted into an issue of additional, new Škoda stock. Yet, Schneider and UEIF lacked the funds to control the stock issue out of their own resources.[67] Therefore, the possibility to dilute French ownership below majority presented itself. H. E. Carter, a director at the Anglo-Czech Bank, reported to British sources that, "The foreign control of this important industry in Czechoslovakia has, I believe, long been distasteful to those interested in the industry and others in that country. I have for some time joined privately in an effort to obtain a break to this control, ... I am now in a position to inform you that arrangements have been made by which the French share control will cease at an early date."[68] As the share capital of Škoda was going to be increased, the Czechoslovak government could purchase the fresh shares, and in this way the Schneider shares would no longer represent an absolute majority.[69]

In March 1930, Eugene Schneider laid out the situation to the Board of the Société Générale. He recalled the conditions, in accord with the French government, that they had purchased the majority of Škoda shares after the war when the company lay in a precarious condition. Even though the Czechs held almost all the administrative positions, Preiss and his Živnobanka were instigating a public campaign against French control of Škoda. Schneider informed the French shareholders that he had spoken to Beneš, who knew the many services that France had provided, in order to disapprove these nationalistic attacks against French influence. Beneš indicated that he envisioned a way to modify the form of control over Škoda to satisfy the nationalists. The French understood that the motives of Preiss to inspire this campaign stemmed from the interests in the metallurgical enterprise ČKD which competed with Škoda and was connected to Živnobanka. Beneš pledged to defend Škoda against these nationalist attacks by suggesting an augmentation of Škoda's capital and increasing the number of positions in the proper hands.[70]

Under the circumstances, the French recognized the need to modify the relationship with Škoda. Clearly, competition for foreign war materiel between the Czechs and French were adversely affecting the relationship, and twice within a few months Škoda had challenged

[67] SG, Box 7526 Škoda piece 01597.
[68] FO 371/14348, H. E. Carter to Vansittart, March 20, 1930.
[69] FO 371/14348, O. E. Barque to Vansittart, March 25, 1930.
[70] MAE, Europe 1930–1940, Tchecoslovaquie. 167, Visite E. Schneider and Saint-Sauveur, March 10, 1930; F. Charles-Roux (Min in Prague) to Briand (MAE), March 10, 1930.

Creusot. The first occasion involved the Turkish artillery order late in 1929. Škoda believed that Schneider's stubbornness had prevented the Czechs from having a chance to obtain this order which consequently went to Vickers and Bofors (see Chapter 2). The recriminations over the lost Turkish orders between the two administrations had escalated. Škoda's agent in Ankara was recalled at the request of Creusot. The second occasion involved Romania. In truth, an accord existed between Creusot and Škoda which granted the furnishing of Romanian war materiel to Škoda. Yet, the French government had asserted that through the preponderant participation of France in Romanian loans, the order in question should revert to French industry. Creusot had invited Škoda to go against their accord and let Creusot furnish the order. Škoda was inclined by the good graces of the two administrations to seek a package of compensations for these orders. Thus, there had been two instances where Škoda has found itself in competition with the French establishment.[71] Regarding the Romanian armament program, "The French Foreign Ministry, in accord with the War Ministry, is charged to make this demand in consideration for Creusot."[72] In May 1930, at the time of the recent passing of Romanian armament orders, Creusot solicited and obtained the benefit of an assurance credit for $16 million payable over ten years in equal installments. In the interval, Škoda gained a Romanian order in an amount far superior. The simultaneous execution of these two orders would overwhelm the immediately disposable Romanian budget, and the two groups presented themselves at first as competitors. Finally, Škoda retired itself, however the Czechs reserved all their rights for the future. Schneider and Škoda intended to settle their respective activities in Romania and finally to avoid a competition that was proving "difficult and inexplicable given the connections which unite the two establishments."[73] The Czechs had the ambition to be the sole suppliers of war materiel to the countries of the Little Entente. Yet the French government considered that since Romania and Yugoslavia could not make their own war materiel, it was in their interests to equip with materiel of French provenance to acquire its reprovisioning in time of war. Within the business, the French noted the time had come to "Transform from a formula of control over Škoda to a form of collaboration," and to "examine the situation of accords

---

[71] MAE, Europe 1930–1940, Tchecoslovaquie.167, F. Charles-Roux to Briand, April 6, 1930.

[72] MAE, Europe 1930–1940, Roumanie. Matériel de guerre. 160, Note, April 17, 1930.

[73] SG, Box 5898 V. I. Lenin á Pilsen, Dossier monographie Bilans Comparés Note au sujet de l'activite du Creusot et des establissements Škoda en Roumanie, May 21, 1930.

between Škoda and Creusot on the subject of furnishing war materials in Central and East Europe."[74]

Revealingly, the French financial groups led by the Société Générale evinced much less concern than the French government about a Czech challenge or losing control of Škoda through the stock expansion. They did not perceive French industrial enterprise as susceptible to suffer competition from Škoda. Creusot would be the most qualified to raise complaints about this, but they generally worked in agreement with Škoda and, in certain areas, in association with it.[75] As Armand de Saint-Sauveur, one of the French administrators in Škoda, expressed it to one of the directors of the Société Générale in May, "Creusot completely controls the Union Européene, and it in turn completely controls Škoda."[76] On the other hand, the French government, especially the Ministry of Foreign Affairs manifested more opposition to the quotation in Paris of the stocks.[77] Nevertheless, plans for the introduction of Škoda stock shares on the Paris market went forward in October 1930 even as the search continued for a method "to find a system to permit the Union Européene to guard the control of Škoda, while lightening the fraction of its participation."[78]

Preiss had not relented in his attacks on the French interests in Škoda. True, he had resigned his position as a director of the Škoda Board on May 28, 1930, and vacated the post of vice president of Škoda in June 1930. But rather than weakening his challenge, Preiss's resignations only emboldened him. Having just left Škoda, he was elected president of the Board of ČKD, in which his bank had controlling interest, and the struggle between the two enterprises continued. With little left to lose in attempting to hurt Škoda now that he had been pushed outside, Preiss sought to inflict maximum damage on the enterprise. Consequently, he and Živnobanka began to sell the large blocks of Škoda shares they had owned since 1919 as intermediary between the Austrians and the French. Preiss arranged for the dumping of 10,000 shares of Škoda stock on the Prague market at very moment Škoda was introduced on the Paris Bourse, causing a sharp drop in stock's price. At the same time,

---

[74] MAE, Europe 1930–1940, Tchecoslovaquie. 167, Note, March 29, 1930.

[75] SG, Box 7526 Škoda piece 01597, Škoda. Conversation of Théodore Laurent with de Meeus, May 14, 1930.

[76] SG, Box 7526 Škoda piece 01597, Meeting Saint-Sauveur and de Meeus, May 20, 1930.

[77] SG, Box 7526 Škoda piece 01597, Škoda. Meeting of de Meeus with Saint-Sauveur, May 17, 1930.

[78] SG, Box 7526 Škoda piece 01597, Škoda, conversation of Lorain with Cheysson, October 1, 1930.

Table 1.3 *Total Sales of Škoda Works, 1925–1929, Converted into Millions of Dollars*

Year	Domestic sales	Arms Exports	Total Sales	Net profits
1925	3.64	1.45	21.36	
1926	2.62	2.69	20.90	1.20
1927	0.87	3.74	24.74	1.30
1928	3.37	3.45	33.18	1.62
1929	1.94	17.34	21.37	2.03

Source: Vladimir Karlický, *Svét Okřídleného Šípu Koncern Škoda Plzeň 1918–1945* (Plzeň: Škoda a.s., 1999), 598–599. Société Générale, Box 7526, Škoda piece 01597.

BUP was issuing a loan to Škoda to convert the $24.3 million loan of 1926 to a lower interest.[79]

The ownership struggle over Škoda between French and Czech interests resolved itself in 1931 in a manner satisfactory to Schneider, UEIF, and the Czechoslovak government but disagreeable to the French government. By mid-October, Škoda confronted a financial crisis caused by the default of the Romanian government on its armaments purchases, and the enterprise's need for capital to sustain operations exceeded the UEIF's financial resources (Table 1.3). Faced with the prospect of having to halt production and lay off some 3,000 workers, Škoda turned to the Czechoslovak government for relief. The Czechoslovak Republic had secured a state loan from France previously and now used those resources to acquire Škoda shares in a stock expansion. While the French government had wanted to force the Czechs to preserve French control over Škoda, Schneider and Leperq were willing to accommodate Czech interests. Ultimately, French business interests diverged from those of the French Foreign Ministry. Instead of serving as a pliant tool of the French government's foreign policy, UEIF and Schneider followed their own business interests in siding with Škoda's biggest and most important customer, the Czech Ministry of Defense. Loevenstein had also managed to bring into the Škoda camp several Schneider representatives, including Yves Rochette, Aimé Lepercq, and, later, starting in 1930, Jacques Cheysson.[80]

The Schneider–Škoda alliance had survived the opportunistic challenges from within and grown into a thriving relationship. Without a doubt, Schneider and the French shareholders benefited directly

[79] Teichova, 211. Segal, 253.
[80] Segal, 141, 255, 263, 276, 291–293; Diestler, 38.

and indirectly from Škoda's prosperity. More significantly, though, the nature of the Schneider–Škoda alliance had changed. Having started as the object of French corporate expansion, Škoda had become the subject of its own strategies in the armaments business. In the process, Škoda transformed from the junior partner into at least an equal partner with Schneider. By the end of the twenties, Škoda had surpassed Schneider as the prime artillery exporter to Eastern Europe. Beginning in 1923, Škoda embarked on the peacetime expansion of the firm's armaments production that would continue until the end of the 1920s. As the figures show, the value of Škoda's arms exports exceeded domestic military sales starting in 1926 and continued thereafter. By 1929, armaments exports reached unprecedented levels. In May 1929, at Škoda's annual share-holders' meeting, the company reported 30,000 employees, and that it had reached the highest point in the accumulation of armaments orders. According to Loevenstein, the firm had in hand enough work to fully occupy the factory for the next two years. Yugoslavia proved Škoda's biggest customer by far. In the period 1923–1930, Škoda exported to Yugoslavia arms materiel worth $43.88 million, which represented 72 percent of the value of all of the firm's arms export from the years 1918 to 1930. By 1930, Škoda employed 32,000, with half working at Plzeň. A total of 4,000 workers were directly involved in war materiel, and war orders in hand would keep the factory fully employed until 1932. Contracts in hand in 1930 included $48.6 million for Yugoslavia (800 antiaircraft guns, artillery, and ammunition with delivery to be completed in 1931), $17.5 million worth of antiaircraft guns, artillery, and ammunition for Romania, and $12.4 million for 124 field guns and ammunition for Turkey. These orders granted generous terms for payment over multiple years for the buyers (ten years for Yugoslavia, five years for Turkey). Within Czechoslovakia Škoda owned three factories engaged in armaments work.[81] As a British Foreign Office observer put it in 1930, "This country (Czechoslovakia) is the arsenal of the Little Entente."[82]

---

[81] RG 165, #2331-II-15 (7) Mil Att John Thomas Jr. to G-2, May 16, 1929; Karlický, 95; WO 190/120, Draft of Minutes of Third meeting of Sub-committee on the Disarmament of CID, May 7, 1931, 12–14.

[82] FO 371/14329, Czechoslovakia, Annual Report, 1929, Macleay to Henderson, February 18, 1930.

2   Disarmament by Default
The British Arms Business in Eastern Europe,
1921–1930

British armaments firms found themselves between the Scylla of disarmament and the Charybdis of industrial depression in the 1920s.
The Washington Naval Treaty of 1922 did serve as an impediment to
the British naval trade. Yet, the negative attitude of the British government toward the arms trade in pursuit of disarmament proved an
even more important factor and went beyond naval systems. Prior to
1914 British firms had exhibited dominance in naval trade, although
they had been unable to land significant military contracts for rifles or
artillery in the Balkans compared to German and French firms. With
the Germans eliminated in the immediate postwar years, British firms
had expected to compete intensely with the French on land and sea,
but unexpectedly faced new challengers from Czechoslovakia and Italy.
British firms generally acted with propriety and dutifully checked with
the British government for official approval or objection before seriously involving themselves in armaments export negotiations. They also
experienced general failure in getting anything from the government in
the way of financial guarantees or support, despite repeated requests.
Thus, over most of the decade of the twenties British armaments
firms experienced a period of reduced orders, low returns, and near
bankruptcy as more often than not, the British firms lost out to European
rivals.

In the pre-1914 era, Britain had ruled the warship export markets,
however, the 1920s brought a stunning decline in the fortunes of British
naval firms. Without a doubt, disarmament played an important role
in shaping the naval trade to French advantage. The Washington Naval
Treaty represented the only disarmament agreement formally enacted
internationally. The Washington Naval Agreement, signed by Britain,
the US, France, Japan, and Italy on February 6, 1922, set the maximum
size of a capital ship at 35,000 tons with maximum gun caliber at sixteen inches. The Agreement also limited aircraft carriers to 27,000 tons
and cruisers to 10,000 tons with a maximum of eight-inch guns for these

Table 2.1 *Naval Sales to Eastern Europe, 1922–1930*

Ship Category	French	Italian	British	Dutch/German
Submarines	12	3	2	2
Destroyers	2	6	-	-
Motor torpedo boats	-	-	4	-
Minelayers and minesweepers	2	1	-	1

Source: Conway's All the World's Fighting Ships, 1922–1946 (London: Conway Maritime Press, 1980), 349–354, 357–358, 360, 366, 405–408.

two classes of warships.[1] The Treaty placed restrictions on the allowed number of larger surface warships, but it left unaffected the smaller classes of naval vessels such as submarines, destroyers, minelayers, and minesweepers. The French would come to dominate the submarine sales to Eastern Europe while also acquiring one-quarter of the destroyer sales to rank second behind Italy in that category for the period (Table 2.1).

In general, Eastern Europe did not figure prominently in British foreign policy. Stanley Baldwin, the Prime Minister in power for most years in the twenties, seemingly had little interest in foreign policy matters.[2] He turned over foreign affairs to Austen Chamberlain, who showed standoffishness toward the region based on his assessment of the inherent instability in the new states. According to Austen Chamberlain, "in Eastern Europe our role should be that of a disinterested amicus curiae."[3] In terms of the Baltic, Britain did not have any strong trade links established until 1934.[4]

Hostility to the armaments business in Britain certainly affected the way British firms conducted the arms trade in Eastern Europe. In the immediate aftermath of the Great War explanations for the origins of the conflict had pointed to arms production and arms competition as largely responsible for causing the war. As Carolyn Kitching has

[1] C. Kitching, *Britain and the Problem of International Disarmament, 1919–1934* (London: Routledge, 1999), 57; R. W. Fanning, *Peace and Disarmament, Naval Rivalry & Arms Control 1922–1933* (Lexington: University of Kentucky Press, 1995), 6–7.

[2] Kitching, 26.

[3] Quoted in E. Goldstein, "The Evolution of British Diplomatic Strategy for the Locarno Pact, 1924–1925," in M. Dockrill and B. McKercher (eds.), *Diplomacy and World Power, Studies in British Foreign Policy, 1890–1950* (Cambridge: Cambridge University Press, 1996), 125–126.

[4] R. S. Grayson, *Austen Chamberlain and the Commitment to Europe, British Foreign Policy, 1924–29* (London: Frank Cass, 1997), 260.

described, "Driven by the twin demands of the Treasury and a public fed on the idea that the arms race had caused the horrors of the war, there was enormous pressure on her, as there was on each of the other victorious Allies, to 'disarm.' There is no denying that in the immediate postwar years Britain did, in fact, make enormous reductions."[5] Along with the demand for disarmament came a demand for the control or elimination of the arms trade, which was viewed internationally as a cause of war and domestically as a waste of money to the detriment of social spending. That interpretation became deeply embedded in general public opinion in Britain and had helped expand the political role of peace groups within the country and their forceful advocacy for disarmament. According to David Edgerton, "the greatest campaign waged by the interwar peace movement was against the private arms industry and the international arms trade."[6] The British public's strong support of disarmament had played a vital role in changing the British government's tepid attitude toward the Washington Naval Treaty into one of energetic support in the early twenties. Over the remainder of the decade various British governments feared provoking public outrage if they were seen as obstructing disarmament talks.[7]

The British League of Nations Union (LNU) emerged as one of the main peace groups pushing for disarmament. With Lord Robert Cecil as chairman of its Executive Committee the LNU initiated activities in December 1920. In 1923, Cecil served within the Bonar Law/Baldwin administration, where he advocated pursuing disarmament through the League of Nations. With private lobbying groups such as the LNU growing and pressuring politicians to support disarmament, electoral success became linked with disarmament. In October 1925, those pressures contributed to Britain and other League countries agreeing to convene a World Disarmament Conference. By December, the Council of the League of Nations had adopted the proposal to create a Preparatory Commission to establish the basis for the Disarmament Conference at Geneva.[8] In meetings of the Committee for Imperial Defence during

---

[5] Kitching, 20.

[6] D. Edgerton, *Warfare State, Britain, 1920–1970* (Cambridge: Cambridge University Press, 2006), 25.

[7] C. Lynch, *Beyond Appeasement, Interpreting Interwar Peace Movements in World Politics* (Ithaca, NY: Cornell University Press, 1999), 62, 66; G. C. Kennedy, "Britain's Policy-Making Elite, the Naval Disarmament Puzzle, and Public Opinion, 1927–1932," *Albion*, vol. 26, no. 4 (1994), 623, 631.

[8] B. J. C. McKercher, "From Disarmament to Rearmament: British Civil-military Relations and Policy Making, 1933–1934," *Defence Studies*, vol. 1, no. 1 (2001), 22–23; T. R. Davies, *Possibilities of Transnational Activism: The Campaign for Disarmament between the Two World Wars* (Boston: Brill, 2006), 64, 69; Kitching, 4.

1926 Cecil had argued that Britain had treaty commitments on disarmament. He also reiterated the views that arms competition leads to war, and that expenditure on arms had detrimental effects on the economy by burdening industry with taxes.[9] Public impatience with the lack of progress by the British delegation to the Preparatory Commission coupled with Cecil's resignation from the government in August 1927 led to increased activities by peace groups. The LNU had held 600 disarmament meetings by the end of the year, its biggest effort to date, and 2 million members signed on with the "Women's Peace Crusade."[10] As the national disarmament movement only escalated during 1928, Lord Cushendon, the new British representative to the Preparatory Commission, expressed fears about being blamed by "a large body of opinion in this country" if disarmament negotiations failed entirely.[11]

In order to inhibit the arms business, the British Trade Facilities Act of 1921 provided for financial guarantees by the British Treasury to loans raised for industrial purposes while specifically excluding loans used for the manufacture of munitions of war.[12] Within the British governments, whether Conservative or Labour, the Treasury and the Department of Overseas Trade consistently expressed the strongest opposition to the armaments trade. The Department of Overseas Trade emerged as a new government office created out of the Foreign Office Commercial Department on March 21, 1918, and tasked with directly aiding British traders and merchants operating abroad. The Board of Trade (BOT) after the war was devoted to restoration of Britain's traditional free trade relations with the rest of the world.[13] The Foreign Office continued to be responsible for political aspects of commercial policy, whereas the BOT acted for the protection of British commercial interests abroad. Overseas Trade also managed an Export Credits Department, dealing with export credits, guarantees, and insurance, until this was constituted the Export Credits Guarantee Department in 1930.

Certainly Treasury's opposition to arms sales rested primarily on financial and commercial grounds, but Overseas Trade expressed an active opposition to the arms trade in favor of disarmament. In a sharply worded enclosure to the Foreign Office in December 1923, C. C. Farrar of Overseas Trade voiced his opposition regarding British armaments sales to the Balkans. He wrote, "We are in principle opposed to arming the small states: a) because it is unproductive b) because it leads to war c)

---

[9] Grayson, 148.   [10] Davies, *Possibilities*, 74, 76.   [11] Quoted ibid., 79.
[12] FO 286/937, E. Keeling to Rendis (Greek Foreign Minister), September 26, 1925.
[13] R. W. D. Boyce, *British Capitalism at the Crossroads, 1919–1932: A Study in Politics, Economics, and International Relations* (Cambridge: Cambridge University Press, 1987), 29.

because, as we may one day have to hit the French a very smart blow over their armament policy, we wish to keep our own record in that respect wholly unsullied... What would they think at Washington, what would they think at Geneva, if we were, for the sake of Armstrong Whitworth, to destroy all prospects of these two advances being consummated?"[14] Farrar recognized that the strong desire among Balkan states to buy arms meant that in all likelihood French firms would garner these sales at British expense, but he rejected the prospect of French gains as sufficient reason for Britain to engage in the trade. He also had very little sympathy for the plight of British armament firms, noting, "We will not be dragooned into taking the Balkan point of view in these matters for the sake of a small financial gain to a class of British industry which, if it had been properly financed, should have made enough money during the war to render it quite independent of such orders as these."[15] Here Farrar rejected arm sales to the Balkans directly in terms of their negative consequences for the disarmament process, and couched his objections in terms corresponding to the criticisms from the peace movements.

Under Ramsay MacDonald's Labour government, the British opposition to arms sales extended beyond new war orders to include even war surplus. In September 1924, a Board of Trade Circular pointed out that while applications from foreign governments to purchase vessels, and arms from Government surplus stocks had been received, "*Transactions of this kind are barred* [emphasis original] by 1) a recent decision of HMG that disposal of Government owned arms and munitions to foreign states, whether directly or through private contractors, should not be sanctioned and 2) article 18 of Washington Naval Treaty."[16] In fact Cabinet decisions of April 15, 1924 and July 19, 1924, had forbidden the sale of surplus government arms and ordered their destruction if they could not be made use of by the armed services or sold to Dominions or Colonies.[17]

In the case of Greece, Farrar not only proved unsupportive of the arms industry, but also tried to thwart Greek purchases in 1923. Overseas Trade raised opposition to Greek sales on multiple grounds. In terms of naval armaments, arming Greece appeared unnecessary because Greece could handle Turkey, and so faced no serious threat from a naval standpoint. Moreover, the Greeks already found themselves in a precarious financial situation. They owed British firms $5.725 million (£1.25 million) for requisitions and had obligations to the International Financial

---

[14] FO 371/11345 Encl C.C. Farrer (Overseas Trade) to FO, December 1923, Dept. of Overseas Trade Extract. Enclosed.
[15] Ibid.   [16] BT 60/26/7 Overseas Trade Circular, September 6, 1924.
[17] FO 371/10975, Cabinet 9 (25), February 18, 1925.

Commission. In the British government's view, naval purchases would prove an extravagance at a time when the vital problem confronting Greece was the refugee problem. While the British government had supported a Greek loan by the League of Nations and from the Bank of England as part of the refugee issue, British policy held that Greece should meet those financial commitments first. Furthermore, British policy sought to avoid Greek attempts to lure in British political support through naval contracts. In Farrar's assessment,

Hatzikyriakos is a Republican. He is also head of the navy. He thinks we are a nation of shopkeepers and can be bought. He knows we don't like his republic but he thinks we do like contracts. He wants to sell one for the other. We do not care for this sort of thing. We know that if Greece becomes a republic she will get into a dreadful mess. Hatzikyriakos, by the bird-line of naval contracts, wants to catch us and attach us to his republic. We won't be caught.[18]

Even if the British government had wished to arm Greece in this way, significant obstacles stood in the way. The Trade Facilities could not apply and no credits could be given. Although Greece had received a credit in 1918, the 1918 Credit would not cover the naval program now suggested, and the US would most likely exercise its veto right as set forth in the 1918 Credit over the assignment of additional Greek security to pay for Greek naval orders. Revealingly, even though the British government did not want to get the contract itself, it was prepared to work to prevent the French from doing so by employing the British veto and the American veto on the pledging of further security under the 1918 agreement, and pointing out to the French that the 1918 credits were not made for such purposes. As a final step to preempt Greek naval purchases, the British could block the League of Nations Refugee Loan unless the Greeks abandoned the whole naval scheme.[19] The official policy of the British government remained "to discourage, as a matter of principle," Greek expenditure on armaments, especially naval construction and repairs, even as the conditions of the Refugee Loan advances already prohibited any expenditure which involved the creation of external debt.[20] Well into 1925, the British position conveyed to the Greek government continued to rest on concern for Greek financial well-being in that "the attitude of HMG in regard to that program (naval) is dictated solely by their desire to see Greek finance reestablished on a firm basis as contemplated by the Geneva protocol."[21] The British Treasury

[18] FO 371/11345 Encl C. C. Farrer (Overseas Trade) to FO, December 1923, Dept. of Overseas Trade Extract. Enclosed.
[19] Ibid.   [20] FO 371/10764 Cheetham to Chamberlain, December 19, 1924.
[21] FO 286/937, F. W. Leith Ross to FO, September 4, 1925.

considered that its first responsibility lay with the British banks, companies, and individuals who invested in that loan. Treasury feared that word of the Greek government financing armament programs in violation of their commitments under the Loan Protocol would bring great indignation on the London market and a consequent collapse of Greek credit and exchange.[22]

Within Greece, British firms faced an uphill battle against powerfully deployed French interests. The Greeks had invited five British firms exclusively at the end of 1923 to tender for repair of the battleship *Averof*. In April 1924, after prices quoted by these firms were allowed to become common property the British firms were told that as a result of protests by the French Minister it had been decided to let French firms tender too. The Greek Naval Ministry subsequently made modifications in the *Averof* contract and invited French, Italian, and British tenders. On the other hand, French exclusivity in military orders went unchallenged as the Greek government had not hesitated to place a contract with Schneider for army guns without asking for British tenders. Clearly, the maneuvers of French diplomacy had caused the withdrawal from British firms of contracts which had already been definitely or virtually earmarked for them. Vickers had held a contract to work on the fire control on the *Averof* worth £16,660 and fire control on a second Greek warship, the *Helle*, in the amount of £15,600. Unfortunately for Vickers, they lost all work on reconstruction of the *Averof* along with orders for four submarines to the French.[23]

Unlike their British counterparts, French military and naval attachés permanently resided in Greece, and the French head of the mission exercised a much greater and more constant pressure upon departmental ministers and technical officials than did British diplomatic representatives. As part of the building of a French security system across Eastern Europe since 1920 roughly 2,000 French officers had been stationed in military missions from the Baltic to Greece. The majority of those missions assisted in the organization and training of native armed forces, and were therefore well placed to apply pressure for armaments orders.[24] In the case of contracts generally French diplomatic representatives baldly offered the Greek government assistance, or threatened them with opposition, in questions of political importance. For instance, the French raised the possibility of intervention for or against Greek interests in an Italo-Yugoslavian rapprochement and the cession of the fourteen Epirus

[22] FO 286/937, Lawford to Cheetham, March 9, 1925.
[23] VA, Microfilm R286, Orders obtained by Agelasto since July 1923.
[24] Jackson, 364.

villages in connection with the granting of the submarine contract to French firms. The British representative in Athens, Milne Cheetham, reported back to London that unless the British government applied pressure equal to the French, British firms would have no hope.[25]

During 1925, several British armaments firms had entered into negotiations with the Greek government, but not without checking with the British government first. For example, Vincent Caillard queried on behalf of Vickers whether there would be any objection for Vickers to sell war materiel to Greece.[26] Similarly, Beardmore had received an enquiry from the Greek Ministry of Marine for thirty-two antiaircraft guns for land defense and five antiaircraft guns for submarine vessels, but before replying to this enquiry that firm sought government instruction as to whether there would be any objection to supplying these guns to the Greek government.[27] Vickers, Armstrong, Thornycroft. Cammell Laird, and John Brown each sought naval orders, whereas Vickers, Armstrong, Birmingham Small Arms Company (BSA), Webley, and Scott tendered for army orders. Vickers was mainly interested in submarines as they have not built destroyers for some time and would only consider competing in that direction if financial facilities were available to make it worth it. Armstrong also was most interested in submarines. They had offered two half-finished vessels to the Greeks in 1924, and Armstrong was prepared to accept deferred payments over four years. Thornycroft most actively pursued destroyers and coastal motor boats. The estimated cost of naval program spread over ten years would amount to more than half a million sterling annually, and it was hard to imagine how the Greeks could find this money in their annual budgets without swelling already large deficits. The attitude of the British government remained negative toward Greek defense spending. Cheetham reported from Athens, "while continuing to discourage expenditure on naval and military reconstruction – particularly the latter, since in any case British manufacturers are unlikely to benefit to any considerable extent in view of the virtual monopoly held by the French in this sphere, HMG might indicate to the Greek Government that they are not disposed to quarrel with any schemes for obtaining financial assistance in Great Britain for public works construction."[28]

The British government's political and financial ambivalence about the arms trade and its conflict with the goals of disarmament was not restricted to Greece or the Balkans, but also clearly could be seen in

[25] FO 371/10764 Cheetham to Chamberlain, December 19, 1924.
[26] FO 286/937, Vincent Caillard to Sir Eyre Crowe, March 10, 1925.
[27] FO 286/937, William Beardmore Co. to FO, December 15, 1925.
[28] FO 286/937, Cheetham to Chamberlain, April 1, 1925.

the case of the Baltic States. A request from the Latvian Government in 1924 for a British military mission had come to nothing because it was linked with the proposal that the Latvian Government should buy munitions from Britain. The Labour Cabinet disallowed the whole project. Only a change in government opened the way for an Estonian proposal for a British military mission coupled with a scheme for purchasing British munitions in 1925. At this point, the Foreign Office believed that "There is no more cheap or certain way of increasing the influence of this country in Eastern Europe than of sending British officers to live and work there with the local administration for a period of months, and on purely military grounds the War Office would certainly favor any scheme designed to increase the efficiency of the Estonian army."[29] In general, the British War Office favored the Estonian proposal due to their anxiety about disposing of war stores and to prevent the assertion of French influence in the Baltic States. The Foreign Office concurred as long as the quantities of supplies were reasonable. However, the British Treasury had a generally hostile attitude toward such projects because sending missions was usually accompanied by suggestions for supplying arms, and Treasury viewed this as reacting negatively upon HMG's general policy of attempting to recover debts from various states, Baltic States included. Treasury also held that arms could only be purchased on an adequate scale by the Baltic States on credit, and there was no chance to secure government credits for this purpose. Treasury raised no objection to supplying states with names of private contractors willing to furnish arms, but would not allow financing.[30] Only in February 1925 did the British Cabinet authorize the armed services to take steps to find markets for the surplus and obsolescent equipment among the allied and friendly powers either directly or through private contractors who were recognized dealers. This policy reversed the decisions of the previous Cabinet.[31]

Perceiving that the British government's hard line on arms export licenses was softening, in July 1925, BSA seized the opportunity and advocated for permission to export on the grounds of economic benefit for British workers. BSA applied for an export license to sell 1,200 machine guns (Lewis) to the Lithuanian government. Withholding the British export license would cost the company an order worth $483,000 (£100,000), which would probably go to the French. BSA estimated that the manufacture for the Lithuanian order would take about nine

---

[29] FO 371/10975 Van Allen. Minute to Vaughn (Riga) to FO, January 12, 1925.
[30] FO 371/10975, Note on Departmental Attitude to Military Missions to the Baltic States, A. W. G. Randall, March 24, 1925.
[31] FO 371/10975, Cabinet 9 (25), February 18, 1925.

months and employ 170 men and generate wages of £19,000 in this contract. The company also believed it had a good chance to obtain a Greek government order for 100,000–200,000 Mannlicher-Schonauer rifles and bayonets, and therefore BSA also requested an export license to Greece. In making its case, BSA pointed out that an order of 100,000 rifles should employ a minimum of 1,125 men per week for two years at an approximate wage of $14.49 (£3) per week, making the total of wages paid per annum nearly $816,270 (£169,000). If BSA should get an order for 200,000 rifles, then the firm would employ about 1,495 men per week for three years making the total of wages paid per annum about $1.087 million (£225,000). These figures concerned direct labor in the BSA factory only, and did not take into account any additional employment created in the supply of raw materials, or transport. The company also requested that the British government grant an irrevocable license for the full period of production (two-three years) rather than the customary three-month period. In the event that the government did not grant an irrevocable license, then BSA requested some form of indemnity to compensate the factory for its loss should the export license be withdrawn.[32] On this occasion, the government gave no promise of an indemnity but raised no objection to BSA licenses for Lithuania or Greece, although it voiced the usual warning regarding Greece that "our only preoccupation is that we should not countenance any evasion by Greece of her financial obligations. So long as she pays for her rifles out of ordinary budget surplus, we have nothing to say."[33]

British officials did take to heart the BSA complaint about the insufficient time limits of export licenses. The Baldwin Cabinet decided in early August 1925 that the BOT should have power to grant firms licenses covering the full period of the contract (not just 3 months). Otherwise, British manufacturers would have to confine themselves to taking only small orders and refusing the most valuable ones. In deciding to now grant long-term licenses, the Cabinet noted that "we shall be putting ourselves in the rather ridiculous position of giving the diplomatic assistance to firms to obtain contracts and then denying them the necessary facilities for carrying them out."[34]

Meanwhile, in Greece, Vickers's and Armstrong's pursuit of military orders once again encountered frustration rooted in Greek financial difficulties and French countermoves. British contracts for Greek machine gun and machine rifle orders held some promise. In February 1925,

---

[32] FO 371/10975, Carr (Riga) to FO, July 18, 1925; FO 371/10975 BSA to BOT, July 24, 1925; FO 371/10975, BSA Director H. W. R. Tarrot to BOT, July 24, 1925.
[33] FO 371/10975, Austen Chamberlain to BOT (Conloffe-Lister), July 30, 1925.
[34] FO 371/10975, Cabinet. Licenses for Export of Arms, August 4, 1925.

the Greek Army dangled the prospect of large rifle orders similar to the BSA discussions. The Greek Army proposed to purchase from Vickers 200,000 rifles, 3,000 machine rifles, and 1,000 machine guns with a contract price around $9.66 million (£2 million). If the British made financing available, the Greeks would add another $9.66 million (£2 million) for artillery. Vickers was to supply 6,000 Berthier rifles with payment to be paid in Greek Treasury bonds. Armstrong and Beardmore also competed, but the Vickers gun had given the best test results. Greek tests determined that the best light machine guns were Madsen, Hotchkiss, and Vickers (Berthier). Among those three, Vickers tendered the best price at $173.88 compared to Hotchkiss's $237.15, and Vickers offered good terms of payment with 25 percent at signing, 60 percent on delivery, and balance due within two years. The British Minister in Athens, Milne Cheetham, made representations to the Greek Prime Minister and Minister of War, General Pangalos, in the interests of Vickers. However, the French appeared as the most dangerous competitors in both weapons categories thanks to the influence they exerted on the Greek military authorities through the French Military Mission. Indeed, General Girard of the French Military Mission also served as the local representative of the Hotchkiss firm, and he actively worked to look after their interests. Such professional support helped ensure that the order for heavy machine guns went to Hotchkiss. Vickers lost out on its contract for 1,200 Berthier automatic rifles and 600 land service machine gun to Hotchkiss owing to intervention of French Military Mission.[35]

When in 1925 the Greek proposal for the reconstruction of their navy contemplated raising a loan on the London market, the British Treasury almost immediately registered its opposition to the Greek program with the British Foreign Office. Under the Geneva Protocol and the prospectus of the Greek Refugee Loan, the Greek government had pledged not to create any charges on its revenues by way of security for any loans except such as for productive purposes or for carrying out its obligations under the Treaty of Peace. Also, under the War Debt Agreement the Greek government could not assign any security for a loan without the consent of Britain, France, and the US. The Greek naval proposal would require a credit of $24.15 million (£5 million) with deferred payments over fifteen to twenty years for four destroyers, four submarines, and four coastal motor boats. The Greeks expressed their desire to place the whole program with British firms if they could find the necessary

---

[35] FO 286/937, Vincent Caillard to Chamberlain, February 23, 1925; FO 286/937, British Legation to C. Goulimy, December 15, 1925; Milne Cheetham to Austen Chamberlain, November 17, 1925; VA, Microfilm R286, Orders obtained by Agelasto since July 1923.

credit.[36] Treasury urged the Foreign Office to "pour the coldest of cold water on this insanity."[37] Realistically, Greece had no chance of obtaining such a loan, but Treasury worried that even talk of the project would affect negatively Greece's financial situation. Greece faced a deficit budget in the next year and had a very dangerous floating debt problem. The mere talk of the naval program could jeopardize Greek financial reconstruction, and therefore Treasury wanted Cheetham, to "dissuade them in the most energetic terms, if you want there to be a Greece."[38] Meanwhile, the Greek Foreign Minister, Rentis, appealed to Cheetham to support the Greek naval program on strategic grounds. Noting the obvious geographic position of Greece as a naval base in the Eastern Mediterranean and Greece's rich maritime reserve, Rentis argued that British interests would be better served if Greece had an effective, powerful navy to assure the security of these territories, and he presented the Greek naval program as an important factor in maintaining the peace and as an instrument "to safeguard European civilization in these seas."[39]

British policy makers fully understood that their opposition to Greek defense orders could seriously undermine British influence in that country. In urging the Greek government to adopt a more modest naval program, Britain made it more likely that at least part of the order would find its way into French or Italian hands.[40] Cheetham reported from Athens that the new Greek naval minister, Admiral Hatzikyriakos, personally inclined toward France, and whichever country secured the present naval contract would hold a preponderance of influence in the Greek Navy with a monopoly of construction. In response, Austen Chamberlain remarked in a confidential note, "You will realize that we anticipate extravagance on the part of new government and do not wish to be the first to encourage that extravagance. League of Nations protocol and 1918 agreement must be strictly maintained."[41]

Treasury played the decisive role in nixing British naval sales to Greece. Strategic arguments held water with the British Admiralty and the Foreign Office, as neither wanted to see Greece fall under the sway of France or Italy. Given the divisions among British policy makers, Treasury, Admiralty, Board of Trade, and the Foreign Office held an interdepartmental meeting in August 1925 to coordinate British policy. The precipitating action for the meeting was a proposal from the

[36] FO 286/937, O. E. Niemeyer (Treasury) to Admiralty, July 24, 1925; FO 286/937, C. Townsend (Head of British Naval Mission Greece) to Admiralty, May 28, 1925.
[37] FO 286/937, O. E. Niemeyer (Treasury) to Harold Nicolson (FO), February 4, 1925.
[38] Ibid.   [39] FO 286/937, Rentis (Greek Foreign Minister) to Cheetham, July 9, 1925.
[40] FO 286/937, E. Keeling (Athens) to FO, July 26, 1925.
[41] FO 286/937, Milne Cheetham to Chamberlain, July 9, 1925.

British shipbuilding firm John Brown to undertake the Greek business if the British government would provide a guarantee. Treasury was first to oppose it, whereas the Admiralty and the Board of Trade supported the Greek business on naval and commercial lines and the Foreign Office supported it on political grounds. Treasury prevailed, and instructed the Foreign Office to tell Browns they could not do it. The Foreign Office lamented handing Greece over to France and Italy, "but the Treasury are adamant on the subject, and we are powerless against them."[42] As a result, the British Foreign Office reminded Rentis in September 1925 that the British Trade Facilities Act of 1921 which provides for financial guarantees by HMG Treasury to loans raised for industrial purposes specifically excluded from its provisions loans used for the manufacture of munitions of war.[43]

The position of British naval firms in Greece was further harmed by difficulties with the Vickers torpedo-boat destroyers. Greek naval officers complained that because Vickers had subcontracted the work for the torpedo tubes to Armstrong, the four ships were incomplete. During a diplomatic crisis with Turkey in 1925, Vickers had pressured the Greeks to accept delivery of the four ships without the tubes. The seriousness of Greek dissatisfaction with Vickers threatened to jeopardize the decision of the Greek Naval Ministry that only British firms would be given naval contracts. Sure enough a few months later the Greek government signed an additional contract in Athens with French firms for three submarines of 710 tons displacement priced at $555,450 (£115,000) with delivery in two years.[44] The Greeks went with the French submarines because they were half the price of British tenders, although smaller vessels. The Greek government adopted the attitude that since the British would not help with financing the bigger program, they had no choice but to fill the minimum naval requirements by purchasing in the cheapest market and "what was good enough for France is good enough for Greece."[45]

At the start of 1926, Armstrong took a turn and approached the BOT about receiving a license for export of war materiel to Greece. In January 1926, the BOT raised no political objection to the Greek sale, just the recurring financial objection.[46] Into the spring of 1926, the Greeks continued to indicate that they would prefer to buy their war materiel

[42] FO 286/937, FO to Keeling, August 10, 1925.
[43] FO 286/937, E. Keeling to Rendis (Greek Minister of Foreign Affairs), September 26, 1925.
[44] FO 286/937, Vice Admiral Webb to ADM, March 9, 1925; FO 286/937, Athens to FO November 17, 1925.
[45] FO 286/937, Milne Cheetham to FO, October 12, 1925.
[46] FO 371/11347, FO to BOT, January 19, 1926, encl. T. H. Dent, Director Armstrong to H. Fountain, BOT, January 14, 1926.

from Britain as they considered the quality of British items the best. At the same time due to financial considerations, the Greeks had to buy in the cheapest market unless they could obtain credit. French and Italian firms consistently undercut British manufactures' prices, and the French and Italians were ready to give credit with little, if any, security. The British government could not assist the British armament firms with credits under the terms of the Trade Facilities Act. Nor would British banks advance money except under adequate security, which the Greeks could not provide on account of the stringent provisions of the Greek Refugees Loan Protocol. The Treasury, however, raised no objection to the sale of armaments to Greece, provided the finance could be obtained and provided that the purchases did not endanger the equilibrium of the Greek budget, which the Greek government undertook also under the Refugees Loan protocol to do their utmost to balance. On one hand, the British government was anxious to assist Armstrong's sale of $7.245 million (£1.5 million) worth of munitions to Greece, if only to relieve unemployment. On the other hand, "There is reason to believe, however, that public opinion in Greece might become indignant at the expenditure of this large sum in England when the goods desired could be obtained more cheaply elsewhere."[47]

In May 1926, C. C. Farrar at Overseas Trade again weighed in against arms sales to Greece. While reminding the Foreign Office that "with a possible exception of certain aviation cases, Overseas Trade has never pressed the Legation to support armament firms in Greece,"[48] Overseas Trade laid out the pros and cons of supporting British armament firms. While acknowledging that British firms were very short of work, and that Greece had shown itself determined to get arms somewhere, somehow, Overseas Trade conceded that certain naval and military advantages might follow from the adoption of armaments manufactured in Great Britain. Nevertheless, the deplorable state of Greek finances meant that it seemed very doubtful Greece could pay for these orders without long credit, which neither the British government nor private firms could provide. Any payments made would be at the expense of numerous private creditors of Greece and HMG, and such expenditure would harm the economic condition of the country. In conclusion, Overseas Trade found that "Lobbying for these orders forms a bad precedent... If we were to attempt to compete with the French etc we should have to stoop

---

[47] FO 371/11345, Foreign Office Minute (Blond) Supply and Munitions to Greek Government by Armstrongs, Whitworths, Encl Blond, March 11, 1926.

[48] FO 371/11345, C. C. Farrar (Dept. of Overseas Trade) to Howard Smith (FO), May 25, 1926.

to degrading methods," and thus ultimately the government's position should be negative.[49]

In the end, the rifle business came to nothing for the British firms. Instead, the Greeks under Pangalos placed their order for 100,000 rifles with an Italian firm at Brescia. The British Foreign Office found it difficult to believe that the Greeks had the cash, and so they would need to arrange of a credit with the Italian government for the purchase of rifles. BOT's prescience proved correct as the Greeks cancelled the order (along with the Schneider artillery order) in April 1926 for reasons of economy. Finally, in January 1928, the Greek War Minister resigned due to inability to obtain sufficient credits for the army and because of delays in delivery of Italian rifles ordered by Pangalos on August 14, 1925.[50] As Farrar had warned about Greece back in 1923, "It seems to me preposterous that the Greeks should affect indignation, in view of their past financial history, if asked to put up a proper security... they will always rescind any contract if it is inconvenient to pay."[51]

Given the reluctance of the British government to support the armaments business, especially on the financial end, British firms found themselves largely left to their own resources. The first half of the twenties appeared particularly bleak. In 1921, the Vickers board glumly noted in its annual report that, "The Armament business of the Company, except foreign order for armor plate received from Japanese government, was virtually stagnant."[52] Vickers experienced a severe depression 1920–1926. With no foreign armament work to speak of except the Japanese order for armor, and the British government suspending work on four battle cruisers to comply with the Washington Naval Treaty of 1922, Vickers had to let workers go. The firm was forced to draw heavily from its carry forward funds in order to survive.[53]

At roughly the same time as Schneider's moves in Czechoslovakia, Vickers looked to take up the struggle for export markets with special attention to establishing plants in Eastern Europe. In 1919, the Polish government had wanted to establish Starachowice as a domestic plant for the production of artillery, rifles and ammunition, and the next year the Poles made agreements with Vickers and Schneider to provide technical and financial assistance to Starachowice. Unfortunately, work did

[49] Ibid.
[50] FO 286/937, Keeling to Chamberlain, August 15, 1925; FO 371/11345, Foreign Office Minute (Blond) Supply and Munitions to Greek Government by Armstrongs, Whitworths, March 11, 1926; FO 371/11345, Cheetham to Austen Chamberlain, June 16, 1926; FO 286/1034, Athens to FO, January 25, 1928.
[51] FO 371/11345, Encl C. C. Farrer (Overseas Trade) to FO, December 1923.
[52] VA, File 1480, Annual Reports and Accounts Vickers Ltd., 1921.
[53] J. D. Scott, *Vickers: A History* (London: Weidenfeld and Nicolson, 1962), 143–144.

not go smoothly there, and as of 1925 Vickers had received only meager contracts totaling $275,310 (£57,000). A similar story played out in Yugoslavia, where Vickers participated in Sartid (Société Serbe Minière et Industrielle Yugoslavia), a joint venture with the Yugoslav government, starting in 1922. Sartid, too, turned out paltry results yielding Vickers profits of $3,600 (£800) in 1923–1924 and $7,072 (£1,600) in 1924–1925. Vickers and Armstrong had recovered their rights in the Ottoman Dock Works in April 1920, but after 1921 that business lost money and Vickers and Armstrong left Turkey in October 1923. By far Vickers's most significant attempt as part of that strategy involved Romania, which Sir Vincent Caillard deemed the best place for British industry to establish itself.[54] Specifically, Vickers involved itself in establishing Romanian armaments works in Copsa-Mica and Cugir (CMC) under the administration of the Resita Engineering Company.

Resita was located on ethnically Hungarian territory of the Banat and had been part of the former Austro-Hungarian State Railway Co. After the war the territory had been transferred to Romania, becoming the only steelmaking place in country. After nationalizing the Railway Company, Romania offered shares to Vickers. The Prime Minister of Romania, the Liberal Party leader Ion Brătianu, and Prince Barbu Stirbey (who was the brother-in-law of the Prime Minister's brother, Vintila Brătianu) believed the time had come for Romania to develop its own arms factory. Adalbert Veith, the Director of Resita, proposed bringing in Vickers, along with Romanian banks, Steyr, Manfred Weiss, Astra Co., and Nobels. Veith's proposal called for Vickers to provide machinery and technical assistance. The Romanian government's plan was designed to lead Romania gradually to independence from foreign armament imports by employing Resita to a certain limited extent, but also applying to England and to France with a view to constructing appropriate armaments works in Romania. These works would be situated as far as possible from a probable enemy frontier, and in locations near to coal and iron mines. The Romanians deemed it prudent to have the support of English and French institutions and capital, but desired that the English and French groups should establish themselves in different parts of the country.[55]

---

[54] Scott, 149; R. P. T. Davenport-Hines, "Vickers' Balkan Conscience Aspects of Anglo-Romanian Armaments 1918–39," *Business History*, vol. 25, no. 3 (1983), 287.

[55] VA, Microfilm R286, Copsa-Mica Company, August 27, 1928. VA, Microfilm R284, Douglas Vickers, Memorandum of Conversation with Mr. Veith on the Subject of his letter of December 4, 1923, December 14, 1923; Davenport-Hines, 295; VA, Microfilm R284, Basil Zaharoff to Douglas Vickers, February 14, 1924.

During 1924, Vickers mulled over the Romanian project while aspects of the proposal and the role of its participants changed. Steyr expressed no interest whatsoever in the Romanian factory. The Austrian firm previously had disposed of a great part of its machinery and now lacked competent foremen to run such a factory. The Romanian government had come to reject the idea of making arms at Resita because of its vulnerable proximity near the frontier in an area not ethnically purely Romanian, i.e., Hungarian.[56] For the Vickers firm, Basil Zaharoff told Prince Stirbey his reservations that "my experience for many years past had been that whenever any of our money had gone abroad we did not easily see it again."[57] Sir Douglas Vickers based his concerns on his assessment that the comparatively small needs of Romania could be readily met from Resita, but building a larger complex of factories would exceed Romania's financial wherewithal.[58] Sir Douglas considered the scale of the Romanian proposal overly grand and ambitious, "but something might be done with advantage to them and to us. The idea is that Resita should occupy the directing position, which is very good from our point of view."[59]

Vickers's involvement in Romania grew with the signing of the Paris Convention drawn up between Sir Douglas Vickers and Veith, the administrator of the Resita Company on January 29, 1925. The initial capital was $15.9 million (300 million lei) for forty years, and Vickers pledged to provide the machinery to equip the two factories in Romania. The first at Copsa-Mica proposed to manufacture guns up to .305, along with shells, and tanks, and the second at Cugir would make, rifles, machine guns, and automatic rifles. The Romanian government also entered into an Agreement of Cooperation with Vickers Ltd. and the Resita Co. to establish works to make armaments and ammunition. Vickers promised to supply old war machinery lying at their works which was not required, Resita would supply machinery for shells, and the Romanian government would supply machinery from the old Hungarian Arsenal at Gyor. Furthermore, the Romanian government guaranteed a dividend of 7 percent for ten years and thereafter 6 percent. Vickers would receive about $3.9 million (75 million lei) and balance in shares. Pending completion of the factory, the Romanian government promised to order any materiel it needed from Resita in the interim. Vickers also pledged to deliver surplus machinery at Copsa-Mica as a new state plant. Given Vickers's financial difficulties 1923–1926, the opportunity

[56] VA, Microfilm R284, Veith to D. Vickers, November 28, 1924.
[57] VA, Microfilm R284, Basil Zaharoff to Douglas Vickers, February 14, 1924.
[58] Davenport-Hines, 298.
[59] VA, Microfilm R284, Douglas Vickers to Zaharoff, February 9, 1924.

to drop depreciated, obsolete war surplus capacity to the tune of roughly $1.5 million (£320,000) served as the most important element in Vickers's Romanian strategy.[60] Keeping foreign rivals at bay also played a role in Vickers's decision as "It was obvious at the time that if Vickers had not entered into the business, their place would have been taken by Škoda or Schneider."[61] In April, the Vickers Board approved taking a share interest in Resita worth $510,633 (£115,528), and Sir Douglas Vickers was elected vice president of Resita in May 1924. The constitution of the Copsa-Mica & Cugir Company, drawn up after the Paris Convention and published on April 1, 1925, placed all management authority in an executive committee rather than the board of directors. As a result, Vickers lacked any formal representation in the executive committee, although Captain E. G. Boxshall, the English son-in-law of Prince Stirbey, informally monitored Vickers's interests in Copsa-Mica.[62]

Despite Vickers's higher level of commitment to its Romanian venture than its other East European ones, the results from Romania proved just as disappointing through 1926. Vickers had been unable to come to a final decision as to rifle machines to be handed to Romanian company at Copsa-Mica because the layout previously prepared was based on the Serbian rifle. Then in 1926, the Romanian government changed its mind and instead wanted the factory to produce the Russian 7.62mm model rifle. Douglas Vickers assured Veith that Vickers hoped to satisfy the Romanian government's request for a complete plant, even at the expense of Vickers's own plant retained at Crayford. Alternatively, Vickers had a large quantity of jugs, tools, and gauges made for the Russian rifle by Pratt and Whitney sitting in storage in America. The Romanian government did not even begin constructing the Cugir works until 1926. In any case, converting old Russian guns did not generate meaningful profits, and the total fees and profits for Vickers from Resita remained trivial. Total orders placed with Vickers in England through CMC for the years 1925 and 1926 only had yielded a profit of just under $192,000 (£40,000).[63]

Whatever woes Vickers was suffering, their rivals Armstrong Whitworth were in even worse shape. In 1925, Latvia had ordered $192,000 (£40,000) worth of surplus artillery from Armstrong, but the firm had

[60] FO 371/12977, Goodden (mil attaché) to British Legation Bucharest, April 16, 1928; VA, File 1368, Minute Book of Board Meeting. Vickers Ltd., February 27, 1925; Davenport-Hines, 300.
[61] VA, Microfilm R286, Copsa-Mica Company, August 27, 1928.
[62] VA, File 1367, Minute Book of Board Meeting, Vickers Ltd., April 27, 1924; Scott, 148; Davenport-Hines, 301–302.
[63] VA, Microfilm R286, Douglas Vickers to Veith, May 26, 1926; Scott, 149; Davenport-Hines, 303.

not built and sold any new artillery since 1918. As their conditions had grown more desperate, the two rivals had begun to cooperate in seeking foreign orders. In May 1924, Vickers and Armstrong had entered a working agreement whereby the two firms acted in concert for armaments orders in South America, Japan and China, Spain and Portugal, Greece, and Turkey. Each firm upon receipt of a foreign enquiry would inform the other before submitting its offer, and the two firms would send separate pricings after having consulted with each other. Any work coming through this agreement would be shared. The meager fruits of Vickers's Greek business thus yielded Armstrong a subcontracted order for Greek torpedo tubes in 1925. In July 1926, the Yugoslav government made a cash offer for two submarines to be built by Armstrong with a total price of approximately $2.2 million (£458,000): 15 percent on order, 10 percent four months later, 25 percent on May 31, 1927, and remaining 50 percent on delivery September 30, 1927, with all payments made in sterling.[64] Unfortunately, as the British Ambassador in Yugoslavia, Howard Kennard, reported in August, "Armstrong have got into a bad mess over this business." Specifically, the Yugoslav specifications called for a diving depth of 250 feet, and the Yugoslav naval authorities insisted on the submarines diving to a depth of 150 feet on trial. However, Armstrong would only accept the Admiralty specification of 100 feet. Armstrong's refusal to dive to 150 feet raised Yugoslav doubts about their product. Kennard continued:

Either their assurances were genuine or if not, they should frankly admit that it would not be safe to go so deep. Supposing as the result of these assurances, all the bigwigs of the Yugoslav Navy went down to 200 feet and never came up again! . . . I do not think that Armstrongs have behaved quite frankly with the Yugoslavs in this matter . . . it is quite possible that they may lose the contract by their evasion. It certainly is uphill work assisting British firms, especially when the competition is so strong and French and other firms are using every kind of pressure. No doubt the latter will offer a diving depth of 300 feet without regard for actual performance, but we have a reputation for straightforward dealing which I fear is not enhanced by these methods.[65]

Ultimately, Yugoslavia did continue working with Armstrong to construct the two submarines at Elswick, and Yugoslavia made regular payments. Nonetheless, Armstrong's difficulties getting and keeping sales fed financial losses so large that the Bank of England effectively took

[64] FO 371/10975, Lloyd (mil attaché) to Vaughn (Baltic), August 4, 1925; Vaughn to FO, September 10, 1925; VA, Microfilm R284 Armstrong – Vickers Working Agreement, May 26, 1924; FO 286/937, Vice Admiral Richard Webb to ADM, March 9, 1925; FO 371/11411, Howardsmith to FO, July 5, 1926.
[65] FO 371/11411, Howard Kennard to Howardsmith, August 17, 1926.

ownership in 1926 when the firm owed \$12.48 million (£2.6 million) and was facing receivership.[66]

By 1926, Britain's two biggest armaments firms, Vickers and Armstrong, faced a crisis. With their armaments factories operating at less than 40 percent capacity, the two firms proposed a merger on June 22, 1927, and sought the blessing and support of the British government. If Vickers and Armstrong did not continue as the primary manufacturers of armaments in the country, Britain would lose the vast skill and experience attained. In the opinion of both firms and their advisers, fusion of the two works coupled with the cooperation of the British government seemed the only solution. The merger would include Vickers's Barrow Works, Sheffield Works, Erith Works, and Dartford Works combined with Armstrong's main works at Elswick, the Openshaw Naval Shipyard, and the Walker Shipyard. The new company, Vickers–Armstrong, desired to have assurance of minimum profits of \$6.125 million (£1.25 million) annually from the government. To achieve that, the companies suggested that the government should pay a rental to retain those portions of the armaments works with minimal staffing. Otherwise those highly valuable skilled departments would have to be dismantled. If the government would agree to pay rent of \$1.47 million (£300,000) annually for five years to maintain the capacity, the companies believed that by the end of that period the internal economies, which should be possible through the rearrangement of works and plant, would enable Vickers–Armstrong to reassume the whole burden after the five-year period. Alternatively, the companies proposed that the government guarantee or purchase profit notes of the new company to the sum of \$1.47 million (£300,000) per year for five years.[67]

The Admiralty recognized the value of preserving the production lines in both firms, but had no interest in the state taking part in the merger. In case of war, the Royal Navy required the retention of the whole of the present gun mounting shops of both firms, and unless the personnel of both firms were kept together and given continuity of employment on this work during peace time, the works would be of little use in the first year of a big war as the skilled men would have lost their capacity both in design and production for rapid and efficient work. The Admiralty therefore deemed it essential that orders in peace time should continue to be divided between the shops at Barrow and those at Elswick. The

---

[66] FO 371/12219, Kenwood to Austen Camberlain, February 2, 1927; Scott, 152, 161.
[67] CAB 27/353, Committee on Armament Firms. Vickers–Armstrong Fusion Scheme. Vickers and Armstrongs. Memorandum re proposed Merger, William Plender, Independent Chairman of the Joint Committee of Vickers Ltd. and Sir Wm. G. Armstrong, Whitworth and Co. Ltd., June 22, 1927.

gun making and gun mounting plant of both Vickers and Armstrong were essential to meet Admiralty requirements. Nevertheless, in Admiralty's view, Vickers, by a more judicious management of their resources and by a successful reorganization after a drastic writing down of capital, now found itself in a sound position to continue its business without any extraneous help, In contrast, the Admiralty had a negative assessment of Armstrong, which "by unfortunate speculations and disastrous fresh undertakings since the Armistice, find themselves in a position where they are faced with liquidation unless some substantial government assistance can be provided. The facts as at present before them do not seem to the Admiralty to warrant the proposed merger . . . Vickers might themselves purchase this essential plant."[68]

The Air Ministry and War Office also opposed any state commitment to the merger. The Air Ministry had less interest in the proposed merger since the branches of the two businesses manufacturing aeronautical materiel, Vickers Works at Weybridge (aircraft) and Armstrong-Siddeley Works at Coventry (aircraft and engines) would remain independent and unaffected by the merger. Moreover, Air observed that Armstrong and Vickers were but two out of seventeen firms, which manufactured aircraft for the RAF, and orders for new machines and engines had for some years been insufficient to secure adequate financial return to all seventeen. The Air Ministry constantly received representatives pleading for help to keep export staff and maintain shops, and therefore Air worried about setting the precedent of a definite monetary subsidy. If Armstrong and Vickers received special consideration, it would be difficult to resist future claims from some of the aircraft firms. If the government took the decision to assist Armstrong, then Air Ministry would "much prefer a solution on the lines recommended by the War Office . . . a definite program of orders extending over a period of years."[69]

In the end, Vickers proceeded into the merger with Armstrong without direct government participation, and Vickers–Armstrong Ltd. came into existence October 31, 1927. Lacking the government guarantee for the merger, the Bank of England arranged for the Sun Insurance Company to issue a policy to guarantee a certain level of profits. Specifically, the insurance policy obligated that if Vickers–Armstrong profits fell below $4.4 million (£900,000) in any given year during the five-year policy

---

[68] CAB 27/353, Committee on Armament Firms. Vickers–Armstrong Fusion Scheme. Note by First Lord of the Admiralty, July 21, 1927.

[69] CAB 27/353, Committee on Armament Firms. Vickers–Armstrong Fusion Scheme. Note by the Secretary of State for Air, July 25, 1927.

term, then Sun Insurance would make up the difference up to a maximum payment of \$980,000 (£200,000) in any one year.[70]

The newly constituted Vickers–Armstrong company continued to encounter difficulties in Greece regarding the destroyer contracts, but this time they lost to the Italians. In April 1928, two representatives from the British firm set off on a journey through southeastern Europe in search of business. Upon arriving in Athens, they met with the British ambassador there. Vickers–Armstrong was ready to make an offer for the Greek naval orders, but that they could not go to their financial people until they knew definitely whether the Greeks were going to do business or not. Subsequently, Sir Percy Loraine, the British Minister in Athens, met with the Greek Foreign Minister and asked unofficially that Greece place its order for four destroyers with British firms as a sign of appreciation for the financial help obtained from Britain. Sir Percy advocated that the superior quality of British-built destroyers more than compensated for their higher prices compared to French or Italian built ships. Unfortunately for Vickers–Armstrong, price and financing once again worked to the detriment of their sales. The Greeks ended up placing contracts with the Italians for all four destroyers.[71]

After having absorbed Armstrong in the merger, Vickers decided to review its foreign commitments in Romania. In February 1928, Sir General Noel Birch, the new head of Vickers, began making arrangements to be immediately co-opted as a member of the Resita Board and the Copsa-Mica Board so as to enable him to take part in next board meeting scheduled for April 1928. From the Romanian side, the president of Resita, Prince Barbu Stirbey, and the Resita Board felt dissatisfaction about liaison with Vickers. Stirbey anxiously desired that Vickers should take some financial interest in Resita and wanted Sir Mark Webster Jenkinson to join the board. Sir General Noel Birch came to Bucharest with Douglas Vickers to attend the annual board meeting of Resita Engineering Co. as new board directors representing Vickers–Armstrong. Having expressed their own dissatisfaction with the Resita agreement as too costly, the men from Vickers were surprised to learn that the Resita Board had been in communication with Škoda and invited the Czech firm to join the combination.[72]

---

[70] Scott, 165–166.
[71] FO 286/1034, Howard Smith to Loraine, October 25, 1928; FO 286/1034, Percy Loraine to Austen Chamberlain, December 20, 1928; *Conway's All the World's Fighting Ships, 1922–1946* (London: Conway Maritime Press, 1980), 405.
[72] VA, Microfilm K612, Capt. Boxshall to Vickers–Armstrong, February 17, 1928; VA, Microfilm K612, Notes on visit of General Birch to Bucharest, April 19, 1928; FO 371/12977, Goodden (mil att) to British Legation Bucharest, April 16, 1928.

Apparently, Škoda had been intriguing for some time to be allowed
to get participation at the Resita Works as part of Loevenstein's strategy for Škoda to establish itself in plants of the Little Entente countries.
Of course, Vickers much preferred to be the sole partner in the artillery
business, but when the Romanian government got into much closer relations with the French government, it became clear that it was not worth
the struggle to keep Škoda out and that it would be best to bring them
in as associates in a friendly way. Škoda wanted in on terms comparable
to Vickers, i.e., to supply machinery which would be paid for in preference shares. Resita and the Romanian government now intended that
all artillery work currently being done at Resita should be transferred
to Copsa-Mica as it started production.[73] After much argument on the
Vickers side, it was agreed to study the idea of letting Škoda in, not as
the Chairman of Resita desired on equal terms with Vickers, but propor-
tional to the amount of money and material Škoda would willingly invest
into the Works. The Chairman of Resita then tried to reduce the percentages, which Vickers considered as the only decent thing agreed upon in
the Paris Convention. Vickers raised no objection to the transfer of work
from Resita to Copsa-Mica as long as some of the work undertaken by
Vickers was actually done by Copsa-Mica. However, Vickers would not
consider a general reduction of its percentages. According to Birch, "I
had a disagreement with Vickers (Douglas). He thought that Škoda was
a fool to come in. Škoda's manager, Levinshtein [sic], is not a fool and
the fact that at Copsa-Mica there is a natural supply of gas which will
save 500 tons of coal a day is one reason for his coming in. Another
is that I think Schneider and Škoda are snowed under with orders."[74]
Birch suggested that Vickers accept Škoda coming in, but on Vickers's
terms. "There is no doubt that Copsa Mica is a future danger to us but
I think it would be wrong to sink another $2.45 million (£500,000), in
spite of the natural gas, as we should, with only two directors, have very
little controlling influence."[75] Despite being extremely resentful of the
Czech interlopers, Vickers's directors conceded and allowed Škoda to
enter into Copsa-Mica and Cugir in first half of 1928.[76] Thus, Škoda
infiltrated what had begun as a British venture to establish a stronghold
in Romania.

The Škoda entry into the Romanian arsenals heralded a general
retreat by Vickers in that country. As of November 1928 the question of
machine guns for Romanian Army remained unresolved. The Averescu

---

[73] VA, Microfilm R286, Copsa-Mica Company, August 27, 1928.
[74] VA, Microfilm K612, Notes on visit of General Birch to Bucharest, April 19, 1928.
[75] Ibid.   [76] Davenport-Hines, 304.

government had held gun trials in May 1927 and the Romanian Military Commission had reported very strongly in favor of adopting the Czech machine gun. But the Averescu government was replaced by the Stirbey and Ion Brătianu government, which ignored previous trials and held a fresh series in November 1927. In the second trials, Praga (ČZB) and Madsen (Danish) gave equally excellent results: Hotchkiss and Châtellerault, and Browning were second class, and the Vickers-Berthier gun broke down.[77] Even though the Vickers gun had performed very poorly, Vickers–Armstrong appealed to the British Foreign Office to push back against French and Czech pressures for the machine gun order. In the view of the company, the Foreign Office should remind the Romanian government that Vickers–Armstrong had invested heavily in Romania by delivering over $1.5 million (£300,000) worth of machinery in exchange for shares in the Copsa-Mica and Cugir Arsenals as well as purchasing for cash a large interest in the Acieries et Domaines de Resita. Moreover, Vickers–Armstrong had an understanding with the Romanian government "that in consideration of this we should have preference in any armament orders which could not be executed in Romania."[78] When the British did not get the machine gun order, it became obvious that Vickers–Armstrong could not expect Romania to hold to its promises, nor should the firm hope that its industrial efforts within Romania would earn it any advantage in the eyes of the Romanian government. In June 1929, when Copsa-Mica & Cugir requested that Vickers ship the outstanding balance of machinery under their contract (plant worth $256,098 had still to be delivered, and it would cost $72,900 in order to recondition this equipment) Vickers had had enough. Taking into account that the Copsa-Mica Company owed Vickers dividends in respect of 1927 and 1928 in the amount of $58,048 (£11,944), Vickers informed Copsa-Mica that no further machinery would be delivered unless Vickers received its overdue dividends. The Vickers–Armstrong Board also decided to close the Resita Co. office in Bucharest. In 1931, Vickers sold its 150,000 shares of the Resita Company and gave up its equity in the venture. In lieu of direct investing, Vickers did entertain the idea of a technical assistance contract based on commission. In fall 1932, Vickers–Armstrong engaged in negotiations with the Resita Company to supply technical assistance in connection with the manufacture of artillery. Vickers–Armstrong would receive a commission of 2 percent on all guns and other materiel manufactured at the Resita Works. Two

[77] FO 371/12973, Greg (Bucharest) to Austen Chamberlain, March 9, 1928; Goodden (military attaché) to Minister Bucharest, April 17, 1928.
[78] FO 371/12973, Vickers–Armstrong to FO, November 9, 1928.

years later, those negotiations still had not yielded a definitive agreement. With nothing to show for its years in Romania, Vickers finally abandoned the field and sold its 328,315 shares in Copsa-Mica in 1936.[79]

By 1928, Vickers–Armstrong had confronted many years of disappointment in East European markets. The company had a pressing need for military orders. The volume of work in heavy gun mounting at the Barrow Works was decreasing, and the howitzer shop was not employed to full capacity. At the Erith Works orders for machine guns showed a very serious drop. Since machine guns had proved an especially remunerative manufacture, "a dearth of machinegun orders will have a considerable bearing on the factory profit."[80] Prospects appeared dark as the Vickers-Berthier machine rifle had only been adopted in Latvia and Bolivia.[81] Surprisingly, the firm found its greatest success at the end of the decade not in naval sales, but rather in land armaments, and the major customer was Turkey.

In spring 1928, the Turkish Army stood on the brink of a major armaments modernization. General Emin Pasha of the Turkish Military Mission informed Birch confidentially, that the Turkish Army had reached a turning point as regards its future armament, and the decisions made about the adoption of standard weapons systems would shape Turkish purchases for years to come. Emin Pasha bluntly told Birch that "financial considerations are not less important for Turkey than the type and quality of the armament . . . the financial considerations might be the determining factors rather than the slight superiority of certain make or type."[82] By July, the Turks formally announced their army purchase program which included 75mm mountain guns, antiaircraft guns, and 105mm field howitzers. The conditions of payment would amount to $4.8–9.6 million (TL 1–2 million) as advance during 1928, 50 percent by time of complete delivery, and full payment of the whole order in six years, with delivery within one to three years. Preliminarily, the Turks had bracketed Vickers–Armstrong with Schneider as first class firms, while they deemed Škoda second class, and Bofors third class. The Turks considered Vickers's antiaircraft materiel the best, but preferred Schneider for field guns. They also highly regarded the Škoda mountain guns. The whole order probably would not go to a single firm. The Turks were

[79] VA, File 1222, Board Minutes. Vickers–Armstrongs Ltd., June 6, 1929; VA, File 534 Foreign Investments; VA, File 167, Factory Reports to Directors, Fourth Quarter 1932; VA, File 172, Vickers–Armstrong quarterly report on Military and Air Armament First Quarter 1934, Sir George Hadcock.

[80] VA, File 148, Vickers–Armstrong Ltd. Factory Reports for the Quarter ended March 24, 1928.

[81] VA, Microfilm R286, Minutes of Army Sales Committee, May 3, 1928.

[82] VA, Microfilm K617, A. Vahid Bey to Noel Birch, March 23, 1928.

moving quickly. By mid-July, they were already fixing up shell orders for 100,000 rounds for 75mm mountain guns with Škoda at price of $15.65 (£3.43) per round.[83]

Hurriedly, Birch and other Vickers–Armstrong representatives left for Turkey. The company board had preapproved payment terms designed to please the Turks: 50 percent contract price by time of delivery complete in three years, 50 percent in equal installments during three years after delivery completion. The estimated value of the contract, including 15 percent profit, amounted to $10.01 million (£2,056,250). The board had instructed Sir Noel Birch that, if he found it necessary in order to secure the contract, he had authority to reduce the contract price by the amount of profit on the contract ($1.27 million or £260,944).[84] This last provision demonstrated how desperately Vickers wanted to gain entry to the Turkish market. The willingness to waive the profit in order to lower the bid price could ensure that Vickers landed the critical initial contract with the expectation that the coming years of Turkish follow-on contracts would more than compensate for the short-term lack of profit.

The first stages of tendering did not auger well for the British firm. Upon arriving in Ankara the Vickers team met with the Turkish Commission of the Trials Department. There the Vickers people encountered language problems as they could not find adequate Turkish terminology for the various parts of the guns, carriages and ammunition, and the Turks made up for their lack of knowledge by use of Krupp specifications. In November 1928, the Vickers–Armstrong Board approved terms of payment for a tender to Turkey for two destroyers and four submarines with a total value $7.96 million (£1,635,000) and built in profit of $1.286 million (£264,000) on contract. Instead, Turkey gave the order to the Italians. Next the Turks sought the mountain gun orders. On December 12, 1928, the Turkish Commission issued its call for prices. The firms submitted tenders as follows: Schneider ($4,650,000), Vickers ($4,230,000 -$4,178,000), Škoda ($4,200,000), and Bofors ($3,757,000). Evidently, price mattered most as the Turks gave the order to Bofors with a further reduction of $150,000. However, surreptitious financial dealings also may have played a role in that Bofors had financing through a certain Mr. Krueger, who made the Turks a loan with a stipulation concerning the match monopoly. According to Bofor's

---

[83] VA, Microfilm K617, Mustafa Abdul Halik (Turkish Minister of National Defense) to Vickers, July 2, 1928; Rept. on Visit to Turkey May–July 1928. Artillery program, July 12, 1928.

[84] VA, File 1222, Board Minutes. Vickers–Armstrongs Ltd., August 2, 1928.

manager, the order for the 75mm mountain guns constituted part of a deal between Krueger and the Turkish government.[85]

Beyond winning the immediate contract, Vickers–Armstrong placed tremendous value in reestablishing relations with Turkey for the supply of naval and military armaments lost since 1914. In May 1929, Sir Trevor Dawson went to Ankara to negotiate for contracts on the antiaircraft and naval orders worth $9.23 million (£1.9 million) including an estimated profit to Vickers–Armstrong of $777,600 (£160,000). Although Turkey's financial position was not the most robust, Vickers recognized that the Turks had never defaulted in respect of payments for munitions of war.[86] Yet, outstanding questions relating to prewar contracts cast a pall over Vickers–Armstrong's business prospects with Turkey. In 1914, the Ottoman government had paid for the battleship *Reshadieh*, but the British government had requisitioned the warship at the outbreak of the Great War. In October 1926, the Turkish government entered an action before the Mixed Tribunal of Constantinople against Vickers and Armstrongs over *Reshadieh*. The court heard the case in December 1928, and rejected the Turkish claim.[87] The battleship was just one of several naval contracts that Vickers and Armstrong had obtained for the Ottoman naval program. The British firms had received payments in the sum of $1.934 million (£397,528) (one battleship, two scouts, four torpedo-boat destroyers, two submarines) minus costs incurred of $491,163 (£100,952). The Turks wanted either the execution of the contract or repayment of the amount received with interest. Vickers–Armstrong knew it had an indefensible position. The British judge on the Mixed Tribunal offered the firm his legal advice that if Vickers–Armstrong contested the case, it would lose the action. Therefore, he urged the firm to settle the matter without delay so as to avoid suffering a great blow to its prestige. In light of those prospects, the Vickers–Armstrong Board determined its best course of action would be to offer to the Turkish government an offset in the range of $1.2–1.46 million (£250,000–300,000) if the Turks would grant them the order now under consideration. Alternatively, the company could execute the original contracts if the Turks were willing to observe all the conditions of the contracts, and also to revise the prices in view of present-day costs. There still remained yet another claim, in this instance by Vickers and Armstrong against Turkey regarding the Ottoman Dock

[85] VA, Microfilm K617, Tillotson, Visit to Angora, July 24 to August 25, 1928; VA, File 1222, Board Minutes. Vickers–Armstrongs Ltd., November 15, 1928; VA, Microfilm K617, Turkish Order. 184 75mm Mountain Equipments.

[86] VA, File 1223, Vickers–Armstrong Ltd. Minute Book of Board Meetings, Minutes, May 1, 1929. Turkish Business. Minute no. 232 (G. G. Sim).

[87] ADM 116/2589, Vickers–Armstrongs to ADM, June 28, 1929.

Company. This matter was heading for final arbitration in Switzerland, with Vickers–Armstrong claiming $2.8 million (£576,576) for expenditures and damages suffered. Realistically, if the firm won its case, it did not expect to receive more than $974,000 (£200,000). Given the importance of securing the new contract Vickers–Armstrong prepared to take over the net liability on these two disputed matters, "the loss being borne out of the profits and fixed charges on the new contract."[88]

Vickers–Armstrong's breakthrough occurred in July 1929 when the Turks awarded the firm a contract for sixty-four antiaircraft guns for the sum of $1.87 million (£385,000).[89] This contract marked the first order for land artillery ever received by the firm from Turkey. With the stakes high, Birch impressed upon management the need to make a very positive first impression by executing the order as efficiently as possible. Birch stressed the importance of establishing Vickers–Armstrong's reputation beyond the naval sphere, as he emphasized, "We have to make our name for army artillery weapons."[90] Even though the Turkish order brought some relief, the Barrow Works still faced financial difficulties. As the factory reported in September, "The recent contract from Turkey for 64 75mm equipments will not have much effect in the shops in retaining the skilled men before the end of the year, as the working drawings have yet to be prepared and material ordered up."[91]

Having finally opened the gate into the Turkish market, Vickers–Armstrong pressed on for more in December. With the firm poised to pick up enormous Turkish orders on land armaments between $9.72 million and $14.58 million (£2 and £3 million), Birch sought the approval and support of the British government. Specifically, he queried the Foreign Office:

Does the rule still operate that the Foreign Office can help us in no way with late enemy countries? Our chances of obtaining the orders in Turkey are about 50/50, and a little push one way of the other might make a great difference. If the rule is still in operation, then the less said about it the better. Of course I cannot tell whether diplomatic pressure would do good or harm, but everybody else is using it in the Mediterranean and they seem to be getting trade through it, though they are using other things behind diplomacy, guaranteeing credits, etc etc.[92]

---

[88] VA, File 1223, Vickers–Armstrong Ltd. Minute Book of Board Meetings, Minutes, May 1, 1929. Turkish Business. Minute no. 232 (G. G. Sim).

[89] VA, Microfilm K617, Noel Birch, July 14, 1929.

[90] VA, Microfilm K617, Noel Birch, Turkish order for Anti-aircraft Equipment, July 3, 1929.

[91] VA, File 154, Vickers–Armstrong Factory Reports for Quarter ended September 20, 1929.

[92] VA, Microfilm K616, Noel Birch to Bland (FO), December 7, 1929.

The Foreign Office raised no objection to doing business in Turkey.[93] Significantly, Birch decided at this juncture not to enlist British diplomatic support for his firm. As he wrote to the Foreign Office, "On thinking it over, I prefer to leave our Turkish prospects alone, especially as you say there will be no obstacle."[94] Rather than subjecting the Turks to a hard sell through diplomatic lobbying, Birch saw the key to Turkish contracts in settling the outstanding debts.[95] That course of action proved highly successful. Under an agreement December 23, 1929, Vickers–Armstrong paid the Turkish government $729,000 (£150,000) in full and final settlement of all matters outstanding.[96] In related developments, Elswick received an order for seventy 75mm guns and prospects were in sight for Turkish field gun orders in the sum of $7.63 million (£1,570,000).[97]

The importance of the Turkish orders in 1929 for Vickers–Armstrong cannot be overstated. Amounting to over $2.9 million (£600,000), these contracts made Turkey the single biggest client for the company in Eastern Europe during the twenties. Besides the magnitude of the orders, their timing also proved crucial. As the following table shows, Vickers experienced sharp drop in its foreign orders from a high of almost $21.87 million (£4.5 million) in 1927 down to under $4.87 million (£1 million) in 1928. Turkish orders comprised over one-third of all the firm's armaments exports in 1929, and helped boost Vickers–Armstrong's flagging sales and provided the company some breathing room. Even more importantly, the Turkish artillery sales served to establish the British firm as a major contender for land armaments in Eastern Europe (Table 2.2).

Certainly Britain lacked an overt multilateral disarmament policy,[98] but the British government's limited technical, financial, and diplomatic backing for British armaments firms effectively contributed to a kind of disarmament by default. Moreover, British laments about bad French behavior in the armaments business, along with Farrar's invocation of Washington and Geneva, bespeak an implicit desire to foster disarmament by example at least as it pertained to the private international armaments trade. Money is the life blood of the arms trade. Yet, on legal and policy grounds the British government repeatedly balked at

[93] VA, Microfilm K616, Bland (FO) to Birch, December 7, 1929.
[94] VA, Microfilm K616, Birch to Bland, December 12, 1929.
[95] VA, Microfilm K616, Birch to Bland, December 18, 1929.
[96] VA File 1369, Vickers Minute Book 1930–1933, January 21, 1930.
[97] VA, File 155, Vickers–Armstrong Factory Reports Fourth Quarter, 1929; VA, File 155, Noel Birch. Quarterly Rept on Military and Air Armament Sales, Fourth Quarter, 1929.
[98] Kitching, 20.

Table 2.2 *Vickers Armaments Contracts in Eastern Europe, 1925–1929, in Pounds Sterling*

	Greece	Latvia	Lithuania	Poland	Romania	Turkey	USSR	All Foreign Sales
1925	2,265	59,494	3,140	5,045	92,882	1,399	52	
1926	32,697	8,711	8,510	35,200	710	29	8,265	1,362,274
1927	9,810	19,216	7,682	148,332	321,971	12,073	1,100	4,457,034
1928	8,326	21,342	75,712	24,907	2,068	6,222	0	931,194
1929	39,619	44,896	17,064	9,794	2,989	604,938	0	1,619,014
Total	92,717	153,659	112,108	223,278	420,620	624,661	9,417	

Source: VA File 533, Armament contracts and expenses 1925–1937.

providing financial guarantees for the armaments business based on the restrictions imposed by the Trade Facilities Act. Left to make their own arrangements for financing, private British armaments firms considered their potential East European customers bad credit risks for making full payments on the short-term contracts desired. Time and again British firms failed to secure the final contracts because they refused to indulge their customers with more flexible payment schedules or lower prices. The French and their Czech partners on the other hand showed themselves willing and able to extend credit for the long-term payment plans preferred by those cash-strapped states.

3   The Škoda Scandal in Romania, 1930–1934

The Škoda scandal broke in Bucharest on March 10, 1933, when investigators from the Office of the Military Prosecutor called at the office of Bruno Seletzki, Škoda's representative in Romania, to probe for alleged financial irregularities. Upon discovering top secret Romanian military files in Seletzki's possession including ciphered documents, top secret ciphers, and the personnel files and evaluation reports of several high-ranking Romanian officers that could only have come from the War Ministry, these investigators notified civilian police, the Military Prosecutor, and the Prefecture of Police. Mihai Popovici, the Minister of Justice, and General Nicolae Uica, the Minister of War, then ordered an immediate halt of the investigation, and they instructed the investigators to replace the files and codes, release Seletzki, and leave the office. Popovici indicated that these instructions came from Prime Minister Alexander Vaida-Voevod. Before withdrawing from Seletzki's office, the investigators drew up a brief list of the kinds of files found in Seletzki's safe, procured some examples, and sealed the rest in the safe before allowing Seletzki to return to his office. Seletzki immediately broke the seal and destroyed most of the documents. Dr. Nicolae Lupu, a leading member of the National Peasant Party, brought the Seletzki affair to public attention when he raised the issue in Parliament two weeks later, thereby initiating a parliamentary investigation and producing a national scandal which would dominate Romanian politics for the next year.[1]

The scandal truly blew up when one of the implicated officers, General Dumitru "Gica" Popescu, committed suicide during the investigation. In 1929–1931, General Popescu, as Secretary-General of the Ministry of National Defense and acting directly under then-Defense Minister General Henric Cihoski, deliberately misrepresented the

---

[1] Larry L. Watts, *Romanian Cassandra, Ion Antonescu and the Struggle for Reform, 1916–1941* (New York: Columbia University Press, 1993), 61–62; see also R. Diestler, *Příběh zapomenutého průmyslníka: život a doba Karla Loevensteina, generálního ředitele Škodových závodů* (Praha: Grada, 2010), 85–89.

competitiveness of Škoda's merchandise by claiming that Schneider-Creusot's prices for the same items were more expensive than Škoda's when in reality, French arms were 1 percent cheaper and their munitions 22 percent cheaper than Škoda's. Popescu also "claimed that it would be impossible to receive better terms from Schneider-Creusot because they were in a cartel with Škoda."[2] The documents found in Seletzki's possession along with the irregularities in the negotiations and signing of the contract convinced the Parliamentary Commission to call for the investigation and trial of the former Defense Minister Cihoski, but the corruption extended beyond Cihoski to King Carol II because the King had granted himself prerogative of appointing the War Ministers. Before he committed suicide, Popescu wrote a number of letters in which he had indicated that General Constantin Stefanescu-Amza, the War Minister 1931–1932, had played a leading role in the scandal.[3]

On the surface, the Škoda scandal possesses all the elements of the "Merchants of Death" image, i.e., manufactured war scares, bribery, corruption, and fat contracts. In April 1933, *Time Magazine* reported that back in 1930 Romania had hurried to purchase large numbers of weapons prompted by a war scare over Soviet Russian machinations in Bessarabia, but now Peasant Party Leader Nicolae Lupu was accusing Seletzki of orchestrating the whole war scare and having bribed Romanian Army officers and politicians, specifically Premier Alexander Vaida-Voevod's son and a nephew of the Finance Minister, to obtain the orders.[4] The Škoda scandal quickly grew into an international *cause celeb* in the antiarmaments literature of the period. Fenner Brockway included it in his book noting the accusation that Seletzki bribed three Romanian ministers $508,800 (£120,000) on an order totaling $76.32 million (£18 million).[5] Other Merchants of Death literature also covered the scandal.[6]

The Seletzki case provides a prime opportunity to examine the operations of a "Merchant of Death" in action. Many of the general processes described by Fenner Brockway pertain in this instance, namely, an armament salesman inducing a small country to buy arms that it could

---

[2] Watts, 63.   [3] Ibid., 64.
[4] "Rumania Scandal without Carol," *Time Magazine*, April 10, 1933, 25.
[5] F. Brockway, *The Bloody Traffic* (London: Victor Gollancz, 1933), 143–145.
[6] H. C. Engelbrecht and F. C. Hanighen, *Merchants of Death: A Study of the International Armaments Industry* (New York: Dodd, Mead, 1934), 5, 194; G. A. Drew, *Salesmen of Death: The Truth about the War Makers* (Toronto: Women's League of Nations Association, 1933); League of Nations Union, *Profits in Arms* (London, 1934); R. Lewinsohn, *The Profits in War: Through the Ages* (New York: Dutton, 1936); P. J. Noel-Baker, *The Private Manufacture of Armaments*, vol. 1 (New York: Oxford University Press, 1936), 159–161, 167–69, 387.

not afford by taking loans from foreign banks.[7] The French government did turn to its banks and guaranteed the payments with the expectation of gaining political, military, and economic influence over Romania. Moreover, Seletzki did act as the culprit who drummed up a war scare and bribed Romanian officials. However, in its particulars the Škoda scandal deviates from the expected narrative in important ways. A thorough reading of the French Foreign Ministry documents, which include translations of the official transcripts of the Romanian deliberations in Chamber, reveals that despite French government advocacy for taking huge Romanian artillery contracts, Schneider-Creusot declined. French money went to purchase Czech weapons while Schneider-Creusot purposefully stood on the sidelines.

The Škoda scandal highlighted a culture of corruption in arms orders as a way of doing business in Eastern Europe generally and Romania in particular. As part of the Nye Committee investigation undertaken by the US Senate in 1934 to look into improprieties in the arms industry, the Committee gathered testimony from the Du Pont Company. Part of the evidence introduced included a letter from Du Pont's representative William N. Taylor assessing prospects for business in Eastern Europe in 1922. Taylor felt flummoxed by the business practices in the Balkans, which seemed so alien from American methods. He wrote:

If you draw a line from Trieste to Warsaw and go east of that line, you find the business and financial conditions run on a set of rules entirely their own, and if we can't conform to the situation, we won't be able to get any business. There, the ordinary business ethics are entirely different from ours and people have no knowledge of ours, they don't know what our business ethics mean . . . They don't much care what they pay so long as they get the graft, which is their main object.[8]

The Romanians held an especially poor reputation regarding graft. As Grant Harward described it, "Romanian stereotypes formed a unique Balkan stereotype: that of the crafty, lascivious, and infinitely corruptible Balkan Latin, a nation ruled by the bribe, morally bankrupt, and utterly incapable of competent self-administration or military competence."[9] Prior to the breaking of the Škoda scandal with the Romanian Army in

---

[7] Brockway, 22–23, 38–50, 202–203, 205, 262.

[8] William N. Taylor to Casey (Du Ponts), October 10, 1922; *Munitions Industry Hearings before the Special Committee Investigating the Munitions Industry, United States Senate Seventy-Third Congress Pursuant to S. Res. 206, A Resolution to Make Certain Investigation Concerning the Manufacture and Sale of Arms and Other War Munitions, Part 11, December 6, 7, and 10, 1934, Chemical Preparations Following the War and Interchange of Military Information* (Washington, DC: US Government Printing Office, 1935), 2595.

[9] G. T. Harward, "First among Un-Equals: Challenging German Stereotypes of the Romanian Army during the Second World War," *The Journal of Slavic Military Studies*, vol. 24, no. 3 (2011), 440.

1933, the other Romanian service branches also experienced brushes with impropriety. In September 1930, General Gorski of the Romanian Air Force related an incident to the British military attaché involving a silver cigarette box which had been sent round to his house. The card inside it was that of a representative of Hawker Engineering Co. and Sauders-Rose Ltd. This gentleman had visited General Gorski a day or two previously, but then disappeared. Because the card bore no address, the General had no way to return the box to him. General Gorski was "furious and said he supposed this was the method adopted in other Balkan countries; I have no doubt that he used the adjective 'Balkan' on purpose as Romanian dislike of being considered a Balkan country is well known."[10] The British military attaché concluded that "While the venality of Romanian administration in many fields is well known and admitted by themselves it appears to be an elementary lack of tact for representatives of foreign firms to be allowed to assume that such a state of affairs is so universal that a Romanian officer can be exposed without any finesse whatsoever to what a British officer would regard as a gross insult."[11] In 1932, the Romanian Navy refused to take delivery of submarine *Delfin* built for them at Quarnaro yard, Fiume, as the vessel failed to pass trials. Serious scandals came to light involving the late Commander-in-Chief Admiral Scodrea and several other naval officers accused of taking bribes from various firms. Admiral Scodrea lost his post and faced the prospect of court-martial. However, the court-martial never took place as, according to rumor, the Italian government brought pressure against court-martial because Italian officials were involved and it would discredit Italian shipbuilding.[12]

A full appreciation of how the massive Romanian artillery order with Škoda in 1930 turned into the Škoda scandal of 1933 requires analyzing the interplay of several sets of interests ranging from the international business domain, the diplomatic realm, and domestic Romanian political concerns. As partially discussed in Chapter 1, the French government and Schneider-Creusot had differing priorities in Eastern Europe. The French government supported a policy of exercising stronger influence and control over the military alliance with Romania and measured the success or failure of that policy in terms of Romanian armaments orders being placed with French industrial enterprises. Schneider-Creusot through its Artillery Convention with Škoda had given Romania to the Czech firm, and the French firm felt pressure from the French

---

[10] FO 371/14437, Sampson (military attaché) to WO, September 9, 1930.   [11] Ibid.
[12] FO 371/16825, Romanian. Annual Report, 1932. Palairet to Simon, March 15, 1933, 36.

government to take up more Romanian business than Schneider wanted. Even though the French government and the Czechoslovakian government were allied, the two states competed with one another for dominance as the supplier of the standardized military equipment for the armies of the Little Entente. Within Romania, Škoda continued to elbow Vickers out of Romanian domestic plants at Resita and Copsa-Mica & Cugir, but as a consequence Škoda provoked opposition from Romanian domestic industrial interests who resented Škoda taking Romanian money out of the country to manufacture armaments in Czechoslovakia. Those disgruntled Romanian interests spurred the domestic political conflict between the Romanian Cabinet and the Opposition over the Škoda scandal.

In order to disentangle the international and domestic threads of the Škoda scandal, it is necessary to explicate the background to the 1930 artillery order. The French War Ministry pushed hard for French dominance over the Czechs in the Romanian market on the grounds of national security. In December 1928, Col. Palasse, the French military attaché in Bucharest, came to Paris and informed Schneider-Creusot that Romania would be realizing a program of artillery and preferred to get French materiel.[13] General Dumitru "Gica" Popescu, Secretary-General of the Romanian War Ministry then visited France at the end of 1929 to obtain from Schneider et Cie communication of prices for materiel.[14] However, Schneider-Creusot exhibited an apathetic attitude regarding the representations of Romania. Schneider refused to communicate their sale prices for materials, and as a consequence Romania prepared to order from other countries, i.e., the Czechs. The French War Ministry urged the Foreign Ministry, "We have an immediate interest to avoid this eventuality. I ask you to convey to Schneider the inconvenience that their attitude presents from the national point of view."[15] Col. Palasse reported in January 1930 that Škoda was on the move in Romania by forcing itself into the Societe Franco-Romanian IAR for construction of airplanes and negotiating the purchase of Romanian shares in the hands of Astra Co. in Arad. Simultaneously, Škoda sought greater involvement in Resita and Copsa-Mica-Cugir. Palasse doubted that Škoda really intended to manufacture war materials in Romania. The Plzeň firm really desired to obtain Romanian orders to

[13] MAE, Europe 1930–1940. Roumanie. 161–163, Note. Roumanie. Commandes de 45 batteries de 105L, October 30, 1931.

[14] MAE, Europe 1930–1940, Tchecoslovaquie. 167, Note sur les relations Schneider–Škoda, January 18, 1930.

[15] MAE, Europe 1930–1940, Roumanie. Matériel de guerre. 159, Min de Guerre to MAE, January 18, 1930.

be executed in Czechoslovakia. Palasse concluded, "I believe it would be prudent to call the attention of the Romanian government to the fact that Czech industry is very exposed, and in case of war, the resupply of the Romanian army would be difficult."[16]

The French government expressed much greater interest in the Romanian artillery orders than Schneider did. In 1927, as part of a loan to stabilize Romanian currency, the French government had set limits on Romania's foreign military purchases and further had required that any such orders had to be placed exclusively in France.[17] The Romanian General Cihoski told Puaux, the French Minister in Bucharest, that if Creusot persisted in its attitude, it would make it difficult for Romania to reserve artillery orders for France. By February 1930, Romania wanted to purchase forty-five batteries of 105mm guns with 2,000 shells each for a sum of $16–17 million. Romanian orders held little interest for Schneider at the time as the factory found itself fully occupied with orders from Mexico, Argentina, Chile, Greece, and Poland. Schneider estimated that Romania would have to wait three to six years for the plant to get around to their order. Moreover, Schneider's agreement with Škoda now granted Škoda the markets of Central Europe and Balkans, and the terms of the Artillery Convention absolutely prohibited Schneider from receiving an order directly from Romania. At the end of February 1930, the French Foreign Ministry made known to Schneider that they believed Soviet incidents on the Bessarabian frontier threatened Romania, and the Romanian coast completely lacked artillery. On March 1, 1930, the French War Ministry, on request of the Foreign Ministry, again called attention of Schneider to the needs of the Romanian Army. Alarmed by the situation, the Romanians wanted armaments quickly. The French government suggested to Schneider that the firm should reduce delivery time and sacrifice other orders to help aid Romania. In the face of these appeals from French ministries, Schneider decided to renounce in Turkey some important business in order to be able to reduce delivery times for a Romanian order.[18]

The French government worked furiously to ensure that Schneider rather than Škoda would secure the Romanian artillery contracts. Much to the chagrin of Paris, on March 17, 1930, Škoda and the Romanian

---

[16] MAE, Europe 1930–1940, Tchecoslovaquie. 167, Lt.-Col Palasse (mil att) to Ministre de la Guerre, January 19, 1930.

[17] P. H. Segal, *The French State and French Private Investment in Czechoslovakia, 1918–1938* (New York: Garland, 1987), 261.

[18] MAE, Europe 1930–1940, Roumanie. Matériel de guerre. 159, Note. Armaments roumains, February 20, 1930; Puaux (Bucharest) to MAE, February 7, 1930; MAE, Europe 1930–1940. Roumanie. 161–163, Note. Roumanie. Commandes de 45 batteries de 105L, October 30, 1931.

War Ministry signed a contract for forty-five artillery batteries in the amount of $31.4 million (CZK 1,035,978,000) with payment terms stretching into 1939. Puaux frantically called for Creusot to submit its proposals to the Romanians, and he urged the French Finance Ministry to insist to Romania that the decision favoring Škoda be suspended. But under the pressing menace of Russia, the Romanian government felt it had no time to lose. Puaux reported to the Foreign Ministry that Romania would like to give the order to France since French financial aid was indispensable to the country. Unfortunately, Creusot's tardiness caused serious problems as the firm was supposed to submit proposals eight months ago and still had not completed them.[19] The Romanian order for 75mm and 105mm artillery, valued at $30 million (F750 million), presently excluded Creusot from furnishing artillery. The French Foreign Ministry requested that the War Ministry "intervene urgently on behalf of Schneider which sent its proposals late to Bucharest."[20] It seemed likely that Romania soon would grant Škoda contracts for the 75mm howitzers and 150mm field guns. For the 105mm pieces, unless the French government provided financial guarantee for Creusot, that order also would pass to Škoda. Puaux mused that "If Škoda is absolutely independent of French banks for financing, we will have other means to pressure the Romanian government such as our decision concerning the agriculture credit."[21]

Schneider's apparent disinterest in Romanian orders stemmed in part from lack of confidence in Romania's ability to pay, and the company would only take the business if the French government provided a guarantee. French financial experts rightly expressed concerns about Romania's ability to meet its obligations since Romanian budget deficits for 1929 and 1930 due to military purchases amounted to over $48 million (RL 8 billion).[22] The French government proved willing to give its guarantee to Creusot only after it established that the resources of the Romanian budget were sufficient to cover the payment for the totality of Romanian orders which would be attributed to Škoda.[23] When Creusot finally tendered for the 105mm guns, it underbid Škoda and

---

[19] MAE, Europe 1930–1940, Tchecoslovaquie. 167, Charles-Roux to MAE, October 17, 1931; MAE, Europe 1930–1940, Roumanie. Matériel de guerre. 159, Puaux to MAE. March 10, 1930; Puaux to MAE, March 11, 1930.

[20] MAE, Europe 1930–1940, Roumanie. Matériel de guerre. 159, MAE to Min Guerre, March 11, 1930.

[21] MAE, Europe 1930–1940, Roumanie. Matériel de guerre. 159, Puaux to MAE, March 20, 1930.

[22] Segal, 262.

[23] MAE, Europe 1930–1940, Roumanie. Matériel de guerre. 159, MAE to Bucharest, March 21, 1930.

secured the contract. Under the circumstances, the French government gave its guarantee to Creusot "without inconvenience," although the government recommended that "It would be good to sign a contract as soon as possible [emphasis in original] to avoid a complete surprise should Škoda or Bofors return to the offensive."[24] Schneider's did sign for the 105mm order with General Peterescu and President Tatatescu on July 18, 1930, in the amount of $10.64 million (F266 million), with interest bringing the total up to $12 million (F300 million). After Schneider signed the contract, Bruno Seletzki, Škoda's sales representative in Romania, invoked the Artillery Convention to acquire Škoda's portion of the order. Consequently, Creusot took only thirteen batteries and 36,000 shells while Škoda received thirty-two batteries, and all materiel and munitions would be Škoda type and price. The French government linked the order of war materiel passed to Schneider with the Romanian stabilization loan of 1930. After Schneider received its $12 million for war materiel, one or another of the foreign competitors would get the rest.[25] In late July, the French minister in Bucharest revisited the question of the program of rearmament with the Romanians. From the French government's point of view, while France supported Romania strongly, Puaux noted that the strength of one country did not rest solely on military equipment, but also derived from its credit. On that score, the Bank of France and French creditors had given the most to Romania to stabilize its money. Since the French government had undertaken to guarantee the advances for French industry to the Romanian government, France wanted Romanian assurances that those agreed upon engagements would not surpass the limit of $6 million (RL 1 billion). The Romanian war minister General Condesco responded that 1 billion lei credit was insufficient for the needs of the army, and Romania would need $24 million (RL 4 billion). As of September 1930, Romanian orders to Škoda amounted to $30.3 million (CZK 1 billion) compared to Creusot's $13.6 million (CZK 450 million). After dragging its feet, Schneider finally entered into discussions with Romania for coastal artillery worth $4 million (F100 million) in November, but only so long as the firm would receive an assurance credit from the French government. The French Commission of the Assurance Credit could legally accept $16 million (F400 million) of risk for Romania.

[24] MAE, Europe 1930–1940, Roumanie. Matériel de guerre. 159, Puaux to MAE, March 22, 1930.

[25] MAE, Europe 1930–1940, Roumanie. Matériel de guerre. 160, Puaux to MAE, July 4, 1930; MAE to Min Fin, July 19, 1930; SA, 01F0155, Schneider contact with Romania, July 18, 1930; MAE, Europe 1930–1940, Roumanie. Matériel de guerre. 159, Puaux to MAE, March 25, 1930.

Currently $5.36 million was already engaged on Romania ($4.8 million for Schneider). By late November, the Commission did accept the new request by Creusot, which raised the assurance credit by $2.4 million.[26] In the end, the Romanian government borrowed $48 million through its 1930 loan. From those fresh funds, Romania placed new artillery orders with Škoda for $21 million, still owed Škoda $6 million on previous orders, and Romania owed Schneider $9 million in France.[27]

Machine gun orders served as another field of French-Czech competition. As discussed previously, the Romanians favored the Praga machine gun manufactured by ČZB and Škoda since the first trials in 1927. Although the Vickers gun (Berthier) had performed poorly in the 1928 trials, Birch reported back to Vickers that the Romanian trials had been very extensive "and Škoda won on his merits."[28] The Danish competitor, Madsen, evinced less confidence in the Romanian process. Madsen's agent, With-Seidelin, complained that the trials had not been conducted in an impartial manner, but favored the Praga, and he related to the British military attaché in Bucharest his suspicion that bribery played a key role in Praga's victory. Specifically, With-Seidelin asserted that "an officer in the Technical Department of the War Ministry, responsible for the trials, approached him and hinted his need for a motor car. His hint being turned down, this officer appeared a fortnight later in possession of a Praga car."[29] Meanwhile, Romanian war minister Angelescu favored the French Châtelleraut weapon, and the French government through its military attaché brought strong pressure to bear on the Romanians to adopt this weapon in connection with the loan negotiations. Even with the insistence of the French Minister in Bucharest supporting the rifles of Châtelleraut, the Praga performed better. The Châttelleraut firing trials did not go well, and so the Romanian committee pronounced in favor of the Praga machine gun.[30] Undaunted, Puaux took up his lobbying directly with King Carol II at the end of July 1930. King Carol told Puaux that Romania would adopt the Czech artillery and machine guns because "the Romanian Army cannot wait for a long time. We need the 75mm to unify the calibers of the Little Entente. The experience of the Praga has been entirely satisfactory and I have sanctioned the

[26] MAE, Europe 1930–1940, Roumanie. Matériel de guerre. 160, Puaux to MAE, July 28, 1930; Charles-Roux (Prague) to Briand (MAE), September 20, 1930; Pour Monsieur Coulandre, November 19, 1930; Note pour Mr. Bargeton, November 22, 1930.
[27] Segal, 262.
[28] VA, Microfilm K612, Notes on visit of General Birch to Bucharest, April 19, 1928.
[29] FO 371/12973, Goodden (military attaché) to Minister Bucharest, April 17, 1928.
[30] FO 371/12973, Goodden (military attaché) to Minister Bucharest, April 17, 1928; MAE, Europe 1930–1940, Roumanie. Matériel de guerre. 160, Note. July 1, 1930; Puaux to MAE, July 24, 1930.

unanimous advice of the commission." Nonetheless, the Monarch did recognize that France had a right to "compensations," and he spoke notably about the coastal artillery and the Hotchkiss model of airplane machine guns as excellent.[31]

Throughout this period, the Romanian government neglected its formal commitment to Vickers–Armstrong. As part of its obligations in Resita and Copsa-Mica & Cugir, the Romanian government was supposed to give armaments orders to those domestic works. If they could not handle the orders, then Vickers–Armstrong should receive the business. Outside of the specific pledges to Vickers, according to Romanian law one-third of state munitions orders ought to go to domestic plants.[32] In March, Vickers–Armstrong complained to the Foreign Office that the Romanian government was about to place orders with Škoda that Vickers could supply, and the British firm wanted a fair opportunity to compete for the orders. Finally, in July the Romanian President of Council, Iuliu Maniu, gave instruction to approach the British firm concerning the complete reequipment of the Romanian Army. Romania had $48 million available for purchases, and King Carol desired that the rearmament of his army be carried out from England. Maniu told Boxshall of Vickers that the army orders would hinge entirely upon financial considerations. Romania sought longer credit terms such as ten to twelve years' credit similar to what Schneider and Škoda had accepted in their contracts for artillery. Maniu claimed that he did not want all Romanian contracts to go to other countries and none to England, but the French and Czech firms had been only too glad to accept Romanian requirements, namely delivery in five years and payment in ten to twelve.[33] Lacking the private means to fund such an order on long credit terms and prohibited from a state guarantee as their French and Czech competitors enjoyed, Vickers–Armstrong found itself effectively sidelined in Romania.

Vickers's marginalization at the hands of the Romanian government and Škoda continued to grow in the years ahead. At Copsa-Mica & Cugir much of Vickers's machinery had been lying for years on the quay at Constantza unpacked and presumably deteriorating. Reports to Vickers's home office revealed consistent mismanagement, internal

---

[31] MAE, Europe 1930–1940, Roumanie. Matériel de guerre. 160, Puaux to MAE, July 30, 1930.
[32] Watts, 62.
[33] FO 371/15268, Vickers–Armstrong to FO, March 31, 1930, enclosed in Vickers–Armstrong to FO, August 27, 1931; VA, Microfilm K612 Noel Birch Resita, February 17, 1928–June 8, 1938; Romanian Business to Birch, July 7, 1930; Boxshall to Birch, July 11, 1930.

discord, lack of state support, and the technical advice given by Vickers–Armstrong has been consistently ignored. As of August 1931, Vickers–Armstrong had still been refused a nomination to the executive committee, and the dividends guaranteed by Romanian government had not been paid for 1928 and 1930. On the other side, Škoda moved into a closer working relationship with the Romanians for domestic production. In addition to greater Škoda participation in Resita and Cugir, by the agreement of February 6, 1931, the Romanian government and Škoda arranged to build a munitions factory in Transylvania and an auto plant in Bucharest. Additionally, talks were on course between Škoda and the Romanian government regarding the installation of a factory for rifles and machine guns at Cugir. Škoda purchased Vickers's stock in Cugir and received the same promise from the Romanian government that artillery production would be reserved in principle for Resita. The Copsa-Mica Company, in which Vickers had shares, filed a claim for bankruptcy at the end of 1932.[34]

Significantly, despite invitation from the Romanian government, Schneider-Creusot chose to steer clear of the Romanian domestic enterprises and leave Škoda a free hand. The Romanian President of Council told Puaux that he would be happy to have French participation in the enterprise. However, in light of Schneider's abstention, Romania did not want to delay further the organization of a factory deemed indispensable for its national defense. Schneider-Creusot indicated that they did not engage in the manufacture of rifles and machine guns. Therefore, the French firm would be happy to see the shares of Cugir passed to Škoda, and they made no competition with the Czechs. Even though the Resita Company had offered participation to Creusot in that enterprise as a replacement for Vickers, Schneider had refused by raising concern that to transform the locomotive factory into a cannon shop would be extremely onerous. Schneider also informed the French government that its accord with Škoda prohibited Creusot from installing works for the construction of artillery materiel in Romania.[35]

The French Foreign Ministry, concerned that Czech industry with the support of the Czechoslovak government was raising a competition to French war industry in other countries of the Little Entente, called

[34] FO 371/15268, Vickers–Armstrong to FO, August 27, 1931; MAE, Europe 1930–1940, Tchecoslovaquie. 167, Puaux (Bucharest) to MAE, January 12, 1931; SG, Box 5898, V. I. Lenin á Pilsen, Dossier Notes et Renseignements, February 6, 1931; MAE, Europe 1930–1940, Roumanie. Matériel de guerre. 160, Puaux to MAE, February 17, 1931; FO 371/16825 Romanian. Annual Report, 1932. Palairet to Simon, March 15, 1933, 22.

[35] MAE, Europe 1930–1940, Roumanie. Matériel de guerre. 160, Puaux to MAE, February 17, 1931; Note. Armament de la Roumanie, February 25, 1931.

in Schneider's Secretary-General Litzelmann for discussions.[36] Accordingly, Litzelmann met with the subdirector for the European section to talk about the Romanian order for coastal artillery. Litzelmann noted that under the terms of the Schneider–Škoda Artillery Convention, the Romanian market was reserved to Škoda. For Creusot to obtain the Romanian order would mean a violation of this accord. If Schneider wanted to take this order for coastal artillery, a new agreement would have to be made with Škoda. Creusot had resolved not to take that risk, but Litzelmann suggested that to avoid this difficulty, the new order could be made directly from government to government. Presently, Creusot was executing some artillery for the French War Ministry, and taking this route the Škoda problem would be defused. For the French Foreign Ministry, "The question is: If we are to abandon the Romanian market to Czech industry while we have another means directly to grip the possible finances of Romania.; if in order to avert this danger . . . it is not suitable to adopt the procedure proposed by Creusot, which would not occur without inconvenience thanks to the direct and apparent intervention of the French government on the occasion of military aid to Romania."[37] The French Foreign Ministry felt some urgency to act because Škoda was talking with Manoilesco, Popovici, and General Samsonivici in Bucharest about the Czech firm selling artillery of all calibers including mountain and coastal guns with payments over fifteen years.[38] In July 1931, the French Military attaché met with Romanian General Rudeanu to convey the French government's displeasure to see Romania on the point of engaging for a major part of war munitions with Czech and Polish industry, when French industry, and in particular Schneider should serve that purpose. Rudeanu responded that "Schneider and Škoda make common action in the country and that it makes no difference to address to Schneider or Škoda."[39]

At this juncture, a clear pattern had emerged in French relations with Romania. The French government sought to keep Romania under control according to its conception of military and economic dominance. Romania's equipage with French war materiel would be taken as proof of Romania's commitment to the French alliance, and sharing the same systems would facilitate Franco-Romanian military cooperation and resupply in time of war (a point continually raised by the French military attaché). To that end, French officials in the Foreign Ministry and War Ministry showed themselves all too eager to leverage

[36] Ibid., Note. Paris. January 21, 1931.
[37] Ibid., Note. Armaments roumaines. January 22, 1931.
[38] Ibid., Laboulayo to MAE, January 26, 1931.
[39] Ibid., Note. Lt. Col. Palaisse (Mil att Bucharest) to French Minister, July 21, 1931.

Romania by applying financial pressure on the Romanian government to keep Romania in the French orbit as conceived in Paris. Meanwhile, the French industrial concern for which French officials lobbied the hardest, Schneider, evinced a marked tepidness and diffidence regarding Romanian business. Whereas the French government worried that France was losing Romania, in truth Schneider had given it to Škoda. Schneider justified their abstention by repeatedly pointing to the Artillery Convention as the grounds for their inaction when the French government pressured the firm to tender for Romanian orders, which Schneider did belatedly. Litzelmann's half-hearted suggestion for the French government to orchestrate a state-to-state artillery transaction to bypass Škoda should be understood in this context as an excuse for Schneider to avoid doing business directly with the Romanians, and in fact, nothing ever materialized out of that ploy. Once again, as had been the case with the struggle over ownership of Škoda, the French government and Schneider had gone in different directions.

As it happened, Schneider's wariness proved warranted, as the Czech firms paid a heavy price for their apparent gains in Romania. By mid-October 1931, Romania missed payments on the order of $41.5 million which had been passed to Škoda for artillery and munitions. As the financial crisis gripped Romania, the government was falling behind in payments, and soon the Romanians stopped paying for orders entirely. The default of its major customer hit Škoda far harder than Schneider, although it did affect Schneider's proportion of ownership in the Czech concern as discussed in Chapter 1. By December, after Romania had not paid Škoda for artillery worth $2.72 million, Škoda detained the materiel.[40] The Škoda order for sixty-six batteries of 100 mm howitzers held the same status. Although six to eight batteries had been manufactured, Škoda would deliver nothing until the money had been received. A financial statement of the Škoda Company made in April 1932 contained a statement to this effect. At the same time as the above orders were given, tentative orders were placed with Škoda for twenty-five batteries of antiaircraft artillery and a number of field guns. According to Czech sources, Škoda only produced the pilot models of these orders because the French banks refused to finance these orders unless the Romanians made a partial initial payment in advance. When the Romanians could not even make partial payment, Škoda held up that order as well. The Romanian government's contract for several

[40] MAE, Europe 1930–1940, Tchecoslovaquie. 167, Note. October 14, 1931; Charles-Roux to MAE, October 17, 1931; MAE, Europe 1930–1940. Roumanie, 161–163, Note. Roumanie. Commandes de Creusot, October 24, 1931; MAE, Europe 1930–1940, URSS. 930, Charles-Roux to MAE, December 9, 1931.

thousand light machine guns and 300 million rounds of ammunition with ČZB also went into abeyance. None of the Brno guns had been delivered although the larger share had already been manufactured, and none would be delivered until paid for by the Romanian government. The first and second payments had come due on January 1 and April 1, 1932, respectively, but to date nothing had been paid.[41] The effects of the Romanian debacle plunged Škoda into a deep financial pit. Škoda's profits plummeted from $2.055 million (CZK 67,831,000) in 1930 to $0.28 million (CZK 9,232,000) in 1931, and by 1932 Škoda's employment dropped from 30,000 workers to just 18,000.[42]

Unable to take delivery of the vast amounts of war materiel ordered from Škoda, the Romanians fought back by disparaging Škoda's products and making overtures to the Poles. After the refusal of Škoda to execute the order for antiaircraft artillery and field guns without any initial cash payment, the Romanians sent a commission to Czechoslovakia which reopened the question of the suitability of the materiel in question and claimed that the Czechoslovakian antiaircraft gun did not have sufficient power and was not modern. They claimed that the field gun was too heavy. According to the American military attaché Emer Yeager, "The first allegation is true in a way, but the Czechoslovakian anti-aircraft gun compares favorably except for its mount with all other anti-aircraft artillery developed in Europe up to the present. The claim about the field gun is entirely justified, as it is considerably heavier than is considered feasible for divisional artillery by leading and competent authorities."[43] Under the provisions of the new version of the Romanian-Polish Defensive Alliance signed in 1931, a joint board of officers for the unification of calibers and armaments in the two armies had begun working in Bucharest. Until recently the Polish military authorities had insisted upon the Romanians taking advantage of the opportunity to support the development of Polish war industry by purchasing such armament and equipment as possible in Poland. Invoking the provision for unification of equipment in the 1931 alliance, the Romanians seized the opportunity to reopen the field gun question and they now deemed the Škoda field gun too

---

[41] RG 165, Entry 77, Romania 6510, #2724-V-52 (2) G-2 Report, Romania, Status of various orders for Armament and Equipment, Emer Yeager (Mil attaché Warsaw), July 24, 1932.

[42] SG, Box 5898 V. I. Lenin á Pilsen, Societe Anonyme des Anciens Establissements Škoda, Communication a la Direction no. 90, September 29, 1932.

[43] RG 165, Entry 77, Romania 6510, #2724-V-52 (2) G-2 Report, Romania, Status of various orders for Armament and Equipment, Emer Yeager (Mil attaché Warsaw), July 24, 1932.

heavy.[44] Claiming that Škoda had not fulfilled certain contractual stipulations, during the summer of 1932 Romania renounced a part of the original order, which included 232 100mm howitzers and 180 150mm howitzers. The failure to carry out this part of the order for 100mm howitzers also affected a further item of 100 75mm field guns, as it was found impossible to make carriages for these of the right dimensions to be interchangeable with the 100mm howitzers.[45]

Ultimately, the Poles did not step into the breach. In a realistic assessment of Romania's condition, the attitude of Poland changed. The Polish Army no longer cared where Romania purchased its new equipment and armaments. France remained the only possible source of credit for this purpose and the Poles hoped that the French financial mission, which was then in Bucharest investigating the Romanian finances would find it possible to recommend loans which could be used for the purchase of the badly needed armaments and equipment. Since in all likelihood France would not give credit unless the purchases were made in France, there was nothing for the Poles to do about it. In case there were credits granted to Romania for the purchase of armaments and equipment, some of the money without doubt would be used to pay for the materiel already ordered and partially manufactured by Škoda, but not yet paid for or delivered.[46] As the Poles had anticipated, this in fact occurred as of August 31, 1932, when Romania passed an order to Schneider for forty-five batteries of 105mm long guns for $10.6 million (F265 million) supported by the assurance credit from the French government. Revealingly, Poland also granted a contract to Schneider for $20 million (F500 million), and Schneider honored the Artillery Convention by retro-ceding the materials for the Polish 155mm and 220mm guns to Škoda "in compensation for the Romanian order."[47] Nevertheless, within the next fiscal year, Schneider completely suspended execution of its Romanian order due to lack of payment.[48]

Having followed the development of Romanian artillery orders in the context of the business dealings with Vickers, Schneider, and Škoda, it is now appropriate to consider the Romanian domestic political context. The future King Carol II had renounced the throne and gone into exile

[44] RG 165, Entry 77, Romania 6510, #2724-V-52 (3) G-2 Report, Romania, Status of various orders for Armament and Equipment, Emer Yeager (Mil attaché Warsaw), November 25, 1932.

[45] FO 371/16825, Romanian. Annual Report, 1932. Palairet to Simon, March 15, 1933.

[46] RG 165, Entry 77, Romania 6510, #2724-V-52 (2) G-2 Report, Romania, Status of various orders for Armament and Equipment, Emer Yeager (Mil attaché Warsaw), July 24, 1932.

[47] SA, 187AQ029–02, Marche des Industries pendant l'Exercice 1931–1932, 45.

[48] SA, 187AQ030–01, Marche des Industries pendant l'Exercice 1932–1933, 42.

in 1925 because he chose to leave his wife, Princess Helen of Greece, to live with his mistress Madame Lupescu. His young son Michael became King under a Regency with the National Liberal Party in power, and the Liberal Party consistently opposed Carol in later years. The main opposition to the Liberal Party came from the National Peasant Party headed by Iuliu Maniu. Maniu emerged as one of the leaders of the Romanian National Party of Transylvania before the First World War. When the National Liberals came to power in 1922, Maniu contested the legality of the election and he remained an adversary of the Liberal Party thereafter. The National Peasant Party, formally founded in 1926, grew out of an alliance in 1925 with the National Party headed by Maniu and Alexander Vaida-Voevod and the Peasant Party under Ion Mihalache. In 1928, a National Peasant government came to power, headed by Maniu, and Maniu brought Carol back from his Parisian exile to become King Carol II in 1930 in order to pull the country together and secure more financial support from the international community. As soon as he could, Carol maneuvered Maniu into resigning, and the King began exercising his personal powers to the fullest by appointing members of the so-called camarilla to government posts. The camarilla functioned as King Carol's informal, extralegal advisory body organized around Madame Lupescu. It included palace favorites such as politicians, diplomats, army officers, and industrialists, most notably Max Auschnitt and Nicolas Malaxa, Romania's biggest arms and steel manufactures. Unable to strike a cooperative stance with the King, Maniu would eventually lead public opposition to the King and his camarilla, and thus he made common cause with his adversaries the Liberal Party against the King. In January 1933, Maniu stepped down as president of the National Peasant Party as he mounted his first press attack on the camarilla.[49]

The Škoda scandal erupted publicly in mid-March 1933, but political moves behind the scenes had begun already in 1932. In April 1932, the Romanian fiscal authorities, probably as a result of an intrigue by members of the Opposition (Liberal Party), received information which led them to believe that Bruno Seletzki was defrauding the revenue in regard to his income tax returns. An enquiry was accordingly ordered, and in December 1932 the decision was taken to search his private papers, although that decision was not put into effect until March 1933.[50] About a week prior to the Seletzki search, the Chamber of Deputies

[49] R. A. Haynes, "Reluctant Allies? Iuliu Maniu and Corneliu Zelea Codreanu against King Carol II of Romania," *The Slavonic and East European Review*, vol. 85, no. 1 (2007), 107–109; Prince Paul of Hohenzollern-Roumania, *King Carol II: A Life of My Grandfather* (London: Metheun, 1988), 111, 139, 148, 160.

[50] FO 371/16825, Michael Palairet to Sir John Simon, April 7, 1933.

entered into debate about war orders and military preparations. As part of that parliamentary process, on March 2 a Liberal Party deputy in interpellation of the Minister of War raised questions about "the national metallurgical factory which could have made war materiel domestically if it had not been neglected three years ago." The Minister of War (Samsonovici) responded that orders were given to foreign firms due to reasons of urgency because it would take too long to adapt Romanian industry for war materiel. Regarding the delays in delivery of Škoda orders he said, "The question can be summarized very simply: If we had the money, we would have all the material necessary."[51] Revealingly, the line of questioning taken in the interpellation foreshadowed the attacks that would be mounted against the 1930 Škoda contract. As we have seen, Romanian manufacturing of war materiel had been neglected much longer than three years. Vickers's long, bitter experience with Resita and Copsa-Mica & Cugir attested that a variety of Romanian governments had accomplished nothing in the area of domestic military production throughout the 1920s. There had also been many orders with Škoda. Why then, did the Liberal deputy specifically reference the three-year period unless to draw attention to the Škoda contract of March 1930? Whether the Liberal deputy was privy to the imminent Seletzki raid or not, the ground was being prepared for a coming political struggle over the Škoda order. The reason for the publicity surrounding the scandal was political since Romanian authorities recognized that they could never afford to pay for the Škoda contracts.[52] The Romanian military budget regularly received cuts, and as a proportion of state expenditures it consistently remained one of the smallest in Europe. In 1931, it constituted only 14.7 percent of state spending, and reached its minimum in 1933. The meager funds were further depleted by notorious corruption and the irrational priorities such as King Carol's passion for a wide range of exotic garments that provided no practical service as military uniforms.[53]

Finally acting on the tip, the Ministry of Finance issued a denunciation of Bruno Seletzki alleging fiscal fraud. Under examination, inspectors found certain papers of a military interest, and the fiscal agents then called upon military authorities, who sent a sentinel to guard the office and apply seals to the locked drawers. Later an order arrived which removed the sentries, and subsequently the seals were found torn open.

[51] MAE, Europe 1930–1940. Roumanie. 161–163, Bucharest to MAE, March 6, 1933.
[52] Watts, 99, n. 9.
[53] A. Statiev, "When an Army Becomes 'Merely a Burden': Romanian Defense Policy and Strategy (1918–1941)," *The Journal of Slavic Military Studies*, vol. 13, no. 2 (2000), 68–69.

Seletzki incredibly claimed his small daughter had torn off the seals while playing. Seletzki's background as an Austrian subject and a former officer in the Austro-Hungarian Army, his rumored connections with persons suspected of being Soviet agents, and his secretary being the sister of an Anarchist named Max Goldstein, who made an attempt against the Senate two years after the war, made easy fodder for adversaries of the government to view Seletzki's actions as a grave act of espionage. On the other hand, good details of the incident remained obscure.[54]

Dr. Nicolae Lupu of the National Peasant Party led the charge against Seletzki in the Chamber of Deputies. On March 20, Lupu fired a barrage of questions at the President of the State Council, Vaida-Voevod. Had Seletzki defrauded the government of tens of millions; what compromising documents had been discovered in Seletzki's flat; who was endeavoring to hush up the scandal which had come to light; how many of the guns ordered from Škoda in 1930 had actually been delivered; and why had the defenses of the country been entirely neglected for two years? In replying, Vaida-Voevod characterized the various rumors in circulation as purely fantastic. He asserted that no secret of national importance had been betrayed, and, moreover, the firm of Škoda had no interest in acting with other parties to weaken the national defense of their customer. Meanwhile, he added, the seized dossier was being examined, and its contents would in due course be communicated to the Chamber. The debate continued the following day when Dr. Lupu again pressed his accusations in greater detail. Lupu alleged that among the documents seized were full reports of the state of Romania's national defense and dossiers containing the habits, acquaintances, and personal weaknesses of all commanding officers and generals in the Romanian Army. Most damning of all, Lupu asserted that authorities had seized Seletzki's private code, which would make it possible to prove that of the $90 million (RL 15 billion) due to Škoda from the Romanian government $24 million (RL 4 billion) had been expended in bribes. In particular, one Minister had been paid $3.6 million (RL 600 million) and $4.2 million (RL 700 million) had been paid to a group of individuals. Dr. Lupu concluded by demanding the immediate arrest of Seletzki. The government replied briefly to the effect that they were most anxious to see the affair cleared up, and they had given orders that the enquiry was to be concluded as soon as possible. Justice would be done, and no guilty party would be allowed to escape.[55]

---

[54] MAE, Europe 1930–1940, Roumanie. 170, Puaux to MAE, March 24, 1933.
[55] FO 371/16825, Michael Palairet to Sir John Simon, April 7, 1933.

Dr. Lupu continued his attacks and was now joined by Liberal Party politicians. On March 23, Lupu conducted a formal interpellation in the Chamber. He spoke against the irregular character of the Škoda contracts to furnish armaments and asserted that different governments had systematically neglected to address national industry, while the largest part of the orders went to foreigners. He enumerated certain pieces found at Seletzki's house which presented the character of national defense secrets. Other documents raised questions about the commissions, and certain names figured on a confidential list: General Samsonovici (Minister of War), Manoilescu (former minister), General Gorski, Buzdugan, and others who were indicated by coded numbers, but the numbers had disappeared. Liberal Party orators Duca, Goga, Georges Brătianu, and Junian all reproached the government for letting Seletzki go free despite the character of espionage, and Duca demanded the fullest possible enquiry into the morass of corruption which had been disclosed In response, the government justified that at the moment when the Pact of the Little Entente was about to be signed, they could not neglect to take this information also to the representative of Škoda. Vaida-Voevod declared that he would hold an inquest, and it would be led by someone whose sole concern would be equity. General Samsonovici finally requested that the Chamber hold a confidential military inquest.[56] Watching from the sidelines, the French Minister Puaux offered his interpretation to Paris. He observed, "It can be believed that the owners of national industry have provoked this incident to divert the Government's system of orders to foreigners, and to call the attention of the country to this. On the other hand, it is notable that Škoda distributed very large commissions. If the inquest discovers the names of these beneficiaries, it could create a great scandal that would have repercussions for the political situation."[57] The role of Romanian industrialists became evident when Nicholas Malaxa, a member of the King's camarilla and the largest shareholder in the Cugir Company, joined the Škoda scandal fray. Malaxa advocated cancelling the Škoda contract and reserving the order for war materiel to national industry with a substitution of Vickers for Škoda for the pieces impossible to make domestically. Malaxa threw his support behind the opposition to engage the battle in Parliament.[58]

Having cast the net broadly in the preceding days, the indefatigable Lupu returned to the Chambers for a fifth straight day of oration on the

---

[56] MAE, Europe 1930–1940. Roumanie. 170, Puaux to MAE, March 24, 1933; FO 371/16825, Michael Palairet to Sir John Simon, April 7, 1933.

[57] MAE, Europe 1930–1940. Roumanie. 170, Puaux to MAE, March 24, 1933.

[58] Ibid., Puaux to MAE, March 27, 1933.

Škoda scandal, but this time he focused on the 1930 Škoda order. In a four-hour speech Lupu recalled that in 1930 alarming rumors were circulated regarding the situation in Bessarabia, and it was said that there were powerful concentrations of Soviet forces on the Romanian frontiers. This information had been a ruse by Seletzki to drum up a war scare in order to influence the Council of Regency at the time to place larger orders with Škoda for munitions to be supplied to Romania. After the contracts were concluded, the rumors of troop concentration ceased, and it afterward became known that they were baseless. Lupu concluded that the contract with Škoda had been approved by the Secretary-General of the Ministry of War, General Cihoski, against the provisions of the law and without the permission of the Munitions Committee of the Ministry of War. Lupu accused the sons of Vaida-Voevod and Popovici of service to Škoda. Both Lupu and Duca insisted that further delay was criminal, that in the meantime the compromising documents were likely to disappear, and that the affair was only as yet in its initial stages.[59]

Two weeks after investigators had visited Seletzki's office, the government finally took action. Seletzki was arrested on March 25 on grounds of possessing documents of interest to national defense, and a judicial enquiry commenced. Debates on the subject continued both in the Chamber and in the Senate. The attempts by the Opposition to use this case as a means to bring down to the government had not succeeded, but public opinion had been deeply stirred by revelations of corruption practiced on such a large scale. Indeed, the whole case was less about espionage than bribery pure and simple. The documents which Seletzki had improperly obtained related not to strategic matters, but rather to questions of the supply of armaments. It should be noted that the Government and the Opposition made special efforts to insist that the Czechoslovak government was in no way involved.[60]

The Škoda scandal claimed its first victim with the suicide of General Popescu at the end of March. Popescu's death energized his defenders to restore his honor and reputation. General Popescu had addressed his last letters to various notables in which he protested that he was completely innocent, but that life had become intolerable to him owing to the attacks made upon him by General Stefanescu-Amza and others. The question was exhaustively discussed in the Chamber of Deputies

---

[59] T 181/40, Royal Commission on the private manufacture of and trading in arms. Document No. 41, April 26, 1935: *Pester Lloyd* newspaper from March 24, 1933; MAE, Europe 1930–1940. Roumanie. 170, Puaux to MAE, March 30, 1933; FO 371/16825, Michael Palairet to Sir John Simon, April 7, 1933.

[60] MAE, Europe 1930–1940. Roumanie, 170, Puaux to MAE, March 24, 1933; FO 371/16825, Michael Palairet to Sir John Simon, April 7, 1933.

on April 1 and 3. The debates were in the nature of a duel between the Government and the Opposition, who failed in their attempt to use the Škoda scandal as a means of bringing about the fall of the Ministry.[61]

In the Senate the matter was lifted on to a higher plane and was discussed from the point of view of the efficiency of the military defense of the country and the administration of the Ministry of War. The Prime Minister, Vaida-Voevod opened the debate by declaring that the government had nothing to hide and desired the fullest enquiry. He therefore demanded that the sitting should be a public one. He was followed by General Rujinski, who urged the necessity for putting an end once and for all to a system of giving orders which led to such corruption as had now been disclosed. He criticized severely General Amza for his share in the Škoda contract, and paid a tribute to General Popescu, who, he declared, had been unjustly accused. General Popovici and General Petala spoke on much the same lines, and the former emphasized the desirability of organizing the Romanian production of armaments so that the country should not depend on foreign factories. General Petala expressed his astonishment at the discovery among Seletzki's papers of documents which should never have left the Ministry of War. General Cihoski, who was Minister of War when the contract was drawn up, and had himself signed it, gave various explanations to prove that the contract was good in itself, but had subsequently become the subject of political intrigues. It had, he said, been suspended three months after the first delivery had taken place, and for the last eighteen months attempts had been made to make a new contract. Nothing had, however, been settled with the result that the whole supply of armaments had been interrupted.[62]

After General Cihoski had justified himself and the Škoda contract, and other orators reproached General Stefanescu-Amza for having stopped the execution of the contract to the detriment of national defense, Marshal Prezan intervened in the discussions and caused a sensation. He, like General Cihoski, severely blamed those who had suspended deliveries under the contract, thus imperiling the defenses of the country. He also stressed the importance of reorganizing the Romanian armament factories with all speed. The Marshal concluded his speech, which was received enthusiastically, by declaring that the accusations made by the deceased General Popescu against General Stefanescu-Amza must be either disproved or substantiated. Marshal

---

[61] MAE, Europe 1930–1940. Roumanie. 170, Puaux to MAE, March 30, 1933; FO 371/16825, Palairet (Bucharest) to Simon, April 6, 1933.

[62] FO 371/16825, Palairet (Bucharest) to Simon, April 6, 1933.

Prezan commanded the highest respect throughout the country and his speech produced a great impression. By paying homage to the memory of General Popesco and charging General Stefanesco, Prezan had strengthened the position of the government.[63]

Finally, it was the turn of General Samsonovici, the current Minister of War, to weigh in on the Škoda scandal. On April 3, Samsonovici made an authoritative statement on the case. He declared that no military secrets had disappeared into Seletzki's dossiers. Such secrets were in the keeping of the General Staff, where no indiscretion had been revealed. The national defense was therefore, in no way impaired, and the alarming reports which had been spread were groundless. The fact that some of the armaments ordered had not arrived in time did not justify the conclusion that the country was disarmed. Steps were being taken, General Samsonivici said, to fix responsibility for allowing Seletzki to obtain copies of confidential (but not secret) documents, and the persons involved would be treated with exemplary severity. No documents, he stated, had disappeared from the Supreme Council of National Defense. The Copsa-Mica works would be reorganized on a new basis and the supervision of factory representatives and military suppliers would be more strictly organized. In the opinion of the War Minister, reliable officials should remain where they were, and, in order to ensure continuity of policy and its execution, War Ministers should not be liable to change once a year, or even more often. Referring to the late General Popescu, General Samsonivici argued that King Carol had entrusted Popescu with a military command after examining the accusations made against him, and the King's actions showed that the accusations against Popescu could not be considered serious. Any guilty person who might be discovered would, he assured the Senate, be severely dealt with. When General Samsonivici had concluded his statement the President of the Council addressed the Senate. The case affected Seletzki, he said, not the firm of Škoda, which enjoyed a worldwide reputation and was fulfilling its contract with the Romanian government. The materiel supplied so far was good. As for the accusations against Seletzki, and the charges of corruption against Romanian officials, he demanded that the fullest enquiry should be made, regardless of all considerations of party politics. As a result of weeks of parliamentary debate and publicity, the government launched three enquiries. The War Council took up the accusations against Seletzki and tried him in a court-martial. General Petrescu led an investigation into the administration of the Ministry of

---

[63] FO 371/16825, Palairet (Bucharest) to Simon, April 6, 1933; MAE, Europe 1930–1940. Roumanie. 171, Puaux to MAE, April 3, 1933.

War, and General Gorski headed an enquiry into the charges brought against General Stefanecsu-Amza. King Carol abruptly brought the interpellation to an end when he issued a decree of Cloture of the Chambers on April 13 which permitted the government to avoid a renewal of the interpellation about the Škoda affair.[64]

Seletzki's court-martial occurred over the summer of 1933. The military documents used to condemn Seletzki included technical information on the factory of the Copsa-Mica-Cugir Company which was competing against Škoda for armaments orders to the Romanian Army, reports of the Council Superior of the army, and secret communications addressed from the Ministry of National Defense to the Etat-major. The defense endeavored to show that the indictment of Seletzki was a political and economic machination, not just to hinder Škoda, but for the great benefit of rival firms and to weaken the party in power and to compromise Iuliu Maniu. The defense again contested the importance of the documents found in the possession of Seletzki. Many former ministers of the Defense Ministry and a great number of superior officers noted the service Seletzki rendered to the country. Four ex–ministers of war testified to the effect that there was nothing confidential in the documents in question. Over the course of the trial accusations and insinuations were also made concerning prominent politicians, including Maniu, whose government first decided to order armaments from the firms of Škoda, Schneider, and ČZB. It was insinuated that Maniu, among other prominent men, had received compensation for his share in securing the contract for Škoda. Significantly, Seletzki was visited in prison three times during the trial and offered acquittal if he would sign a document saying money had been paid to Maniu. This visitor, Col. Georgescu, had indicated that Seletzki's only chance of avoiding a severe penalty lay in divulging the names of the civilians who had received commissions. At one point, the prosecutor introduced alleged evidence of Maniu's connivance, but it was quickly discovered that the attorney had doctored the evidence by handwriting the damaging portion of the testimony into the document to make it seem like Seletzki's own words. Such actions indicated that the instigators came from the Lupescu camarilla who hoped to please the King by ruining Maniu. At the final sitting on August 16, 1933, the court found Seletzki guilty of breaking seals placed on his engineering office and of procuring military documents affecting the security of the country during the state of siege. The Council, who considered that there were extenuating circumstances,

---

[64] FO 371/16825, Palairet (Bucharest) to Simon, April 6, 1933; MAE, Europe 1930–1940. Roumanie. 171, Puaux to MAE, April 17, 1933.

exonerated him from blame for breaking the seals on his private office. These verdicts were passed by three-two vote. Sentence of five years imprisonment was then passed on Seletzki under article 258 of the Code of Military Law and article 8 of the law regarding espionage.[65]

In response to the scandal and conviction of Seletzki, Škoda launched a major public relations campaign to restore the firm's reputation. In an official statement from Škoda to the Romanian public, the company asserted that Seletzki's trial had actually vindicated the company "since it was declared by the most competent authorities and by the most authorized specialists whose opinion is above all doubt that, in furnishing supplies to the Romanian State, the Škoda firm invariably proceeded in the most correct manner, fulfilling the most comprehensive conditions and furnishing goods of the highest quality. This declaration makes it clear to every impartial person that in order to secure orders in Romania, the Škoda firm had no need to adopt extraordinary means." Acknowledging that Škoda's reputation had been damaged in Romania and beyond, the company's Directorate solemnly declared "that we have never used extraordinary means to gain the favor of the authorities and that we have relied solely on the quality of our products and upon the most correct commercial agreements," and concluded that "We consider this our declaration to be necessary out of esteem for the name of Czechoslovak industry and out of esteem for the good renown of Romania abroad."[66] For its part, the Czechoslovak government reaffirmed its continued good relations with Romania. The official *Prager Presse* wrote that "this regrettable affair is not the interest of the Czech State, and, as has been expressed in the Romanian Parliament, does not affect the official relations between the two allied states. Škoda, a private enterprise, is solely responsible for its representatives who are employed abroad."[67]

Škoda's internal review following the trial speculated that the scandal had been led by King Carol not against the company, but against the politician Iuliu Maniu. Several members of the management group traced the source of the misunderstanding about Škoda's pricing to a personal meeting between Yugoslav King Alexander and King Carol where the two monarchs compared the prices of Škoda's arms deliveries,

---

[65] MAE, Europe 1930–1940. Roumanie. 171, Ormesson to MAE, August 21, 1933; FO 371/16825, Palairet to Simon, August 30, 1933; Watts, 64–65; VA, Microfilm K612, Vickers to Birch, Romania, October 6, 1933; SA, 187AQ584–05, Telegram from L'Union Européenne Industrielle et Financière to Schneider et Cie, August 19, 1933.

[66] FO 371/16825, The Škoda Factories to the Romanian Public, enclosed in Palairet to Simon, August 31, 1933.

[67] MAE, Europe 1930–1940. Roumanie. 171, Lèon Noël (Prague) to MAE, April 7, 1933.

and those for Yugoslavia seemed to be significantly lower. While both countries had issued government bonds to cover repayments, in the case of Yugoslavia these had been issued in two tranches, one for the capital and the second for the interest. In contrast, in the case of Romania there had been only one issue, whose interest was included in the price, and this had caused a false impression that the Romanian prices were higher. The Romanians subsequently deemed this explanation satisfactory.[68] Nevertheless, the Seletzki affair did adversely affect Škoda. Out of fears of espionage, Little Entente partners had banned the entry into their territory of some Škoda workers, including the number two man in the group, Vladimir Fiala, who stood for arms deliveries to the Balkans and commissions for them. Fiala served as the second-in-command under Loevenstein, and he eventually became architect of all the major trade concluded primarily in the states of the Little Entente. Within Škoda, Fiala had a reputation for highly aggressive tactics and stopping at nothing in order to secure transactions. Fiala, like Seletzki, seemed to view representatives of foreign countries as employees of the Škoda Group. Most assuredly, paying commissions to foreign officers as part of contract signings had not been limited to Seletzki. In Romania, Seletzki's predecessor, Jesma Maglič, had built in commissions of 5 percent on Škoda contracts for Romanian officials. Seletzki had doubled their rate of commission to 10 percent.[69] In the aftermath of the Seletzki trial, Škoda management needed some housecleaning, and so Fiala had to step down. As reported in the minutes of the Executive Committee of Škoda on December 13, 1933, "We announce that the current Deputy Director General, Mr. Engineer Vladimir Fiala came to retire."[70]

Remarkably, Škoda suffered no lasting damage in Romania. Škoda found the means to rebuild the relationship because the Romanians really desired to convert the old orders on more favorable terms rather than cutting Škoda loose. In September 1933, the Romanian War Ministry firmly resolved to transform the contract with Škoda into a convention whereby part of the materiel would be manufactured in Romania. Romania renewed the Škoda contract preliminarily as of March 9, 1935, with certain ameliorations in favor of Romania. The original 1930 contract had been held in abeyance during the long scandal until November 1934, when the committee of the General Staffs of the Little Entente urged Romania to take immediate steps to

---

[68] V. Karlický, *Svět Okřídleného Šípu Koncern Škoda Plzeň 1918–1945* (Plzeň: Škoda a.s. 1999), 173.

[69] R. Diestler, *Příběh zapomenutého průmyslníka: život a doba Karla Loevensteina, generálního ředitele Škodových závodů* (Praha: Grada, 2010), 39–40.

[70] Karlický, 174.

rehabilitate the army in respect of fire power weapons. So Škoda for various reasons was again sought with a view to a modified contract. The original contract in all had called for 612 pieces of various calibers and 181,000 projectiles. In the renewed contract, Škoda agreed to make at Resita the small 75mm (196 pieces and 98,000 rounds) and fill the contract for larger guns and howitzers at its home works. Caissons would be made in Romania. Škoda lowered the original contract price of $31.5–18.36 million On the original 1930 contract, Romania had paid $1.2 million (200 million lei), balance to be paid by annual installments over six years. The modified contract addressed the complaints raised in the parliamentary interpellation. The new contract included a provision that materiel furnished would have to meet required technical standards and tests set by the Romanian Ordnance Section of Military Technique, it reduced the price, it placed roughly one-third of the amount of material ordered to be manufactured in Romania, and it arranged for Škoda to grant a license to manufacture this portion in Romanian plants at Resita and Copsa-Mica-Cugir under the technical direction of Škoda experts. Up to the end of 1932, Škoda had completed twenty howitzers of 100mm and 21,000 projectiles; these were, however, not delivered, as Romania had paid only $1.2 million (CZK 40 million). A feature of the new contract provided that Romania now accepted these items and paid the amount still due. The original contract had obligated Romania to pay in gold. Under the new contract, Škoda accepted payment in non-interest bearing Romanian Treasury bonds, which Škoda could use as a credit reserve and which Romania would redeem periodically, or rather bonds with which Czechoslovakia could pay for purchases of Romanian agricultural raw materials as needed. The new contract specified 5 percent interest on all portions of the order delivered, but not fully paid for at time of delivery. The Romanian Chamber of Deputies approved the contract with Škoda on April 8, 1935, and financed it through a credit to be paid off over eleven years by compensation deals in oil and cereals. General Cihoski was acquitted in February 1936. The Romanians conditionally released Seletzki in September, and he retired to Vienna.[71] Observing the process in Romania, the American military attaché Lt. Col. Whitley remarked that "Romania has achieved a remarkable success out of the Škoda mess of four years' standing, a success which is due in a large measure to the energy and ability of Tatarescu, the

---

[71] VA, Microfilm K612, Boxshall to Vickers–Armstrong, September 13, 1933; RG 165, Entry 77, Romania 6510, #2724-V-60 (3) G-2 Report, Romania, Renewal of Škoda Arms Contract, Lt. Col. F. L. Whitley (Mil attaché Belgrade/Bucharest), March 20, 1935; FO 371/20431, Romania. Annual Report, 1935. Hoore to Eden, February 14, 1936, 34; Diestler, 89.

soldier-politician who reversed the usual order in Romanian politics by placing the welfare of the country superior to the lust for graft."[72]

Regardless of the prosecutorial chicanery at his court-martial, unquestionably Seletzki had paid bribes and "commissions" to a host of Romanian Army officers and politicians over his years in the country. In retrospect, it seemed unnecessary. Škoda pretty much had the field on its terms. Therefore, the likely explanation for starting a war scare and paying massive bribes was not simply to get orders for Škoda, but to generate massive demand on an unprecedented scale. Major W. H. Oxley, the British military attaché in Czechoslovakia, had anticipated the situation for Czech war industries aptly when he had observed in 1930 that "true to say that this country is the Arsenal of the Little Entente, but a point must eventually be reached when the Little Entente will become more or less saturated and unless some convenient market like China is then forthcoming it is a little difficult to see how this large munitions industry can be kept alive. It therefore seems fair to assume that we may expect intensive efforts on the part of munitions firms here to undercut foreign rivals and to use every means possible to extend their markets."[73]

Škoda's financial difficulties began in 1931 with the Romanian fiscal implosion and continued thanks to the aggravation of the Seletzki scandal in 1933, but beyond Romania the Great Depression struck other customers. Škoda's Yugoslav business plummeted from $1.85 million (1929–1931) to a mere $81,000 in 1932. Similarly, Turkish orders fell from $3.7 million in 1930 to barely $14,424 in 1932. Even the China business declined from $1.9 million in 1930 to $0.29 million in 1931 and $14,090 in 1932.[74] As the orders dried up, unemployment rose starkly. By the end of 1931, Škoda had dismissed 9,000 workers from its Plzeň factory and the remainder had been put on short time. By May 1932, another 4,500 workers have been dismissed, and remaining workers had their wages and salaries cut 10–20 percent.[75]

The domestic repercussions of the crisis of Czech war industries served to strengthen Škoda's position. To preserve Škoda as the country's main defense supplier, the MNO placed artillery orders worth $13.67 million (CZK 451 million) in 1932 to be executed 1933–1937 (Table 3.1). Due in large measure to these Czech Army orders, Škoda's

---

[72] RG 165, Entry 77, Romania 6510, #2724-V-60 (3) G-2 Report, Romania, Renewal of Škoda Arms Contract, Lt. Col. F. L. Whitley (Mil attaché Belgrade/Bucharest), March 20, 1935.

[73] FO 371/4329, Major W. H. Oxley (mil attaché) to Ronald Macleay (British Legation Prague), March 6, 1930.

[74] Karlický, 141–142.   [75] FO 371/15899, Addison to Sir John Simon, May 31, 1932.

Table 3.1 *Arms Sales of Škoda Works, 1930–1934, Converted into Millions of Dollars*

Year	Domestic Arms Sales	Arms Export Sales	Total Sales (Includes nonarms)	Arms Exports as Percentage of Total Sales	Domestic Arms Sales as Percentage of Total Sales
1930	5.36	16.95	49.5	34.0	10.0
1931	4.09	7.85	36.5	21.0	11.0
1932	2.45	2.04	19.8	10.0	12.0
1933	2.98	3.58	22.88	16.0	13.0
1934	12.04	3.72	32.92	11.0	37.0

Source: Karlický, 598–599.

crisis culminated in 1933.[76] The company's situation remained far from ideal in December 1933 due to Yugoslav and Romanian difficulties, but Škoda's domestic rival ČKD was in even worse shape. Therefore, Jaroslav Preiss as head of ČKD initiated negotiations with Loevenstein about a cartel. ČKD would recognize Škoda's monopoly in artillery, munitions, and aircraft bombs for sale to the Czechoslovak government. However, domestic orders for tanks, ammunition, military wheeled and tracked vehicles, tractors, aircraft, and aircraft engines were to be evenly divided between the two firms. On November 19, 1934, Škoda/ Loevenstein accepted the proposal from ČKD/Preiss to share armored vehicles ordered from the MNO including tanks on an even basis 1:1. The deal pertained to domestic orders only and exempted exports. The cartel with ČKD was signed December 29, 1934, and took effect July 9, 1935.[77] Also in 1934, Škoda increased its holdings in ČZB (Brno) through the purchase of $0.75 million (CZK 18 million) of new shares.[78]

The Škoda scandal reaffirmed that Schneider did not pull the strings as a puppet-master over Škoda. Poor Popescu proved correct about the Schneider–Škoda cartel. Given the strength of the Schneider–Škoda Artillery Convention by this time, Romania really could not use Schneider as a competitor against Škoda. More to the point, Schneider had not aggressively sought Romanian orders despite much prodding from the French government. As the Seletzki case developed, Schneider passively watched the spectacle from the wings because the French had no connection to Seletzki whatsoever. He was Škoda's man.

[76] Karlický, 148, 157.   [77] Karlický, 221; Diestler, 80, 82–83.   [78] Diestler, 91.

4   Limited Modernizations and Surreptitious Rearmaments
The Aircraft Business in Eastern Europe, 1920–1930

The French military aviation industry had enabled the French Air Force to occupy pride of place as the best and biggest in the world by the end of the war, and the dominance of French firms in the combat aircraft export business largely held throughout the twenties. As of May 1923, the French Air Force counted 1,178 aircraft compared to Britain's 371. The French Potez 25 proved the most successful aircraft sold with 7,000 produced, of which licensed manufacture accounted for 3,000, and Potez became the premier French aviation producer during the interwar era.[1] East European states eagerly sought the development of a domestic military aviation industry. Czechoslovakia, Poland, Romania, Greece, Yugoslavia, the Soviet Union, Turkey, and Bulgaria each tried to join the ranks of Britain, France, the US, and Italy as domestic producers of military aircraft during the twenties. Joint ventures served as the most common vehicle for domestication of the aircraft industry. Usually the host government partnered with a foreign private company to establish a production facility in country, train native workers, and provide licensing and technical agreements to complete the technology transfer. Overall, these various efforts did not yield substantial results, and most of the countries remained dependent on foreign suppliers for their aircraft. However, two of the contenders, Czechoslovakia and Poland, did achieve self-sufficiency in military aviation production and transformed into serious competitors as exporters of military aircraft in their own right during the period.

The military aviation rearmament efforts in the Soviet Union, Turkey, and Bulgaria exposed part of a larger problem, namely surreptitious

---

[1] E. Chadeau, "Schumpeter, l'État et les capitalistes: entreprendre dans l'aviation en France (1900–1980)," *Le Mouvement social*, no. 145, La France et l'Aéronautique (1988), 10–12; C. Kitching, *Britain and the Problem of International Disarmament, 1919–1934* (London: Routledge, 1999), 66; D. Edgerton, *Warfare State, Britain, 1920–1970* (Cambridge: Cambridge University Press, 2006), 43; L. Berger, "Henry Potez et Marcel Dassault, Constructeurs Aéronautiques de la Grande Guerre," *Gnuerres Mondiales Et Conflits Contemporains*, no. 209 (2003): 54.

rearmament through the circumvention of disarmament restrictions established by Allied armament controls. The Inter-Allied Military Control Commission consisting of French, British, Belgian, Italian, and Japanese officers supervised the execution of the military clauses of the Versailles Treaty while the Inter-Allied Aeronautical Commission of Control exercised a similar role regarding combat aircraft. The Conference of Ambassadors had supervisory power over the Control Commissions. The Conference of Ambassadors originally had charge to settle Allied disputes over German disarmament, but subsequently it gained oversight over disarmament questions for all the postwar treaties: St. Germain (Austria), Trianon (Hungary), Neuilly (Bulgaria), and Sèvres (Turkey). With the exception of Turkey, who negotiated a new treaty after the Greco–Turkish War, all the other defeated Central Powers were strictly forbidden to export or import arms and war materiel. By the end of 1922, with Germany effectively disarmed and its capacity to produce armaments eradicated, the Aeronautical Control Commission was eventually replaced by the Aeronautical Committee of Guarantee in 1922–1927. The Conference tasked the Military and Aeronautical Control Commissions with distinguishing between war materiels considered a security threat and those that could have peaceful use, i.e., dual use.[2] In the case of aircraft, this meant permissible civilian aircraft that could be converted easily for military use. The problem stemmed from the possibility that aircraft parts could be produced in modest shops in multiple sites and then assembled only when they were needed for military service. Surreptitious distribution of orders would make it possible to build five thousand machines in a couple of years in a populous and highly industrialized country without detection. The close similarity of certain commercial and military aircraft, and the similarity in all cases of certain parts such as the wings, constituted another problem in that a country could easily amass equipment for an air force under the guise of commercial activity.[3]

The provisions of the Versailles Treaty prohibited Germany from maintaining an air force. German desire to get out from under the Versailles restrictions found willing collaborators as the German firm Junkers established plants in the Soviet Union and Turkey. In this case, German military-industrial interests dove-tailed nicely with Soviet and Turkish interest in developing a domestic military aviation industry. Despite being under a similar military aviation prohibition imposed

---

[2] R. J. Shuster, *German Disarmament after World War I: The Diplomacy of International Arms Inspection, 1920–1931* (London: Routledge, 2006), 26–33, 41, 56, 69.

[3] E. P. Warner, "Aerial Armament and Disarmament," *Foreign Affairs*, vol. 4, no. 4 (1926), 627–628.

by the Treaty of Neuilly, Bulgaria too sought to evade its imposed disarmament. The willingness of French and Czech interests to look the other way and treat with Bulgarian business over British objections highlights one of the problems of enforcing the disarmament.

Soviet rearmament efforts in the mid 1920s adversely affected League of Nations disarmament negotiations at Geneva. Preparatory meetings for a new Arms Traffic Convention began in February 1924, in December the League Council agreed to set the opening of a Geneva Conference on the issue for May 4, 1925. As Basil Zaharoff had foreseen in 1918, the nonproducing smaller states quickly rose to defend their sovereignty, and some of the loudest voices for the unfettered arms came from East European delegates. Greece's delegate to the League, Vassili Dendramis decried "a kind of condominium of the great States will be set up over the small nonproducing States, which will, in reality, come under the control of the great. They will be at their mercy; they will be subjected to such economic and political conditions as may be imposed on them."[4] while Turkey's Mehmed Tevfik Bey advocated that "freedom to export ... should be complete and unrestricted."[5] The USSR's neighbors opposed the publicity provisions of the Arms Traffic Convention. As David Stone has argued, the issue of publicizing arms-trading raised issues of security as publishing arms imports and exports meant that the supply of national defense forces of the small states would be compulsorily revealed, and this problem was worst for states bordering on the Soviet Union. The Soviets had declined even to attend the Geneva Conference in 1925, and Eastern European states, especially Romania and Poland, thus refused to ratify the convention as they regarded the unilateral publication of their own munitions trade to be an unmitigated intelligence disaster.[6]

The switch from wood to metal construction of airframes was the most important technical change in aircraft manufacture in the twenties. Similarly, the international development of more powerful engines incorporating special metals and lubricants and sophisticated accessories such as injectors and compressors between 1925 and 1935 affected aircraft motor production. Metal production allowed for better large-scale production of homogenous quality parts with longer use life.[7] These

---

[4] Quoted in D. R. Stone, "Imperialism and Sovereignty: The League of Nations' Drive to Control the Global Arms Trade," *Journal of Contemporary History*, vol. 35, no. 2 (2000), 223.

[5] Quoted in Stone, 224.   [6] Stone, 221–224, 226–229.

[7] Chadeau, 12; P. Fearon, "The Formative Years of the British Aircraft Industry, 1913–1924," *Business History Review*, vol. 43, no. 4 (1969), 486.

technological changes reinforced French advantage to the detriment of British firms. According to Peter Fearon, one of the premiere historians of the British aircraft industry, merely designing and preparing drawings for a British military machine of metal construction in 1925 could easily cost more than actually building a similar machine of wood. Additionally, the lack of demand at home discouraged the rapid application of new techniques. These factors caused British producers to lag behind the French in the use of metals in aeronautics by 1925. The relative backwardness of British producers struck foreign engineers visiting British factories in the mid 1920s who often reported surprise at the lack of special machine tools for aero engine building.[8] Consequently, French firms were the ones to beat, and British firms had trouble keeping up even as new entrants from Czechoslovakia and Poland were waiting in the wings.

The end of the war and consequent sharp drop in war orders created an immediate problem of overproduction for the British military aircraft industry. Roughly 200 British firms had engaged in aircraft construction prior to the outbreak of the war in 1914, and during the war that number had reached 1,529 by October 1918. The following postwar drop in demand had reduced the British aircraft industry to just thirteen firms by 1920.[9] For example the British firm Airco, the largest aircraft manufacturer, had been producing 250 planes a month in 1918. By 1920, Airco had been driven out of business because of lack of new orders from the British government. As Fearon observed, "The general desire in Parliament and the country for disarmament, and the government aim of cutting expenditure on the armed forces naturally had a depressing effect on military orders."[10] For its part, the government favored reconditioning older craft rather than spending for new ones. Facing a lack of domestic demand British aircraft manufacturers looked for salvation in exports. However, the massive excess quantities of aircraft and parts meant that such exports would consist of war surplus rather than newly produced machines. The British Ministry of Munitions had established a Disposal Board in 1919 to manage the overstock, and in 1920 the private firm Handley Page Company took over the entire affair through the creation of the Aircraft Disposals Company. By this means Handley Page acquired 10,000 airplanes, some 30,000 aircraft engines, roughly 350,000 spark plugs, and 1,000 ball bearings for the price of $3.81 million ($£1$ million) and 50 percent future profits. Given the lack of new orders, the $22.86 million ($£6$ million) in profits derived from the

---

[8] Fearon, "Formative Years," 486.
[9] B. Coombs, *British Tank Production and the War Economy, 1934–1945* (London: Bloomsbury Academic, 2015), 9–10.
[10] Fearon, "Formative Years," 494.

Aircraft Disposals Company kept Handley Page from going out of business. Throughout the first half of the 1920s, exports of war surplus made up the largest part of the business for British military aircraft companies.[11]

Complicating the military aviation competition, new competitors from Czechoslovakia and Poland joined the fray in the latter 1920s. Škoda was poised for further diversification and expansion within the Czechoslovak armaments sector. While giving a nod "to the general world situation marked by the striving for the restriction of armaments in almost all countries," a Škoda company publication in 1925 indicated coming moves into the aircraft business, noting that, "the Škoda Works pay the greatest attention to all technical improvements in this direction and are therefore watching the progress in aviation very carefully."[12] Škoda's moves into the aviation business did proceed apace. In 1923, Škoda had initiated the manufacture of Hispano-Suiza airplane motors under French license to meet an order from the Czechoslovak government that was expected to reach 300. By November 1924, Škoda had completed 150 airplane motors with thirty-five motors delivered to the Czechoslovak government, and the rest in reserve. Having introduced aircraft engine production successfully, in August 1926 Škoda received an order from the Czechoslovak government for twenty-five all-metal airplane bodies of the French Dewoitine type based on Škoda's license. This contract represented the first order for all-metal planes ever placed by Czechoslovak government as well as the first large order for flying equipment ever placed with Škoda. The Plzeň works completed all these Dewoitines by January 1928.[13] As a means to support military aviation expansion, Škoda purchased the existing aeronautical works of Milos Bondy in 1926 and transformed it into a newly established, wholly owned subsidiary company Avia in 1927.[14] Avia in Prague produced 195 planes, including 160 pursuit aircraft for the government by its first year. By the end of the 1920s, Czechoslovakia found itself virtually independent in aircraft production with the government only importing two

---

[11] Ibid., 480, 482, 490–493.

[12] *Twenty-Five Years of the Limited Company Formerly The Škoda Works in Plzeň* (Plzeň: Škoda, 1925), 8–9.

[13] RG 165, #2281-II-3 Harry Coates to G-2, November 6, 1923; SA, 01G0075-A-477bis, Rapport Mission of Caillet to Škoda, November 1–13, 1924; RG 165, #2726–59, Major H. W. T. Elgin to G-2, August 9, 1926; SA, 01G0015-A-03, Situation des Industries des A. K. Škoda, January 1, 1928.

[14] A. D'Angio, *Schneider et Cie et la naissance de l'ingénerie* (Paris: CNRS Editions, 2000), 176; M. Hauner, "Military Budgets and the Armaments Industry," in M. C. Kaser and E. A. Radice (eds.), *The Economic History of Eastern Europe 1919–1939* (Oxford: Clarendon Press, 1986), 78.

planes in 1928 and none in 1929.[15] The Czechoslovak government also entered the aviation field. The state-owned Airplane Factory at Letna under the very able direction of Alois Smolik, had developed a series of pursuit, observation and bombardment planes (Smolik series), and those planes met with considerable success in various foreign competitions held in 1928. In the Turkish competition, Letna had landed an order for four Smolik S-14s, and delivered half of another Turkish order for forty-one type S-16 planes by the end of 1931. By 1930, the Czechoslovak state Aircraft Factory employed 350 workers, and its chief foreign orders on hand included twenty day bombers S-16 for Lithuania, fifteen day bombers S-16 for Bulgaria, Turkey four day bombers S-1 for Turkey, and one S-16 for Yugoslavia. The Aero works had 650 workers, and Avia (Škoda) had 250 workers with orders for Belgium and Yugoslavia.[16]

In northeastern Europe, Czech firms truly dominated the military aircraft market, and British producers were stymied in the Baltic. Although it is true that Latvia ordered eight new planes in Britain and ten from France in 1925, during 1926–1927 Lithuania bought eight training aircraft and a series of fighters from the Czechs. They also purchased twenty Smolik day bombers type S-16 in March 1930.[17] Watching from the sidelines, British Ambassador Rennie in Helsinki lamented that the stinginess of the British government cost British firms aircraft contracts. Rennie argued that his government should bear the salary cost for British air officers as part of an Air Mission to Finland. He noted that the French did not charge the host government to send their flying officers abroad because Paris understood that French firms would most likely benefit from the resulting aircraft orders. He wrote, "It must be remembered that the result of the engagement of a British flying officer may be placing in England of orders for aircraft to the amount of several hundred thousand pounds in the near future, and that ultimately Finland will not implausibly place herself in the hands of Great Britain in the matter of aircraft construction. It would, therefore, be very short-sighted policy to risk the loss of such orders for the sake of a few hundred pounds in connection with the salary of a British flying officer."[18] Meanwhile

---

[15] RG 165, #2331-II-18 (2)Military Attaché H. W. T. Eglin to G-2, January 11, 1927; SA, 01G0015-A-03, Situation des Industries des A. K. Škoda, January 1, 1928; AIR 5/1179, A.I.8., May 29, 1933; FO 371/14330, Addison to Henderson (Prague), May 6, 1930.

[16] RG 165, #2726–71 (2) Mil attaché Vienna to G-2, February 19, 1929; AIR 5/1179, Aviation Report Czechoslovakia, December 22, 1931; FO 371/4329, Major W. H. Oxley (mil attaché) to Ronald Macleay (British Legation Prague), March 6, 1930.

[17] FO 371/10975, Lloyd (Mil attaché) to Tudor Vaughn (Baltic), August 4, 1925; AIR 5/1179, A.1.8. Lithuania, August 5, 1932.

[18] FO 371/10990, Rennie to FO, December 22, 1924.

Major-General Kirke viewed a British military mission to Finland as a means to break the "French air monopoly and help our own constructors."[19] The Finnish Air Force had intended to buy Bristol fighters in 1926, but the adverse criticisms of that plane in the House of Commons debates deterred them. They thus bought instead Czech Smoliks, which were $5,000 (200,000 Finnish Marks) cheaper than the Bristol Wapiti (Westland Co.).[20] Concerned about the upcoming visit by the Curtiss Circus to Helsinki, Rennie sought out the head of the Finnish Air Force, Col. Vuori to "counteract the effect of their propaganda." Rennie was pleased to hear from Vuori that the Finns understood that the object of the American circus was to increase sales, and that Vuori had pro-British sympathies.[21] Perhaps as a result of those sympathies, the Finnish Air Force signed a contract for Armstrong-Siddeley engines in 1931.[22]

Problems with engine orders opened the door to multiple British competitors entering the Finnish market. In mid-December 1931, the Finnish Socialist newspaper *Suomen Sosiali-Deomokrati* leveled charges that the Finnish Air Force had purchased inferior Jupiter motors for $500,000 (FIM 20 million), and Finnish air authorities had wasted $42,500 (FIM 1.7 million) for eight Koolhaven bombers because to poor Jaguar motors had to be scrapped. On the heels of the engine revelations, a representative of Bristols turned up in Finland offering for the first time British-built Bristol engines. Now with two British firms involved, Bristol and Armstrong-Siddeley, the British Consul adopted a neutral position so as to avoid the appearance of favoring one over the other.[23]

In British eyes, the Czechs had replaced the French as the chief rival in the Baltic by 1930. With increased Czech competition to British trade in this part of Europe, little Estonia had taken on surprisingly great importance to British trade, and in particular the aircraft market. The Estonians had wanted to order planes in England worth $121,250 (£25,000) in 1925, but nothing came of it. In January 1930, Estonia sought to decide on its new single-seater fighter and had narrowed it down to either the Bristol Bulldog or the Smolik S-31. The British Consul in Tallinn paid a call on the Estonian Assistant Minister for Foreign Affairs, Schmidt, to advocate for the British purchase. The Consul reminded Schmidt of

[19] FO 371/10990, Rept of Major-General W. M. St. G. Kirke on the British Mission to Finland, July 1924–March 1925, April 4, 1925.
[20] FO 371/14809, Rennie to Henderson, April 26, 1930.
[21] Ibid.   [22] FO 371/15562, Seymour to FO, April 9, 1931.
[23] FO 371/15562, Burbury to FO, December 15, 1931; FO 371/16286, C. B. Jerram to Burbury, May 10, 1932.

Estonian assurances during the negotiations on tariff questions at the end 1929, that it was their wish and intention to place orders in Great Britain, as Britain was Estonia's best customer. The Air Adviser had assured Estonian authorities that although the Smolik was 16–17 percent cheaper, the Bristol Bulldog was far more suitable. While the Bristol had been thoroughly tested and adopted by the British Air Force, only two machines of the type Smolik S-31 had ever been constructed. No air force in the world had adopted the Czech aircraft, and the Estonians were not in a position from a financial, technical, or a practical point of view to indulge in experiments to test the Smolik properly. When the Estonian Chief of Air Defense proposed to buy twelve Bristol Bulldogs the next day, the proposal met with opposition in the War Council and resulted in a stalemate. The Estonian resolution of the competition involved splitting the contracts between aircraft and armaments. Estonia signed a contract with Bristol for twelve Bulldogs but ordered the twenty-four machine guns for the Bulldogs with the Czech firm Boemische Waffenfabrik, Strakowice, which manufactured a modified Vickers gun. The Bristol order opened up Estonia for other British sales, and the next year Estonia signed a contract with Hawker for eight Hawker Hart aircraft.[24]

Like many countries in Eastern Europe, the Polish Air Force initially consisted of mostly French aircraft. In the period 1922–1926, Poland's French purchases included 30 Farman-Goliaths, 300 Blériot-Spad-61 fighters, 200 Breguets, and 200 Potez XV. Az planes with 400hp Lorraine-Diétrich engines, and another thirty Henriot trainers with Rhône engines. In all, Poland had ordered some 2,000 aircraft engines from French firms.[25] These purchases under General Wlodimierz Zagorski generated much controversy within the Polish General Staff. Poland lacked trained pilots and crews, or hangars for these enormous purchases, and Poland had to take out loans with France to pay for them.[26] Using a French licensing agreement, the Polish airplane factory

---

[24] FO 371/14779, (Tallinn) Jerram to Walker (Riga), January 29, 1930; FO 371/10975, Vaughn to Austen Chamberlain, January 4, 1925; FO 371/14779, C. B. Jerram to Walker (Riga), January 13, 1930; FO 371/14779, Consul Jerram (Tallinn) to Air Ministry, January 14, 1930; FO 371/14779, Walker to Arthur Henderson, February 10, 1930; FO 371/14779, Jerram to Dept of Overseas Trade, March 12, 1930; FO 371/16263, Knatchbull-Hugesson (Riga) to FO, January 11, 1932; FO 371/16263, Hawker Engineering to FO, January 4, 1932.

[25] RG 165 Entry 77 Poland 9510 Aviation Exports and Imports, Rept. Military attaché Paris, #11, 783-W, December 21, 1926; FO 371/11005, Poland, Annual Report, 1924, Muller to Austen Chamberlain, October 16, 1925.

[26] M. A. Peszke, "The Forgotten Campaign: Poland's Military Aviaition in September, 1939," *The Polish Review*, vol. 39, no. 1 (1994), 53–54.

at Biala Podloaska turned out its first machine, a Potez type XV.A.2, at the end of June 1925.[27]

Zagorki's successor, General Ludomil Rayski led the drive for a Polish aircraft industry to ensure self-sufficiency, and in 1927 Poland decided to emancipate itself from foreign sources of airplane supply. Initially, Rayski's policy showed early promise as Polish fighter squadrons were the first in Europe to be equipped with an all-metal monoplane designed and built in Poland.[28]

Henceforth airplanes for the Polish Army would be built domestically near Warsaw by Zakłady Lutnicze Frankopol, a factory in which Škoda had acquired the controlling interest in late 1926. The Poles were looking to import the engines in the short run, and sought to adopt the British Napier 600hp water-cooled and Bristol Jupiter 200hp air-cooled engines by acquiring the licenses for construction in Poland. At roughly the same time Škoda acquired shares in the Polish-French Car and Aircraft Company in Warsaw which became Polske Zakłady Skody or Warsaw Škoda Works in 1927. The Poles subsequently placed their order with Škoda for 2,000 Hispano-Suiza and Lorraine-Diétrich engines to be delivered by 1929. Based on the satisfactory results, in 1929 Škoda concluded a ten-year contract with the Poles to supply American Wright Whirlwind engines to be manufactured under license in the Warsaw Škoda Works.[29]

Soon the Poles would join the Czechs as serious competitors to the French for aircraft exports. By 1931, the Poles had achieved self-sufficiency in domestic aviation production from their state factories, most notably Państwowe Zakłady Lotnicze (PZL), and began pursuing Romanian export orders. Several Romanian commissions visited Poland, and eventually an order was placed in Poland for 120 airplanes, but the economic crisis intervened and Poland suspended delivery due to Romanian nonpayment. Late in 1931, the Polish authorities informed Yeager, the American military attaché, that they had signed a contract for sixty pursuit airplanes with Romania, but it still remained to decide upon the engine type. However, the French exerted financial pressure on the Romanian government to block the Polish order and support

---

[27] FO 371/11001, Mil attaché Warsaw, July 1925. Notes on Polish Army to FO, May 1, 1925.

[28] Peszke, 54–55.

[29] FO 371/12579, Overseas Trade to Austen Chamberlain, February 9, 1927; FO 371/12579, Br Legation (Warsaw) to Austen Chamberlain, December 20, 1926; FO 371/12579, Overseas Trade to Austen Chamberlain, February 9, 1927; RG 165 Entry 77 Poland 9510 Aviation Exports and Imports, Rept Military attaché Paris, #12, 233-W, April 29, 1927; AIR 5/1179, A.1.8. Poland, August 5, 1932.

the purchase of a French pursuit plane instead.[30] The Poles understood clearly that it was a question of credits. The Polish state company could not extend sufficient credit to the Romanian government to cover this order, and so the French company would win out. According to Yeager, while he was visiting the Center of Aviation Training near Bucharest, the commanding officer in discussing Polish aviation stated that the new Polish pursuit plane was the best in Europe at present. The Romanian officer then turned to the Romanian General Staff officer and said in Romanian, "the Polish plane is the best but we are going to buy the French planes."[31] At last, in 1933 the Romanian government did acquire from Poland fifty planes fitted with French Gnôme engines.[32]

Romania

As in the case of land armaments, French and British concerns went head to head in competition for aircraft sales in southeastern Europe. France had moved first into the Romanian aircraft market. The first postwar arms deal was signed in December 1920. At that time the French military attaché in Bucharest, General Victor Petin, had arranged a contract for the delivery of French war materiel in exchange for payment with Romanian oil instead of currency. The contract also called for the French to construct an aircraft factory in Romania in partnership with a Romanian company. Even though the Romanians had officially agreed upon the French aircraft factory in 1921, as of 1923 nothing had come of the project due to Romanian financial constraints. The French legislature refused to provide the $7.7 million (F100 million) advance to Romania, and French private bankers had grave doubts about Romania's ability to make payments.[33]

Romania had depended on French imports to equip its air force. Following the loss of forty-four new French aircraft when their hangar was destroyed in a storm in February 1921, Col. Ruginski, Director of the Romanian Air Force, looked for French replacements, but his

---

[30] FO 371/ 16825, Romanian. Annual Report, 1932. Palainet to Simon, March 15, 1933, 34; MAE, Europe 1930–1940, Pologne. 313, Ambs Warsaw to MAE, December 2, 1931.

[31] RG 165, Entry 77, Romania 6510, #2724-V-52 (2) G-2 Report, Romania, Status of various orders for Armament and Equipment, Emer Yeager (Mil attaché Warsaw), July 24, 1932.

[32] FO 371/16825, Palairet to FO, June 17, 1933.

[33] M. Thomas, "To Arm an Ally: French Arms Sales to Romania, 1926–1940," *The Journal of Strategic Studies*, vol. 19, no. 2 (1996), 237–239.

subordinate Col Popovici advocated successfully for British planes.[34] In August, the Romanian government signed a contract with the British Aircraft Disposal Co. for sixty planes and parts in the amount of $502,320 (£120,750). Having only paid $65,520 (£15,750), Romania gave treasury bills payable at fixed dates as security, but then refused to honor those treasury bills upon presentation.[35] Thus, began Romanian aviation's bumpy ride through Anglo-French rivalry and Romanian fiscal difficulties.

According to Romanian Crown Prince Carol, the future king who since 1924 served as the Inspector General of the Romanian Air Force and headed the Aviation Supreme Directorate,[36] the Romanian government was "tied up with the French credits and loans, which were used by the French to ensure that contracts shall be placed in France."[37] For reasons of economy, Romania would have to terminate the British naval mission. As compensation to Britain for losing the naval mission, the Crown Prince suggested placing a large aviation order with Armstrong and bringing that firm in as a partner in the establishment of an airplane factory in Romania.[38] The Romanians complained about higher British prices. When the Prime Minister remarked to the British Ambassador Dering that "a cheap watch which went satisfactorily was to him every bit as useful as one costing three times the amount," Dering countered that lives did not depend on the accuracy of a watch whereas with airplanes "only the very best could ensure the safety of Romanian aviators."[39] Even with the Crown Prince backing Armstrong-Siddeley, the French air attaché succeeded in taking half of the share of Romania's orders for aircraft for a French firm. Armstrong-Siddeley received an order for half the sum available for airplanes while the French firm Potez took the remainder. Romanian aviation officials raised seemingly endless technical objections to the British planes, and Colonel Ruginski, recently decorated by France and of noted French sympathies, launched a press campaign against the Armstrong manufacturers and praising the French. The Liberal politician Duca tried to assure Dering "that the British contract will not be allowed to be overthrown by rival action of French or other interests."[40] By April 1924, Romania had

[34] R. P. T. Davenport-Hines, "Vickers' Balkan Conscience Aspects of Anglo-Romanian Armaments 1918–39," *Business History*, vol. 25, no. 3 (1983), 291–292.

[35] AIR 5/274, Aircraft Disposal Co., London to Air Ministry, November 9, 1922.

[36] A. Statiev, "Antonescu's Eagles against Stalin's Falcons: The Romanian Air Force, 1920–1941," *The Journal of Military History*, vol. 66, No. 4 (2002), 1086.

[37] AIR 5/274, Dering to FO, January 5, 1924.   [38] Ibid.

[39] AIR 5/274, Dering to MacDonald, February 15, 1924.

[40] FO 371/10806, Romania. Annual Report, 1924, Dering to Austen Chamberlain, March 5, 1925, 12.

signed a contract with Potez for 120 aircraft for a total contract of roughly $1.13 million (F21 million), and an additional contract with Lorraine-Diétrich worth $130,000 (F2.4 million) for twenty-four military aircraft.[41] Meanwhile, neither the 120 Potez reconnaissance planes nor the sixty Armstrong-Siddeley scout planes had actually arrived in Romania due to construction and payment problems.[42]

The negotiations between Armstrong-Siddeley and the Romanian government for aircraft sales dragged on into 1925. The Romanian air officers continually made alterations and modifications in the contract, leaving Armstrong-Siddeley with the distinct impression that the Romanians were maneuvering to deprive the British firm of its portion of aircraft orders so as to give the whole of the order for airplanes to the French firm Potez. The British firm's prospects suffered a further blow when Major Sanatescu of the Romanian Air Force died in a crash near Coventry while flying an Armstrong-Siddeley Siskin airplane. Romanian papers published a number of articles depreciatory of the British and praising the French machines. The British Air Ministry investigated the circumstances of the accident, but the Romanians deemed the findings unsatisfactory. Distrustful of the aircraft, the Romanian government therefore refused to accept the completed airplanes as specified in the contract, and accept only the engines. After further protracted negotiations in November 1925, the Romanians finally agreed to allow Armstrong to supply seventy Jaguar engines together with extra equipment and spare parts. Of note, the Potez aircraft played a role in at least six fatal accidents and death of twelve Romanian airmen without raising any public outcry. Following the cancellation of the Armstrong-Siddeley contract, the Romanians placed a hasty contract for fifty planes with the Dutch firm Fokker. The Fokkers proved equally problematic because upon arrival the Romanians discovered that while the planes were new, the engines were old. The resulting scandal led to the arrest of several officers responsible for taking over the airplanes under accusations of taking bribes. The Romanian government then cancelled the Fokker contract, and the members of the commission were brought before a court-martial. Though eventually more or less exonerated, several senior officers were relieved of their posts. Pending the creation of a national airplane factory the Romanian Air Force ordered a further 100 planes from France, this time Spads from the firm of Blériot.[43]

---

[41] Thomas, "To Arm," 237–239.

[42] FO 371/10806, Romania. Annual Report, 1924, Dering to Austen Chamberlain, March 5, 1925, 38.

[43] FO 371/11428, Romania. Annual Report, 1925, Herbert Dering to Chamberlain, March 6, 1926, 23, 41.

The Romanian government did strive to develop a domestic military aircraft industry. In 1921, Romania's initial efforts were based on assembling reconnaissance aircraft from parts captured in Hungary.[44] The Romanians had given their approval for Armstrong-Siddeley to manage a national airplane factory in 1924. Yet, the Romanians proceeded to redirect that plant to the French firm Lorraine-Diétrich and Blériot together with Arad Engineering Works. This new company, Industrie Aeronautique Roumaine (IAR) formed in 1925, took charge of the Romanian airplane factory at Brasov. There IAR inaugurated a three-year production program with a quota for 100 Spad airplanes in the second year of operation (1927).[45] Over the years up to the Second World War, Brasov did manage to turn out fighters, bombers, reconnaissance/light bombers, and trainer aircraft. Most commonly, the works employed foreign manufacturing licenses whether from French, Polish, American, German, or Italian sources. Nevertheless, Romania's aviation manufacturing capabilities remained small and did not attain self-sufficiency. In 1939, Romania produced only 125 reconnaissance/light bomber aircraft and 25 fighters, and generally Romanian models fell behind developments in other countries.[46]

Greece

At the same time that Armstrong-Siddeley competed for the Romanian business, they and other British firms sought to make inroads in Greece at French expense. Prior to 1925 French firms had held unchallenged dominance in the Greek aviation market. The Greek military Air Service consisted of fifteen instructional machines, thirty-five reconnaissance (Breguet), and five fighters (Nieuports) all of French construction. As a result of a Greek mission to France in 1925, the Greeks bought thirty more aircraft including fifteen Breguets. Despite the tough going, the British firm Blackburn Aeroplane appeared to pull off something of a coup when it secured the contract to operate the old Phaleron factory, which the Greeks hoped would become their domestic supplier. Blackburn had the support of the British government all to itself since the only other British firm that showed serious interest was Gloucestershire Aircraft Co. of Cheltenham, which concluded that the Greek terms were not

---

[44] Statiev, "Antonescu's Eagles," 1086.
[45] FO 371/11428, Romania. Annual Report, 1925, Herbert Dering to Chamberlain, March 6, 1926, 41; FO 371/12229, Goodden (mil attaché Romania) to Legation Bucharest, October 13, 1927.
[46] Statiev, "Antonescu's Eagles," 1086–1087.

sufficiently attractive. From the commencement of negotiations in 1924 for the operation of the Phaleron Aircraft Company the British representative, Milne Cheetham, had recommended Blackburn energetically to the Greek government. The French Legation pushed for a French contract at least as aggressively, but Blackburn landed the contract due to the attractive terms which they offered. Under the agreement with Blackburn signed December 27, 1924, the company committed to equip the Phaleron factory for the construction and maintenance of aircraft. The Greek government promised to purchase a minimum of £25,000 output, but probably more like £100,000 annually. In April 1925, the Greek government and Blackburn concluded another contract for Blackburn to build six scout planes, six two-seater fighters, nine torpedo planes, and six single engine heavy bombers at Phaleron for the Greek Navy.[47]

However, pro-French sympathies within the Greek Army impeded the Greek government from placing any army orders with factory, only naval orders. It took eighteen months to persuade the army to participate, and another six months to obtain their signatures to the special contract for building French Breguet machines, and a further five months to deliver two of three sets of required drawings. With insufficient work given to factory, Blackburn had suffered a loss of $268,400 (£55,000) as of April 30, 1929. On May 1, 1929, as a result of an interview between Prime Minister Venizelos and Mr. Blackburn, a new contract was agreed upon between the company and the Ministry of Marine, "which brings no profit to the company, but at any rate has the advantage of avoiding a continuation of the losses."[48]

The results by the end of 1929 confirmed the split between the pro-British Greek Naval Air Arm and the pro-French Greek Army. The navy did continue to purchase British materiel, including ten more Atlas machines to be manufactured at Phaleron under license, and six Hawker Horsley Condor Torpedo bombers contracted with Hawker Engineering Co. and Rolls-Royce. In 1930, Greek naval aviation purchased $534,600 (£110,000) worth of air equipment from England, and the next year bought ten Fairey 111F seaplanes and twelve AVRO 504N aircraft. Meanwhile, the Greek Army continued to buy French and made purchases worth $423,208 (£87,080) in 1930. The army

---

[47] AIR 40/1404, Greece. Relations with France; FO 286/937, Milne Cheetham to Chamberlain, January 6, 1925; FO 371/13662, Greek Agreement, encl in Burton to Balfour, December 8, 1929; FO 286/937, Keeling (Athens) to FO, April 17, 1925.
[48] FO 371/13662, Greek Agreement, encl in Burton to Balfour, December 8, 1929.

bought eighteen Morane 130s and twenty-four Potez 25s, followed by twenty-four additional Potez 25s purchased in 1931.[49]

Even with the Phaleron factory concession, British firms had not decisively broken into the Greek aircraft market. By December 1929, Blackburn's representative, Maurice Burton, called at the British Foreign Office on behalf of his firm and drew attention to their claim against the Greek government. His company had not yet decided whether it was worth it to tender for a new contract after the expiration of the current contract. Burton indicated that "from a business point of view their enterprise in Greece had not proved a success. On the other hand, if the interested departments of HMG held the view that it was to the advantage of British interests that the company should continue to work in Greece, they might decide to tender for the new contract."[50] The Foreign Office held the opinion that Great Britain benefited both politically and commercially by having the Phaleron factory operated and controlled by a British firm. While recognizing that Blackburn had good reason to be discouraged by the treatment which they had experienced in Greece, the Foreign Office encouraged Blackburn to stay.

Yugoslavia

Having had some modicum of success in Greece, Blackburn looked to neighboring Yugoslavia. General Festing, a representative of Blackburn Aircraft, arrived in Yugoslavia in December 1925 to meet with Yugoslav naval authorities regarding the supply of naval aircraft. The British Ambassador in Belgrade, Kennard, advised that Blackburn should offer facilities for training and for building an aircraft factory in Yugoslavia in order to make the Blackburn offer more attractive. Otherwise, the Yugoslavs might find the Blackburn aircraft too expensive. The main difficulty for British firms centered on the Yugoslav requirement for easy financial terms as the primary consideration. Conducting business with the Yugoslavs meant that supplier firms had to be prepared to accept small payments spread over a number of years, and British interests rarely showed eagerness to do so.[51]

---

[49] FO 371/13662, Harvey to Henderson, September 2, 1929; FO 286/1045, Oliver C. Harvey (Commercial Secretary Athens) to FO, December 5, 1929; AIR 40/1404, Greece. Relations with Great Britain, December 10, 1932; AIR 40/1404 Greece. Relations with France.

[50] FO 371/13662, FO to Dept. of Overseas Trade, December 9, 1929.

[51] FO 371/10795, Kennard (Belgrade) to Austen Chamberlain, December 18, 1925.

In Yugoslavia, France had a virtual monopoly on military aviation. Through the twenties up to 1931 Yugoslavia had acquired 40 Dewoitine fighters and 400 Breguet observation bi-planes (partly built in France and part in Yugoslavia at Kraljevo).[52] Amid signs of Yugoslav dissatisfaction with these French products, the Yugoslav government had placed an order for three monoplanes with Hawker (British), orders for two bombers each with Junkers and Dornier (German) and two Fokkers made in Czechoslovakia. The French Air Ministry made known to the Foreign Ministry the danger that the French aeronautical industry was about to lose the Yugoslav market to these foreign firms. The Air Ministry therefore requested that the Foreign Ministry use its influence on the government in Belgrade to make them understand the bad effect that would be produced in France by abandoning the orders of the French aircraft industry and using the funds from our loans to profit foreign firms. The Air Ministry further expressed that "The emotion would be even worse if French money went to Germany for the construction and export of military material prohibited by Versailles."[53] The prospects appeared even more grave when the French embassy reported back to Paris that the Yugoslavs were about to purchase 150 Hawker fighters.[54] Immediately the Foreign Ministry applied pressure on Belgrade and succeeded in making Yugoslavia quash the potential order with Hawker. Nonetheless, the Foreign Ministry remained on guard as the Yugoslav Air Force still harbored partisans of the Hawker "despite its known faults," and "There is no rest to the intrigues against our material . . . If for the moment these maneuvers are paralyzed, they will be renewed."[55]

Soviet Union

In stark contrast to the rest of Eastern Europe, the Soviet Union did not serve as a battleground in the Anglo-French competition. As a self-proclaimed socialist state that had abandoned the Allied cause during the war and then been subjected to foreign intervention during the Russian Civil War, the Soviet Union was effectively an outcast from the Paris Peace Settlement. Their exclusion and isolation from the established political order of postwar Europe made the Soviets a sympathetic, potential partner for the other major pariah state in Europe, Germany. The Soviets first turned to German firms rather than French or British ones. Starting in 1919, German-Soviet contacts led to

[52] Chadeau, 28–29.
[53] MAE, Europe 1930–1940, Yougoslavie. 151, Min Air to MAE, June 15, 1931.
[54] Ibid., Dard to MAE, November 14, 1931.
[55] Ibid., MAE to Min Air, November 21, 1931.

military discussions by 1921. In contravention of Versailles, Germany began to send military and technical aid to the Soviets in order to manufacture airplane engines, poison gas, and Krupp armaments on Soviet soil. By summer 1920, the Allies knew of these German actions. The British government learned from Polish sources in July 1920 that a ship with 400,000 rifles and 200 million cartridges bought by Bolsheviks in Germany was about to sail from Germany to Estonia. In August 1920, French military intelligence reported 89,000 German workers, including specialists from Krupp, had emigrated to Kolomna, an industrial city southeast of Moscow.[56]

In June 1921, unofficial, secret talks began between the German firm Junkers of Dessau and the Soviets concerning the construction of a plant in Russia to produce aircraft and motors.[57] Junkers seemed an especially good choice because that firm, along with Fokker, had pioneered the change from bi-plane to monoplane, which would prove one of most important structural alterations in the twenties.[58] In December, two representatives of Junkers and two officers of the German Army flew to Moscow as part of a military-technical commission to negotiate with Trotsky. In Moscow, Junkers and the Soviet government signed an agreement on November 26, 1922. The agreement granted a concession to Junkers to establish a company for the manufacture of aircraft and aircraft motors for a term of thirty years, and for that purpose Junkers received a lease to use the former Russo-Baltic Aviation plant in Fili near Moscow. The production program set the ultimate goal of 300 aircraft annually, and the Soviet government promised to purchase 60 planes annually. Aircraft output was to begin no later than October 1, 1923, and motor production was to begin one year from the confirmation of the agreement. By January 29, 1924, Junkers was obligated to a production level of 75 aircraft and 112 motors and by January 29, 1925, the factory was to achieve the full level of production with 300 aircraft and 450 motors annually. In fall 1923, bilateral talks turned into concrete agreements with the Junkers Company on delivery of aircraft and erection of factory buildings in USSR. The German side assumed

---

[56] Shuster, 60; WO 190/126, Armament Firms in Europe with connections in Germany, July 24, 1931.

[57] For discussion of Soviet–German collaboration, see H. W. Gatzke, "Russo-German Military Collaboration during the Weimar Republic," *The American Historical Review*, Vol. 63, No. 3 (1958), 565–597; H. W. Gatzke, *Stresemann and the Rearmament of Germany* (Baltimore: Johns Hopkins University Press, 1954), 72–88; M. R. Habeck, *Storm of Steel: The Development of Armor Doctrine in Germany and the Soviet Union* (Ithaca, NY: Cornell University Press, 2003), 71–116.

[58] P. Fearon, "The British Airframe Industry and the State, 1918–35," *The Economic History Review*, New Series, vol. 27, no. 2 (1974), 238.

the entire financial risk of this venture, 600 million marks, whereas the Soviet side granted it the right to establish aircraft factories in Fili and Kharkov to make planes and engines. Although initially the talks had concerned wooden aircraft, with Junkers's consent the Soviets changed this to the production of all-metal aircraft. On the Soviet side doubts crept in about the quality of Junkers aircraft, and on December 20, 1923, the Soviets concluded an agreement with the Dutch firm Fokker for delivery of 200 aircraft (125 D-XI and 75 C-IV). In April 1925, 150 Fokkers aircraft were ready for delivery. To preserve secrecy, the planes were loaded on a ship addressed to Rio de Janeiro, and then later readdressed to a private firm in Leningrad so as not to reveal their destination as a Soviet state institution.[59]

Junkers managed to set up a factory with 1,300 personnel relatively quickly, but had difficulties preparing the motors, which turned out to be underpowered and therefore unacceptable. Also, as time went on the Fili plant fell further behind the production schedule. By the end of January 1924, the plant only had produced twelve planes and no motors. One year later, the factory had manufactured 75 planes and not a single motor when the agreement quota called for 300 planes and 450 motors. The planes that had been produced had generated cost overruns of approximately 6,000 rubles per plane. In spring 1925, a twin-motor airplane built by Junkers in Dessau flew to Moscow where it was demonstrated by company representatives with a proposal to convert it into a bomber. At the invitation of Junkers's directors, the Soviets visited Dessau in March 1925 to examine production facilities. Although holding a generally favorable impression of the organization of the work at Dessau, the lack of mechanization, especially for engine building, surprised the Soviets, and they rated it as far behind Italian engine-building factories. The disappointing results by 1925 led some Soviet officials to call for a reexamination of the Junkers concession, and perhaps even its dissolution. Meanwhile, Junkers faced bankruptcy at its home works in Dessau by October 1925, causing production at Fili to cease. By the end of 1925, Junkers Fili had turned out 170 aircraft, of which 120 had been accepted by the Soviets. Considering that total Soviet aircraft production 1924–1925 amounted to 264 planes, Fili had been the single largest producer within the Soviet Union.[60]

[59] Y. Dyakov and T. Bushuyeva (eds.), *The Red Army and the Wehrmacht: How the Soviets Militarized Germany, 1922–33, and Paved the Way for Fascism* (New York: Prometheus Books, 1995), 18, 127–128, 222; S. A. Gorlov, *Sovershenno sekretno Moskva-Berlin 1920–1933, Voenno-politicheskie otnosheniia mezhdu SSSR I Germaniei* (Moskva: IVI RAN, 1999), 94–97.
[60] Gorlov, 98–103; Dyakov and Bushuyeva, 132, 209–211.

In March 1926, complaints began to reach Stalin concerning the extravagant costs of foreign airplanes imports and the binding of Soviet aviation production to the concession agreement with Junkers. Specifically, the Soviets had given the order to Junkers for D-11 type fighters even though the Soviet technical commission had determined that model unfit for adoption during preliminary tests. Nevertheless, the Soviet government had ordered 125 units that arrived in the USSR in such a state that they had to be repaired on the spot. The Junkers order for 100 metal planes also had been accepted without preliminary testing at the Scientific and Experimental Aerodome. After almost the whole of the order had been completed, at last two airplanes were transferred for testing, and these did not conform to the agreement and failed to meet the requirements as military aircraft. Despite having the proper competent authorities render a negative judgment, the airplanes were adopted. The order for Fokker airplanes cost 3.6 million rubles and the order for Junkers airplanes cost 2.5 million rubles. Having spent 6.1 million rubles the Soviet Air Force found itself in possession of low-quality planes that only could be categorized as ordinary training planes, since the Junkers and Fokker planes lacked equipment for arranging and dropping bombs and had no sets for firing through propeller disks. In all, 1923–1924 the Soviet government had spent a sum of 11.7 million rubles for foreign orders including 160 BMW motors in Germany, 200 motors of Lorraine- Diétriech in France, 200 Siddeley-Puma motors at government depots in Britain, and 500 war surplus American Liberty motors. The BMW motors proved especially disappointing as they were low-powered and useless for combat. In 1924–1925, Soviet foreign purchases amounted to a further 11 million rubles plus 3.6 million rubles for twelve Junkers bombers. Expensive imports had created a crisis for the Soviet domestic aircraft industry. The amount of money expended over three years on the foreign market had yielded a disastrous result on providing factories with currently needed materials as well as on development of the aircraft industry in the future.[61]

In April 1926, the GPU (secret police) ascertained that there were connections based on bribery between foreign companies, in particular Junkers, and responsible persons in the Soviet Air Force. In all likelihood, persons playing a large role in the air force influenced not only the purchase of inappropriate airplane and motor types at companies in which they were interested, but also the acceptance of faulty material and low-quality products of foreign companies. At least one Soviet engineer had taken bribes from foreign companies, and it had come to

[61] Dyakov and Bushuyeva, 130–132.

light that the persons who drew up the agreements for proto-types of the JuG-1 and flotation gear had accepted bribes from representatives of the Junkers Company in Moscow. As a result, the disadvantageous agreement had increased the price. Based on calculations, Junkers obtained 325,000 rubles in excess.[62] The Soviets considered Gotthard Sachsenberg, one of Junkers's directors, "a cheat," and even the German Ministry of Defense contended that though the German government had paid Junkers to help complete the plant at Fili, Junkers had misused the funds to suborn Soviet officials and refurbish its plant in Dessau.[63]

Standing on the edge of financial ruin, at the end of January 1926 Junkers decided to pursue arbitration regarding the dispute over the disappointing production at Fili. Meanwhile, the German government had bailed out Junkers with a credit for $4.04 million (RM 17 million). However, because Junkers lacked major aircraft orders, the firm required $3.1 million (RM 13 million) just to maintain normal functioning. Junkers's overinvestment in Russia hurt the company's financial condition so badly that when the German government made available the necessary $2.38 million (RM 10 million) to pay firm's debts and gave the company $1.67 million (RM 7 million) more to increase its capital stock, two-thirds of this stock was to remain in state hands. On March 4, the Politburo discussed Junkers's request to liquidate the concession. The Soviets too wanted to reexamine the conditions of the concession and possibly negotiate converting it into a technical aid agreement.[64]

Junkers representatives traveled to Moscow to talk directly with the Soviets in June 1926. Otto Von Schlieben, a member of Junkers's Board of Directors, acknowledged that serious clashes had occurred between the Soviets and representatives of the Junkers Company. In order to restore confidence, the company had fired one employee and transferred another to other enterprises of the Junkers Company so that he would have no more interactions with the Soviet Air Force. Schlieben stated that, "It is self-evident that in doing so Junkers does not admit any guilt, but for the atmosphere to be more clear all the above-mentioned persons were put out from here."[65] Junkers had received a letter from the concession committee containing the proposal of terminating the concession, but the company hoped to resolve the matter through personal talks.

---

[62] Ibid., 133, 140–143.

[63] W. E. Braatz, "Junkers Flugzeugwerke AG in Anatolia, 1925–1926: An Aspect of German-Turkish Economic Relations, Part II," *Tradition: Zeitschrift für Firmengeschichte und Unternehmenbiographie*, vol. 1975 (1975), 30–31.

[64] W. E. Braatz, "Junkers Flugzeugwerke AG in Anatolia, 1925–1926: An Aspect of German-Turkish Economic Relations," *Tradition: Zeitschrift für Firmengeschichte und Unternehmenbiographie*, vol. 1974 (1974), 39; Gorlov, 118–121.

[65] Dyakov and Bushuyeva, 134, 137.

Junkers was open to having the Fili factory resume operation under the management of the Soviet government but with financial and technical aid from Junkers Company.[66] Schlieben indicated that the company was developing new airplane models, and the political and economic interests of Germany and the USSR coincided in supplying the Soviet Air Force with airplanes of the latest models. Favorable outcome should also be found on the agreement for bombers and motors. Schlieben did not want to discuss old deliveries, but he promised that Junkers Company would strive to remove all existing shortcomings, including the issue on arming airplanes in the shortest possible time. Junkers would not be able to adhere to the agreement punctually, but the company pledged to eliminate technical defects. Schlieben concluded that, "As for subornation of some Russian officials by representatives of Junkers Company, this, to my knowledge, took place after concluding the agreement for airplanes, and Junkers Company will hardly be able to make a concession on the agreement price. The company made an entire calculation and it is of no use for it to operate at a loss. But my statement regarding possibilities of reducing the agreement price does not mean that talks on this matter are impossible."[67]

As part of the negotiations to liquidate the concession, Junkers agreed to give up claim for damages and to form a parity commission to determine the amount of compensation under a new agreement, provided that bomber prices were not be reduced. In October 1926, when the company requested compensation from the Soviets for the bombers and the factory in amount of 4 million rubles, Soviets offered in response 1.4 million rubles. In haggling over the compensation, Junkers dropped to 3.5 million and the Soviets upped their offer to 2.4 million rubles. While wrangling continued, the factory at Fili had been idle for two years and had not been well maintained. The shops lay covered in a snowdrift and machine tools were rusting. Voroshilov wrote to Stalin on January 26, 1927, "In connection with Junkers Company systematically not meeting obligations of the concession and unsatisfactorily fulfilling current deliveries of bombers under separate agreements with the Soviet Air Force, a decision was taken to liquidate the concession and to cancel the delivery agreement."[68]

At this point, Trotsky weighed in with a remarkable statement. On February 3, 1927, Trotsky advised the Politburo:

We are faced with the necessity of deciding today without fail either to pay 3.5 million for the concession and the bombers instead of 2.5 million proposed by our side or to enter the arbitration court. The arbitration court means for

[66] Ibid., 134, 137.   [67] Ibid., 138.   [68] Ibid., 145.

us the possibility of surprises only in the direction of deteriorating rather than improving conditions of the liquidation. Lawyers discussed the question of whether we can take the factory in our hands based on considerations of state necessity and came to a conclusion that neither the concession agreement nor the Soviet–German treaty gave any opportunity for us. In other words, our unilaterally taking possession of the factory would mean a diplomatic conflict and additional payments associated with the arbitration court. Thus, if we apply to the court, which will drag on several months at the minimum, the fate of the factory will hang poised in mid-air for this time. Or we take the factory in our hands unilaterally at the risk of additionally paying an imposing sum for this. The last question remains: if not going by the law, is it possible to gain anything by peaceable way? Since the opposite party poses the question alternatively: either 3.5 million or the arbitration court, no place remains for trading, in my opinion, the more so as we have made the last attempt of squeezing out some fairness between the rough copy of Junkers' letter and its final draft, but we have obtained nothing. The attempt of evading the arbitration court and continuing the trade shall only reveal our weakness. Taken together this leads me to a conclusion that we have to consent to the payment of 3.5 million rubles so as not to risk the payment of the large sum and delay the matter of the factory.[69]

Given the Soviet government's nationalization of industry and lack of squeamishness regarding terror and brute force in the past, Trotsky's concerns about legality and arbitration appear jarring. Yet, the Soviets adopted this position and offered Junkers 3.5 million rubles. Still without a resolution, Voroshilov recommended demanding from Junkers either finally to accept or decline the latest offer from Soviets, which the firm did when the Junkers concession was formally liquidated on February 26, 1927.[70]

Turkey

South of Russia across the Black Sea, the Turkish government pursued a parallel program of domesticating aircraft production. In 1924, Turkey imported a variety of foreign models. In May 1924, the Turkish Council of Ministers had approved the purchase of sixteen French Breguet planes, and Turkey took delivery of these bombers from Marseille in January 1926. By October 1924, the Turkish Minister of National Defense had decided to reorganize its military aviation along French and Italian lines, and hence contracted for sixteen French military aviation instructors, and placed an order for twenty Savoia hydroplanes from Italy. Surprisingly, the Turks also signed an agreement with the USSR in December 1924 for the Soviet Taganrog State Aviation Factory to build for Turkey five planes of Italian models (two Caproni night bombers

---

[69] Ibid., 148–149.   [70] Dyakov and Bushuyeva, 146–147; Gorlov, 197.

and three Savoias Model S57) for 85,000 gold rubles with delivery scheduled for 1926.[71]

Not content to be dependent on imports, the Turkish government showed interest in developing its own manufacturing capabilities. Accordingly, in January 1925 a representative of Junkers in Ankara, an ex-officer of Turkish aviation, proposed terms to the Turkish government for Junkers to erect an aircraft manufacturing plant in Turkey. They proposed to make planes suitable for military purposes. The Turkish government would need to agree to purchase from Junkers a fixed number of planes over a six-year term. The Turkish government would also concede an aluminum mine to the company.[72] The major objective of the Turkish government was to build up the country's ability to protect itself, but Turkey could not afford heavy capital outlays. Rudolf Nadolny, the German Ambassador to Turkey communicated Turkish interest, and by late March 1925 the Turkish and German governments had begun talks. The Turks wished for a German firm to establish munitions and weapons plants in their country. The German Foreign Ministry instructed Nadolny to stall the Turks because of Junkers's financial troubles in Russia conducting similar operations. The Turks persisted, however, and a Turkish trade mission along with the Turkish Foreign Minister arrived in Germany and met with German industrialists to discuss munitions plants, armaments, and aircraft. As part of this mission, Tevfik Bey, General Secretary of the State Presidency in Turkey, visited Junkers in Dessau. The Turks expressed their willingness to grant Junkers a monopoly on Turkish aircraft orders if the firm would establish and manage an aircraft plant. In late June, Sachsenberg communicated to Tevfik Junkers's willingness to take on the proposed plant. Major Fischer of the German Ministry of Defense encouraged the Junkers proposal as a means to offset the financial risk of Junkers's work in Russia. Formal support from the German Ministry of Defense was of critical importance because Professor Hugo Junkers had begun the Russian venture at the urging of that ministry with only verbal pledges of support that the German government would underwrite a large part of costs, and by now Junkers found itself on the hook for $2.86 million (RM 12 million). Having received the formal backing of the Ministry of Defense and the Foreign Ministry, Junkers pursued negotiations with the Turks. As the first fruits of these negotiations, in July 1925 the Turks bought

---

[71] RG 165, #2094–15 (2) mil attaché Constantinople to G-2, May 28, 1924; RG 165, #2094–15 (5) Mil attaché Constantinople to G-2, January 30, 1926; RG 165, #2094–21, mil attaché Constantinople to G-2, October 31, 1924; RG 165, #2094–34, Trevor Swett (Mil att Riga) to G-2, October 28, 1926.

[72] RG 165, #2094–13 (9) Mil attaché Constantinople to G-2, January 14, 1925.

ten Junkers airplanes from Germany of civilian type that conformed to the restrictions laid down by Inter-Allied Aeronautical Committee of Guarantees in Berlin. The Turks also ordered more powerful engines from Junkers factories outside Germany and machine gun mountings. Once materials had arrived in Turkey, they transformed the civilian planes into military aircraft, thereby evading provisions of Versailles.[73]

As envisioned by Junkers, the plans for the Turkish aircraft plant at Kayseri required $1.67 million (RM 7 million) with each side putting up half. However, the Turkish government's share would not be due all at once but instead spread over several years up to the opening of the plant. Turkey would buy all its planes from Dessau until Kayseri began operations. The Turkish government would pay Junkers a lump sum of $0.95 million (RM 4 million) to purchase Junkers patents. This last point angered the Turkish Cabinet, who considered it an excessively expensive demand. After some convincing by Germanophile officers that the German planes were truly superior, Turkish President Mustafa Kemal supported the project, and the Turks agreed to pay the lump sum over five years at 5 percent interest. Lacking the $0.83 million (RM 3.5 million) of its own, Junkers asked the German government to name a bank willing to extend a loan. The Foreign Ministry approached Deutsche Orientbank, which was willing to fund Junkers $0.48 million (RM 2 million) conditionally as long as the Foreign Ministry deposited that amount with the bank. In any case, the German government refused to back Junkers for the entire amount.[74] On August 15, 1925, the Turkish Minister of Finance Hasan Hüsnü Bey concluded agreements with Junkers for the establishment of the aircraft plant at Kayseri to be operated by the firm Tomtasch (Türkische Flugzeug- und Motoren AG) capitalized at $1.67 million (RM 7 million). When fully operational, Kayseri expected to turn out 250 planes annually.[75] Junkers would have sole claim to bauxite and petroleum in Turkey. When Sachsenberg requested an advance of $238,000 (RM 1 million) from Deutsche Orientbank in order to build planes for the Turks at Junkers's Dessau plant, the bank and the German Foreign Ministry refused to endorse this request as they did not want to see the money squandered. Since the Foreign Ministry could

---

[73] Braatz, "Junkers Flugzeugwerke" (1974), 31–33; Political Archives of the German Foreign Office, 1920–1936, US National Archives, Microcopy T-120, roll 2349, frames E174990–175004, Aufzeichnung über die Türkischen Rüstungspläne, December 29, 1925–January 1926; FO 371/10856, Horne to Austen Chamberlain, July 15, 1925; WO to Rendel, November 17, 1925.

[74] Braatz, "Junkers Flugzeugwerke" (1974), 34–36.

[75] Political Archives of the German Foreign Office, 1920–1936, US National Archives, Microcopy T-120, roll 3711, frames K015908–015910, Agreement between Junkers and Turkish Government.

only guarantee $0.48 million (2 million), it wanted the money spent for the project in Turkey not for Junkers's home plant in Dessau. Word leaked out to other German aircraft firms, who saw the Turkish project as a cover for Junkers to get public subsidies to retool its Dessau plant.[76]

Facing deep financial difficulties rooted in its Russian venture, the Junkers Board desperately needed the Turkish plane orders in Dessau to sustain the firm. That desperation fostered a bribery scandal in Turkey that broke right around the same time as the bribery charges in Russia. In late April 1926, the Turkish Minister of Defense, Recep Bey notified Hans Sachsenberg, the managing director of Tomtasch, that an agent of Junkers (Oskar Wolff) had attempted to bribe Captain Mouchli Bey, Chief of Air Division in Istanbul. Wolff apparently acting on his own initiative determined that Mouchli Bey could be bought, and had offered the officer a monthly payment of $44 (TL 80) to use his influence in the Turkish Air Force to place orders for aircraft with Junkers in Dessau. On behalf of the Junkers Board, Schlieben had sent Wolff to Turkey to scrutinize the financial records of Tomtasch for signs of impropriety. When Mouchli Bey complained to the Germans about Wolff's behavior, Schlieben had ignored the Turkish officer's story and insisted that Sachsenberg had exaggerated it to cover up his failure to obtain orders for Dessau. As a result, the Dessau orders never materialized, and company borrowed money to produce inventory.[77]

The opening ceremonies at Kayseri on October 5, 1926, took place against a backdrop of Junkers's financial crisis. Junkers's debt of $1.19 million (RM 5 million) had increased to $4.29 million (RM 18 million), and Tomtasch was experiencing financial troubles too. In December 1925, the Turks had authorized payment to Junkers in the paltry amount of $130,950 (£27,000). However, the bulk of Turkish orders promised as part of the August 1925 agreement had not gone through, and without the money for those orders the viability of Kayseri relied heavily on the German government's support for Dessau. Tomtasch never succeeded in digging out of the hole. Over the protests of the German ambassador, a Turkish court declared Tomtasch bankrupt in December 1928. Although the German government was prepared to offer material assistance to renew the concession, the Turks preferred to cancel the concession or buy out German interests. Ironically, Turkey ended up purchasing some Junkers aircraft from the Soviets. Following up on an enquiry from the Turkish military attaché in Moscow on

[76] Braatz, "Junkers Flugzeugwerke" (1974), 37–38.
[77] Braatz, "Junkers Flugzeugwerke" (1975), 25–28.

December 16, 1926, the Turks signed an agreement with the Soviets on January 4, 1927, for six Junkers planes to be delivered in June.[78]

As an adjunct to state purchases, the Turkish Aviation Association, founded in 1925, played a key role in helping the government acquire foreign aircraft. While the Turkish government carried on with the task of developing military aviation and engaged in negotiations with foreign firms to acquire aircraft and motors, the Aviation Association concerned itself with raising money to pay for aviation material through popular subscription. Initially, the Association's efforts appeared more coercive than popular. In May 1925, requests for subscriptions really took the form of demands from government officials in certain instances. Certain classes of business men met the exactions with great promptness out of fear of reprisals if they refused. Officials made veiled demands for subscriptions of foreigners, and Jews, in particular, were regarded as highly desirable subscribers. The Chief of Police of Izmir and his aides seemed to be particularly active in obtaining funds. The Governor of Izmir Province called a conference of foreigners and Levantines and extorted contributions. The American military attaché reported that, "Notwithstanding the character of the requests made of Turks, Jews of Turkish nationality, foreigners, and protégés in the form of Levantines, this office does not anticipate any difficulty in regard to the matter. To give seems to be almost as much a maxim of life as is to exercise patience: they are merely ordinary requirements in Smyrna for peace, business, and residence."[79] In July 1925, the Aviation Association demanded contributions from all foreign commercial interests. The chairman of the local committee paid a call to the local manager of Standard Oil and demanded that a contribution of $16,500 (T£30,000) to be paid in three days, and he made a similar demand for a contribution of half that amount from the Vacuum Oil Co. and other oil companies. The Standard Oil manager agreed to contribute $1,100 (T£2,000) rather than T£30,000.[80] The Turkish government also hit upon an effective and useful means to raise money for its purchases of airplanes by establishing a permanent Aviation Lottery. The Lottery caused genuine excitement, and in fact, eagerness for the Lottery led to riots in Mudania that nearly

---

[78] FO 371/10856, Lindsay to Austen Chamberlain, December 19, 1925; Braatz, "Junkers Flugzeugwerke" (1975), 29, 32, 34, 39; FO 371/13098, Harold Woods (Overseas Trade) to FO, December 5, 1928; RG 165, #2094–35, Mil att Riga to G-2, April 25, 1927.

[79] RG 165, #2094–25 (1) Mil attaché Const to G-2, May 25, 1925.

[80] RG 165, #2094–25 (3) mil attaché Const to G-2, July 23, 1925.

cost the newsagent his life as people rushed to get their hands on the latest newspaper to learn the winning numbers.[81]

From this unsavory start, the Turkish Aviation Association turned into one of the best, genuinely popular organizations of the country. By 1927, the Association claimed membership of 200,000 and had raised $6.5 million. In 1928, the Association could point to the delivery of twelve Junker training planes, and five more trainers and ten combat planes ordered and funded through popular subscription. On August 30, 1929, the Aviation Association officially presented two French Dewoitine pursuit planes, newly acquired out of funds subscribed at Istanbul, to the Turkish Army at San Stefano. By 1934, the Aviation Association had estimated annual proceeds of $1.6–2.2 million raised in support of Turkish military aviation, and on Turkey's Aviation Day (August 30, 1934), local branches of the Association from the Beykoz, Kadikoy, and Kortal suburbs of Istanbul presented three new Czech Smolik airplanes to the army.[82]

With the collapse of the Junkers operation at Kayseri, other foreign competitors stepped up to replace the Germans. The British Chancery in Istanbul reported decent prospects for airplane orders in November 1927, but in order to supplant Junkers and overcome the French, German and Italian "'sweetening' that goes for to persuade them of the superlative value of the planes shown to them," British manufacturers needed agents on the spot in Ankara, ready with specifications, price-lists, short-time credits, and who could, "go in for hospitality and personal contact with the Turkish deputies and Cabinet on an extensive scale."[83] The Chancery also advised that all these materials should be printed in Turkish, and the British Air Ministry must be more forthcoming and ready to extend invitations. The Chancery mused that if Britain could gain the Turkish market, then Britain could use that position "to minimize Turkey's next warlike adventure by delaying her if not new supplies of engines at least spare parts for those she already possessed. Of course Turkey recognizes this and therefore favors Germany which can be relied upon to play her no such tricks; but much can be done to overcome this fear by the judicious use of 'palm oil' which

[81] FO 371/12323, Chancery at Constantinople to Br Embassy Constantinople, November 14, 1927.

[82] RG 165, #2094–13 (16) Mil attaché Constantinople to G-2, Turkey (Economic), December 1, 1928; RG 165, #2094–25 (11) J. D. Elliott (mil att Constantinople) to G-2, August 28, 1928; RG 165, #2094–42 (1) mil att Const to G-2, October 5, 1929; RG 165, #2094–56 (2) J. A. Crane to G-2, April 26, 1934; RG 165, #2094–59 J. A. Crane to G-2, September 7, 1934.

[83] FO 371/12323, Chancery at Constantinople to Br Embassy Constantinople, November 14, 1927.

need neither concern His Majesty's Government nor reduce the profits of the manufacturing companies to vanishing point."[84] The Chancery in Istanbul concluded, "The need of our manufacturers of airplanes is great and the importance of keeping skilled labor at work in case of emergency is weighing upon the minds of the Air Ministry."[85] However, the Turks showed themselves justifiably wary of buying from Britain based on the bitter experience with the battleship purchases prior to the war. Overseas Trade believed that "the Turks are alleged to be so suspicious of the intentions of HMG that all the military purchasing departments are understood to have been tipped the wink in the past not to buy such material from British sources."[86]

Another stumbling block for British aircraft firms in Turkey involved technical certification. Individual British manufacturers spent considerable sums of money in trying to get their goods accepted by the Turks, but the issue of reception of the aircraft in Turkey before trials always hindered the process. The Turks insisted that aircraft should be constructed and sent out to Turkey to undergo their trials before taking acceptance. This did not sit well with the British firms because they feared that the Turkish personnel flying aircraft and using primitive instruments for testing performances would probably decide that the aircraft were not up to specifications, and after breaking two or three, would renounce the contract. In other words, the British firms could not afford to gamble on acceptance of aircraft by the Turks in their own country. British manufacturers felt that the Turks should recognize British airworthiness certificates issued by the British Air Ministry as the only basis for acceptance conditions in contracts.[87] British officials also had doubts that the Turks would be willing to purchase aircraft at British or American prices, and this gave cheaper French machines an edge. On the other hand, "there is always the question of national prestige and the desire of the Turks to possess the latest thing in military armaments."[88]

It looked as if the French would gain the first advantage in the wake of the Junkers debacle. After all, in previous years the Turkish Air Force had purchased a variety of French aircraft including twenty-nine Moranes (built 1920–1925), sixty-six Breguet 19s bought in 1925, twelve Dewoitines in 1928, and twenty Breguet 19-7s in 1930. The

[84] Ibid.   [85] Ibid.
[86] FO 371/12323, E. Cowe (Overseas Trade) to Oliphant, December 20, 1927.
[87] FO 371/14582, Boyle to Rendel, May 20, 1930; Commercial Secretary Harold Woods to Dept. of Overseas Trade, June 11, 1930, (Enclosure) Meeting of Members of Society of British Aircraft Constructors, Dept. of Overseas Trade, Air Ministry, and FO in connection with Aviation in Turkey sent to FO, June 16, 1930.
[88] FO 371/14582, Commercial Secretary Harold Woods to Dept of Overseas Trade, June 11, 1930.

Turks had recently placed an order for twelve Gordon-Lesseure pursuit and night operations planes. Unfortunately for the French, the Turks refused to accept delivery as the aircraft did not meet speed requirements. The Turkish War Office then took up legal action and sued the company for the original guarantee deposit placed in the Ottoman Bank. The French failure opened the door to American entrance, and the Curtiss-Wright Corporation hoped to receive the order for their plane in lieu of those rejected from French company. In April 1930, the Turks asked the Curtiss group to tender for fifty planes, and the Turks put under consideration turning to the Americans for planes and training.[89]

In 1930, the American firm Curtiss-Wright entered the Turkish market in highly dramatic fashion. Through the US State Department, the American Embassy in Turkey secured permission in April for the demonstration airplanes of Curtiss-Wright to visit Turkey. Under this permission four airplanes visited Constantinople on May 19, 1930. The group was under the direction of Major Melvin B. Hall, vice president of the Curtiss-Wright Export Corp stationed in Paris, and the Chief Pilot of the mission was Major James H. Doolittle on leave of absence from the US Army. The squadron was composed of a standard army pursuit plane, an observation plane, a training plane, and a three-place cabin monoplane for commercial and private flying. These planes were shipped from New York to Greece where they were assembled at the Tatoi Airdrome, near Athens. The Curtiss-Wright Flying Circus made a tour across Eastern Europe. From Greece they then visited Sofia, Belgrade, and Bucharest, before arriving in Turkey. After Turkey, other stops on the itinerary included Budapest, Vienna, Prague, Warsaw, Kovno, Riga, Reval, and Helsinki. The squadron made an extremely favorable impression in Turkey. At Ankara, they were extensively feted and they took the Turkish Prime Minister and his family up for flights over the city. The Turkish Aviation Association paid the entire expenses of the Curtiss-Wright Mission while in Turkey. The demonstration flight reflected great credit on the American Air Service, as well as being an excellent advertisement for the Curtiss-Wright Company. Major Doolittle demonstrated the strength of the American planes by flying vertically for a great distance.[90] Previous to this event the Curtiss-Wright Company paid the entire expenses for a Turkish Mission to visit their factories in America where they witnessed demonstrations and were extensively entertained by the Curtiss-Wright Company. In addition,

---

[89] RG 165, #2094–58 F. D. Mallon to G-2, September 4, 1934; RG 165, #2094–41 (2) J. D. Elliott mil att Const to G-2, December 9, 1930; FO 371/14582 O'Leary to Edmonds, April 5, 1930; FO 371/14582, Chancery to Rendel, May 20, 1930.

[90] RG 165, #2094–47 (1) J. D. Elliott (Const) to G-2, June 14, 1930.

Major Hall kept in constant contact with the Turkish War Office, making numerous visits to Ankara. In November 1931, these efforts bore fruit and the Turks signed a contract with Curtiss-Wright to reopen the old Junkers plant at Kayseri under an American chief engineer and assistants and the sale of ten training planes (Fledglings) to be assembled in Kayseri. During the latter part of February 1932, Curtiss-Wright got another contract for twenty-four Hawk pursuit planes (eighteen shipped from US, six to be assembled in Kayseri under American supervision). The American military attaché in Istanbul observed with satisfaction that, "In view of the fact that several countries were in the market for this order, I believe that the assistance by our office and the G-2 section in Washington, which freely furnished all information relative to the tests of our planes, was of great assistance to the Curtiss-Wright Company," and he hoped that Curtiss-Wright would return the favor by providing accurate information about the Turkish Air Service.[91]

The Curtiss-Wright concession made the works at Kayseri functional for the first time. Up to this point under Junkers the Kayseri factory had never actually operated, not even in the repair of airplanes. The construction at Kayseri was much more expensive than one could buy the same plane in Germany. The machines and apparatuses brought to Kayseri by the Junkers firm could only construct Junkers airplanes, and several million Turkish lira have been spent on this factory for no purpose. In 1933, Curtiss-Wright Co. established for Turkey at Kayseri a factory to make planes. Practically all material had to be imported, and the engines were purchased from Curtiss-Wright. In September 1932, the Turks ordered twenty-four Hawks and eighteen Fledglings from Curtiss-Wright. As of April 1934, Turkish contracts with Curtiss-Wright totaled $583,000 for sixteen Hawks and parts. By July 1934, the Kayseri aircraft plant under the management of Curtiss-Wright had been in operation eighteen months, and Turkey was making a great effort to obtain orders for Curtiss-Wright planes to be made in the factory.[92] Even under Curtiss-Wright, Kayseri only managed to assemble a few planes from imported components, and Turkey continued to rely on foreign aircraft suppliers for the next decade.[93] The American firm duly apprised US intelligence about the strength of the Turkish

[91] RG 165, #2094–47 (2) Lt Col J. D. Elliott (mil att Const) to G-2, March 11, 1932.
[92] RG165, #2331-T-13 (1) mil attaché Constantinople to G-2, November 6, 1931; RG 165, #2094–18 (20), mil attaché to G-2, March 5, 1934; RG 165, #2094–47 (7) Major J. A. Crane mil att Const to G-2, September 23, 1932; RG 165, #2094–57, J. A. Crane to G-2, April 24, 1934; RG165, #2331-T-13 (3) J. A. Crane mil attaché Istanbul to G-2, July 30, 1934.
[93] G. Leiser, "The Turkish Air Force, 1939–45: The Rise of a Minor Power," *Middle Eastern Studies*, vol. 26, no. 3 (1990), 383.

Air Force. As of December 1932, a representative of Curtiss-Wright in Turkey estimated the full Turkish Air Force at 217 planes, of which 40–50 were Junkers. This figure included eighteen Hawks recently delivered by Curtiss but not twelve planes to be assembled at Kayseri.[94]

Bulgaria

British willingness to adhere to the rules of disarmament again placed them at a disadvantage, this time in Bulgaria where once again the French and Czechs proved most successful. The Treaty of Neuilly strictly controlled Bulgaria's ability to acquire aircraft. Under article 79, the manufacture of arms, munitions, and war materiel could only be carried on in a single, state-owned factory. Article 81 forbade the importation into Bulgaria of arms, munitions, and war materiel of all kinds. Article 92 prohibited the importation or exportation of complete aircraft as well as aircraft parts and engines. Major Johnston, a representative of Bristol Aeroplane entered into negotiations with a Bulgarian commission for the purchase of ten planes for postal work. The Bristol Co. airplanes would have conformed to the Nine Rules restrictions on military aircraft which had been imposed on Bulgaria by the Allies. The Nine Rules placed limitations on aircraft speed, range, altitude, and carrying capacity in order to prevent Bulgaria from acquiring any military aircraft. Certain French firms, namely Manriot, Potez, and Morane all offered the Bulgarians airplane models that could be used militarily, thereby not conforming to the Nine Rules. The contract for these machines was signed in 1925 with the French. Consequently Bristol lost the contract because it carried out the orders of the Allied governments while the French did not. Later, Bulgaria signed an agreement with the Czech firm Aero for the establishment of an aircraft factory at Kazanlyk in April 1927. Kazanlyk violated the disarmament provisions as it constituted a second Bulgarian aircraft factory since the Bulgarian government with the support of German engineers had already established the State Airplane Workshop at Sofia by decree in 1924–1925. Kazanlyk received few orders and the project was ultimately sold in 1930 to the Italian firm Caproni. Nevertheless, Bulgaria had 5 million leva worth of aircraft engines on order with the Czech Walter Company in 1930.[95] Regarding Czech aircraft sales to Bulgaria, the British Air Ministry observed that while the Smolik S-16

---

[94] RG165, #2094–37 (3) Mil att Istanbul J. A. Crane to G-2, December 24, 1932.
[95] FO 371/10671, Pigott, Air attaché Paris to Air Ministry, November 23, 1925; AIR 5/1179, Air Intelligence 8. Bulgaria. August 4, 1932.

was a military aircraft, the factory also produced a civil prototype and possibly Bulgaria had acquired that type. Therefore, the Air Ministry did not recommend protesting violation of Article 81 of Treaty of Neuilly against the Czechs because it could not establish definitively that the aircraft being manufactured for Bulgaria were military type.[96]

Bulgaria attracted far more attention that its small market warranted. The American Curtiss-Wright Flying Circus performed in Sofia in early May 1930. To the delight of the crowd, the pilots took up several passengers including the King's brother, Prince Cyril, and *La Bulgarie* newspaper praised the skills of Major James Doolittle the next day. The Curtiss visit did not receive an official reception from the Bulgarian government, unlike the French aviation visit later that month. The British representative in Bulgaria, Waterlow, expressed a high degree of skepticism that Bulgaria could provide much of a market. The government would only buy cheap goods, and any purchases would serve the eventual building up of a Bulgarian Air Force in contravention of the Treaty of Neuilly. Waterlow concluded that "It may be thought that this last consideration should deter HMG from encouraging British firms to push their goods here."[97]

Conclusion

In terms of the export markets, French firms still occupied the top position by the early thirties, but Czech producers had gained considerable ground. Across Eastern Europe, the attempts by various governments to establish domestic production showed mixed results for the period 1920–1930. On one hand, the Poles had secured domestic self-sufficiency and stood on the cusp of successful exports too. On the other hand, the Romanians at Brasov (French), the Greeks at Phaleron (British), the Bulgarians at Kazanlyk (Czechs), and the Turks at Kayseri (American) had achieved only modest capabilities to assemble components at best, and those countries would continue to rely on foreign purchases.

As of December 1928, the Junkers aircraft plant had brought the USSR very little. Junkers did not carry out its obligations concerning delivery of metallic aircraft or the construction of an aircraft plant. Amazingly, Junkers unofficially raised with the Soviet military attaché in Berlin the question of resumption of its work in USSR and, in particular erection of an aircraft plant on a concession basis.[98] The Soviets had

---

[96] FO 371/4329, Air Ministry to FO, April 28, 1930.
[97] FO 371/14326, Waterlow to Henderson, June 4, 1930.
[98] Dyakov and Bushuyeva, 69, 74.

learned their lesson. In the future under the Five-Year Plans, there would be no such corporate concessions as the socialist economy would tolerate no private industrial enterprise. Instead, the Soviets restricted themselves to technical aid agreements and direct purchases of foreign military equipment models and licenses to foster domestic production.

5   Soviet Rearmament, Great Depression, and General Disarmament, 1930–1933

The period 1930–1933 witnessed the biggest push for disarmament as the Geneva conference played out. The developments in the disarmament process leading to the Draft Disarmament Convention in 1930 and the further negotiations of the World Disarmament Conference at Geneva through 1934 had a palpable effect on the armaments business by forcing firms to react in anticipation of reductions in sales and pending qualitative and quantitative restrictions on types of armaments. Although it is true that the Disarmament Conference ultimately ended in failure, the reverberations from the ongoing negotiations and popular pressures from the disarmament movement did echo in the board rooms. In particular, Vickers–Armstrong found itself buffeted by the three great currents of the time: Soviet rearmament, the Great Depression, and general disarmament. In an ironic twist, just as the Great Depression and disarmament threatened to close them down, Vickers found a life support in the rearmament of the socialist Soviet Union as Stalin initiated the building of socialism through centralized state economic planning. In developing their domestic military-industrial base, the Soviets employed the specialist skills of Western defense enterprises through purchases, technical agreements, and licensing deals. In particular, Soviet interest in tanks and tractors created opportunities for large orders at a critical moment.

Rearmament began in the Soviet Union under Josef Stalin during the implementation of the Soviet First Five-Year Plan 1928–1932. Stalin was keenly aware of the role that military and industrial weakness had played in the collapse of tsarist Russia. The Soviet Union that he ruled in 1928 was economically and militarily weaker than tsarist Russia had been in 1913. What would become known as "Stalinism" started as a mobilization strategy to harness all aspects of society for the goal of "Building Socialism." The Soviets initiated that mobilization, a kind of war mobilization in time of peace, beginning with the First Five-Year Plan. In the drive to industrialize, Stalin saw the backward Soviet Union racing to catch up to the capitalist states in economic and technological strength.

143

While Soviet ideology called for the workers of the world to unite, they feared that the capitalist powers of the world would unite and make common cause to invade and destroy the lone socialist state. The defense of socialism required that the Soviet Union build a military-industrial base to become completely self-sufficient in its armaments needs. In this way, state economic planning was the same thing as planning a war economy. When Stalin initiated the First Five-Year Plan in October 1928, part of the declared goal was to develop "all the necessary technical and economic prerequisites for increasing to the maximum its defensive capability to enable it to organize decisive resistance to all and any attempt at military intervention from outside."[1]

The Soviet goals were extremely ambitious. On July 15, 1929, the Politburo adopted its first resolution on rearmament. The document described the vulnerable state of the USSR. The Red Army had fallen far behind the capitalist armies in military technology and mobilization planning. By the end of the Plan (1932), the fully mobilized Red Army should field 3 million soldiers, be armed with 2,000 tanks, 10,000 artillery pieces, and 180,000 motor vehicles. As Maiolo notes, such expansion would make the Red Army the most formidable force in the world by doubling the size of the mobilized French Army, which in 1929 was the world's largest. The Soviet Union would also possess more combat planes than either the British or French air forces.[2] Soviet capital investment in the armaments industry amounted to 7.5 percent of all capital investment in industry. From 1930 to 1932, armaments production increased much more rapidly than Soviet industrial production as a whole and accounted for 11 percent of the total production of the machine-building and metalworking and chemical industries by 1932. By the end of the First Five-Year Plan, the armaments industry proper employed nearly half a million people and armaments production alone amounted to 3.1 percent of gross and 5.7 percent of net industrial production.[3]

Whereas the Soviet Union could not build factories fast enough, the Great Depression raised the specter of massive unemployment for Vickers. While the warship trade declined (see below), aircraft, tank and armored vehicle production offered new prospects for the firm. Up to

---

[1] Quoted in S. Melnikova-Raich, "The Soviet Problem with Two 'Unknowns': How an American Architect and a Soviet Negotiator Jump-Started the Industrialization of Russia, Part I: Albert Kahn," *The Journal of the Society for Industrial Archeology*, vol. 36, no. 2 (2010), 58–59.

[2] J. Maiolo, *Cry Havoc: How the Arms Race Drove the World to War, 1931–1941* (New York: Basic Books, 2010), 13–14.

[3] R. W. Davies, "Soviet Military Expenditure and the Armaments Industry, 1929–33: A Reconsideration," *Europe-Asia Studies*, vol. 45, no. 4 (1993), 585, 589–590.

this point, Vickers had been noticeably absent from the aircraft export business. At the beginning of 1930, Noel Birch recognized that the fortunes of Vickers's air armament sales depended on the development of Vickers Aviation. As Birch laid out the prospects to the board he stated, "It is necessary to emphasize that this business is a gamble, and that therefore the future prospects of sales must be regarded in that light... The sale of air armament will be handicapped until Vickers Aviation get into the world market."[4] As had been the case for Vickers's breakthrough into land armaments, Turkey served as the first major customer for Vickers Aviation. In 1933, the Turkish government planned a major augmentation of the Turkish Air Force. The Turks expected to expend $30,000,000 (T£60 million) over five years to acquire 75 bombers (Douglass Dolphin), 45 seaplanes (Vickers Supermarine), 175 pursuit planes (Curtiss Hawk), and 250 observation planes. As part of this plan, Turkey contracted with Vickers for six flying boats worth $765,000 (£150,000). This Vickers sale of flying boats was the very first Turkish purchase of British aircraft and was made against keen foreign competition.[5]

In entering the tank and armored vehicle field, Vickers would first have to overcome the entrenched position of the French producer Renault. Renault's emergence as an armaments producer began in 1917 when the firm designed a small armored tractor "tank," FT-17, and rushed it into production. During the last two years of the war, Renault manufactured about 3,000 tanks.[6] In the immediate aftermath of the war, many of the East European states used Renaults as the core of their new armored units. As late as 1932, Yugoslavia had sixteen old Renault tanks and ten old armored cars all of WWI vintage.[7] In 1919, the Romanian Army acquired seventy-two Renault FT-17 tanks to serve as the backbone of its new armored forces. As of 1935 Romania still had these same Renault tanks, which had become obsolete and decrepit.[8] The Polish First Tank Regiment, which had originated as the French 505 Tank Regiment, had 120 Renault FT-17 tanks at its creation in 1919.[9] By 1934, Renault offered twenty-four different armored vehicles for export, and

---

[4] VA, File 532, Sales prospects for 1930. Land and Air Armament, January 6, 1930.
[5] RG 165, #2094–53 (1) Major J. A. Crane Istanbul to G-2, January 6, 1933; RG 165, #2094–54 (2) Lt. Col. Cortlandt Parker to G-2, November 14, 1933; RG 165, #2094–54 (1) Lt. Col. Cortlandt Parker (Mill attaché London) to G-2, February 4, 1933.
[6] J. J. Clarke, "The Nationalization of War Industries in France, 1936–1937: A Case Study," *The Journal of Modern History*, vol. 49, no. 3 (1977), 412.
[7] RG 165, #2281-V-29 (1) Hazeltine to G-2, November 15, 1932.
[8] A. Statiev, "The Ugly Duckling of the Armed Forces: Romanian Armour 1919–41," *The Journal of Slavic Military Studies*, vol. 12, no. 2 (1999), 220.
[9] A. Jońca, *Polish Tracks and Wheels*, vol. 1 (Sandomierz: Stratus, 2009), 3.

Schneider supplied the weaponry. However, price and security concerns greatly impeded Renault's success as an exporter. Poorer states could not afford Renault's tanks and richer states opted to produce their own. The French government also blocked Renault exports on grounds of national security. The War Ministry did not want its latest armored technology falling into foreign hands, and into 1932 at War Ministry insistence Renault could only export items from the war era. Because Renault's designs addressed French Army specifications and made improvements based on input from army personnel, the government viewed these collaborations as a joint venture where the private firm should not profit from state expense. The War Ministry also sought to ensure that foreign customers did not acquire new equipment before the French Army did.[10]

A significant opportunity for Renault presented itself in Poland. The Poles had undertaken several attempts to upgrade their old Renault tanks by fitting a new turret and modifying the running gears during the 1920s. Having given up on modifications, the Poles decided to modernize with new machines. Naturally, the Poles looked to the French based on their ties of alliance and the availability of French credits.[11] Earlier on January 8, 1924, France had opened to Poland a credit of $21.6 million (F400 million) to complete its armament. Of this, the Poles had only taken $16.2 million (F300 million). At the start of 1930, the Polish government requested the remaining funds, and this was granted by France. In July 1929, in anticipation of the evacuation of the Rhineland, the Polish government solicited a new request of $60 million (F1.5 billion) to complete its armament to reinforce its means of defense in light of the return of Germany. Specifically, the Poles wanted two-thirds of the loan to acquire war materiel in France and a second issue of the other one-third to use for Polish military-industrial orders. Under an agreement with France of January 24, 1930, the Poles received $75 million (F1.897 billion). By May 1930, Renault took part in discussions with the Polish government about creating a national automobile industry in Poland. The French Ambassador in Warsaw noted the risks of competition given the activity of FIAT to take Polish orders, and urged Renault to make a prompt reply to these talks out of French military interest. The French military attaché in Poland indicated that if Renault did not make the necessary effort, it risked seeing itself shut out from more Polish orders. Believing that Poland lacked the means to pay for its military needs, Renault dragged its feet and showed a complete disinterest in the

[10] Clarke, 413–415.
[11] A. Jońca, *Polish Tracks and Wheels*, vol. 2 (Sandomierz: Stratus, 2011), 3–7.

Polish automobile business. Consequently, the Poles made their agreement with FIAT.[12] In 1931, the Poles expressed interest in Renault's armored cars. The French Foreign Ministry strongly desired to see the Polish Army provided with French materiel "so that it will be homogeneous, in order to assure and continue the deliveries by French industry and to open the way for resupply of a powerful ally in time of war."[13] When the Poles finally made their armored car order, they renounced the American Christie armored car and British models in favor of the Renault materiel. However, in demanding certain modifications to the model, the Poles sought to take advantage of all the ameliorations of this materiel which were developed over the course of study and experimentation for the French Army. Therefore, the War Ministry preempted the Renault sale on the belief that "the necessities of our national defense absolutely oppose that our factories should provide armored car modifications for a foreign power. Despite the desire to unify as much as possible war materials of France and Poland, it is indispensable to respect certain necessities of our proper armament."[14]

As Renault stalled out as a tank supplier to Eastern Europe during the 1920s and early 1930s, Vickers–Armstrong persevered through the hard times and maintained profits thanks to the firm's research in tanks. For the period 1926–1934, the most significant development in armored vehicles internationally came from the Vickers tank, which was fast, mobile, and reliable.[15] The Carden-Loyd Tankette (machine gun carrier), designated as the Mk VI series in 1928, was a turret-less vehicle weighing 1.5 tons and operating at 22.5 hp. The Vickers–Armstrong 6-ton tank came in two types. Type A weighed 7.2 tons and was armed with two machine guns, whereas type B was slightly heavier, 7.4 tons, and carried a 47mm gun.[16] Based on the technical success of its armored vehicles, Vickers superseded the French producers as the leading tank exporter. Almost immediately Eastern European buyers showed interest in Vickers's tanks. The Poles had desired to purchase fifty Vickers Mark C medium tanks in October 1925, but the British government had

---

[12] MAE, Europe 1930–1940, Pologne 311, Note pour Le Ministre. September 25, 1930; Minute. Expedie. Demandes de la Pologne. May 29, 1930; Minute. Expedie. Demandes de la Pologne. May 29, 1930; MAE to Min War, May 15, 1930; Ambassador in Poland to MAE, May 15, 1930; Laroche to MAE, August 13, 1930; Commercial attaché pol to Ministre de Économie Nationale, April 2, 1931; Amb Poland to MAE, December 2, 1931.

[13] Ibid., Ambassadeur in Poland to MAE, May 5, 1931.

[14] Ibid., Min War to MAE, June 2, 1931.

[15] M. R. Habeck, *Storm of Steel: The Development of Armor Doctrine in Germany and the Soviet Union* (Ithaca, NY: Cornell University Press, 2003), 295.

[16] VA, File 895 Tanks and Armored Cars built by Vickers 1919–1942.

prohibited the sale because the British Army used that model. Since the British Army had no interest in the 6-ton tank, Vickers would be permitted to export it. In 1927, the Poles sent their first military mission to Britain to examine the chassis of the 6-ton tank among other Vickers products. The Poles considered placing an order for thirty Vickers tanks at that time, but financial limitations intervened resulting in no contract. By 1929, the Soviets also expressed interest in the Mk VI tankette and Vickers's light tanks.[17]

In January 1930, Birch had laid out to the Vickers Board the importance of the tank market. The new 6-ton tank already had demonstrated technical success, and with it Birch foresaw the possibility of sales for the continental market where Vickers had never previously competed. Price would be of critical importance, and the factory was doing all that it could to get the costs down. Birch thought that if they could get the cost down below $3,645 (£750), their medium tank could generate reasonable orders. The prospects for the Carden-Loyd tankette also appeared promising. Tank armament offered the additional benefit to increase machine gun sales, which otherwise were becoming increasingly difficult. In February, Vickers considered granting a ten-year license to ČKD to manufacture the Carden-Loyd Mark VI armored vehicle for Czechoslovakia and also to grant the Czech firm the rights to produce those vehicles for sale to Yugoslavia on the understanding that Vickers would receive 50 percent of the work secured. In October, the Vickers Board approved the license concluded with Českomoravská to make the Mark VI for Yugoslavia on terms that ČKD would pay royalties to Vickers on the first ten vehicles ordered by Yugoslavia, and for subsequent orders for vehicles, ČKD would purchase from Vickers a minimum of one-half of total orders and pay on total orders received one-half of royalties. Orders received and completed during the first quarter of 1930 included four Carden Loyds for Czechoslovakia. At the same time the board also gave its approval for granting a license to the Poles to make the Mark VI through their state works Państwowe Zakłady Inzynierji for a lump sum of $48,600 (£10,000) under the condition that the Poles also order parts from Vickers in the amount of $84,564 (£17,400).[18]

The opening of the Soviet Union as an overt buyer for Western defense products proved the most significant development for the tank market. The establishment of the industrial base to support a modern armored

[17] A. Jońca, *Polish Tracks and Wheels*, vol. 3, 3; Jońca, vol. 2, 9; Habeck, 115.
[18] VA, File 532, Sales prospects for 1930. Land and Air Armament, January 6, 1930; VA, File 1222, Board Minutes. Vickers–Armstrongs Ltd., Minutes. February 27, 1930; VA, File 156 Vickers–Armstrongs factory Reports First Quarter 1930; VA, File 1222, Board Minutes. Vickers–Armstrongs Ltd., Minutes. October 2, 1930.

force was a key element in Soviet defense planning. The only tanks manufactured in the USSR into 1928 were Soviet copies of the Renault FT-17 light tank built at the Sormovo factory in Nizhnii-Novgorod (later Gorkii), and the total complement of tanks available numbered only 144.[19] In 1927, the Soviets had bought two KH50 tanks from the Czechs, and a Soviet Commission had visited the FIAT Works in Italy to purchase 100 tank motors.[20] In March 1930, the Soviets got combat vehicles from FIAT of type 3000, which was a modified version of the Renault FT-17.[21] Such purchases only served to modify existing tank production.

The Soviet Union eagerly sought the acquisition of Vickers tanks as models to jump start Soviet domestic production and build a modern armored force. In February 1930, the Soviets, through their state trade company, Arcos Ltd., initiated negotiations with Vickers to purchase tanks. Specifically, the Soviets expressed their desire to buy fifteen to twenty Carden-Loyd Mark VI vehicles, fifteen to twenty 6-ton tanks, and fifteen to twenty 12-ton tanks. Birch emphasized the need to establish credit terms, and if those proved agreeable, then the firm would seek permission from the War Office to export the items. Because the details and specifications of Soviet requirements differed from existing Vickers tanks, the firm anticipated incurring considerable expenses to meet Soviet demands. As the negotiations with Soviets for tanks approached the point of reaching a favorable conclusion, Vickers sought assurance from the War Office that in the event of signing a contract to supply tanks to the Soviets permission to export would not be withheld by the British government. Export of war materiel to the Soviet Union had been a risky business, and Vickers worried understandably that they might be left hanging by the British government. After the war, it had been forbidden to send arms to Soviet Russia until 1924. Vickers had obtained licenses in 1924 for the export of certain machine guns and parts to the Soviet government, but when the Conservative government came to power it reimposed the embargo on arms for Russia in December 1924. Labour lifted the embargo again in 1929. The reversal of government policy in 1924 involved revocation of one license and refusal to renew three others, and Vickers was prevented from completing their contracts and made

---

[19] Habeck, 30; G. G. Govan, "The Tank Builders: A History of Early Soviet Armor Research and Development" (US Army Institute Report, Garmisch, Germany, 1979), 2.

[20] RG 165, #2281-D-58 (2) Mil attaché Warsaw to G-2, October 10, 1928; #2281-D-70, Swett (mil attaché Riga) to G-2, January 14, 1928.

[21] MAE, Europe 1930–1940, Russie. Matériel de guerre. 930, Helleu (Moscow) to MAE, March 31, 1930.

claims for compensation, which were refused.[22] Vickers wanted 15 percent of the whole contract up front followed by payments of 25 percent on individual deliveries with the balance spread over a maximum of three years. The Soviets found those terms generally acceptable and in March promised to place orders with Vickers worth $996,300 (£205,000) for fifty large tanks broken down as follows: Mark VI (twenty), six-ton tanks (fifteen), and twelve-ton tanks (fifteen). The closing terms of the purchase involved the Soviets making the initial payment of 15 percent in cash, followed by 10 percent in twelve months with no interest. Then as each consignment shipped, the Soviets paid 15 percent of the value of each consignment with cash. The remaining 60 percent value of each consignment would be divided into five equal bills maturing at intervals of twelve, eighteen, twenty-four, thirty, and thirty-six months bearing a fixed interest at 6 percent annually on the outstanding payment.[23]

Soviet tank orders caused quite a bit of controversy for Vickers at home and abroad. The President of British Board of Trade stated in the House of Commons on May 28, 1930, that a license for the export of twenty twelve-ton tanks, twenty six-ton tanks, and twenty Carden-Loyd light armored vehicles, consigned to Soviet government, was issued on May 21.[24] When questioned about the tank export in the House of Commons on July 11, 1930, William Graham, the President of BOT replied: "The 40 tanks and 20 light armored vehicles were built to the design of messrs. Vickers–Armstrong, and that no objection to the issue of a license for their export to Russia was raised by the War Office."[25] Winston Churchill then queried, "Are the Labour Government definitely adopting the position of making profits by the sale of armaments to countries which may be involved in war with their neighbors?" To which Graham replied that "This is a license granted by the Board of Trade to an order executed by a private firm."[26] The British government remained leery of technical agreements which might enable Soviet citizens to gain instruction in British firms. The armed services worried that the Soviets would use such personnel to establish communist cells in British armaments factories to foment unrest or sabotage in case of mobilization. Therefore, "in respect of the USSR the Services Departments anticipate danger from the introduction of communist personnel into British firms

---

[22] CAB 27/551 BOT Rept. November 14, 1933.
[23] VA, File 1222, Board Minutes. Vickers–Armstrongs Ltd., Minutes. February 27, 1930; Board Minutes. Vickers–Armstrongs Ltd., Minutes. March 13, 1930; VA, Microfilm K612, Russia, February 19, 1930, Visit of Soviet Trade Representatives; Russia, July 29, 1930, Russian Business; VA, Microfilm K616 Birch to WO, February 25, 1930.
[24] RG 165, #2281-D-77 (2) Thomas to G-2, May 29, 1930.
[25] RG 165, #2281-D-77 (3) Thomas to G-2, July 14, 1930.
[26] GFM 33/4539, British Tanks, frame L192868.

who either in peace manufacture war materials, or are designated for the production of munitions of war."[27] Almost immediately upon learning about the large Soviet acquisition in March 1930, the Poles called in the Vickers representative for Eastern Europe and the Balkans to explain this order.[28]

Throughout 1930, the Soviet Union was the most important customer for the Elswick plant. All Vickers's military orders for the first quarter totaled $1.65 million (£338,883) of which Russian tanks accounted for roughly two-thirds. By August, Arcos engaged in negotiations for further supply of thirty Mark VI, twenty 47mm. guns, and twenty 6-ton tanks. Of greater significance for the Soviet industrialization, negotiations proceeded for technical assistance to enable the Russians to make their own tanks domestically. Combined with the supplemental tank orders, the technical agreement meant an additional $1.34 million (£275,000).[29] However, negotiations with Vickers–Armstrong to buy a heavy tank during the second half of 1930 failed due to Soviet technical specifications because the firm was unable to meet Soviet demands for an extremely heavy tank that could travel 30kph with two huge guns.[30] The Tank Department at Elswick provided the majority of work for the Machining shops, and the Soviet orders kept the plant occupied. The sale of tank motors helped prevent the shutdown of the Vickers Works. By the end of October practically all the Mark VI vehicles had been dispatched and the first of the six-ton and twelve-ton tanks were nearing completion for shipping in the fourth quarter. During the first quarter of 1931, the Soviet tank contract yielded profits of $21,702 (£6,440) out of total net profit of $82,049 (£24,347). By late July 1931, the Soviets placed an order for fifteen Carden-Loyd tractor trucks at $3,370 (£1000) each to transport artillery. Vickers produced its amphibious tank for first time by the end of 1931, and immediately the Soviets placed an order for eight light amphibious tanks at a cost of $78,184 (£23,200). By June 1932, the first of these light amphibious tanks for Soviet contract had been completed, tested, and shipped. Soon thereafter, the Soviets initiated domestic production at Leningrad. For the year 1932, Soviet contracts generated $163,737 (£49,920) in profits, thus representing

---

[27] CAB 48/6, CID.Special Sub-Committee on proposals re Technical Aid Contracts with USSR. Report June 3, 1932.

[28] RG 165, #2281-D-77, Emer Yeager to G-2, March 31, 1930.

[29] VA, File 156, Quarterly Rept Military and Air Armaments Sales First Quarter 1930; VA, File 1222, Board Minutes. Vickers–Armstrongs Ltd., Minutes. August 14, 1930; VA, File 160, Quarterly Rept. on Military and Aircraft Armament Sales, for First Quarter 1931.

[30] Habeck, 131.

about one-fourth of Vickers's military and air armaments net profits that year.[31]

Due to Soviet domestication of the Vickers's designs, the company could not expect any more major sales to the Soviet Union. By the third quarter of 1931, the Soviet tank contract at Elswick was drawing to a close. At the end of the quarter, only one twelve-ton tank remained, and this was subsequently accepted. As a result, the Tank Erection Shops faced the prospect of running out of work.[32] The Soviet Union built the Vickers 6-ton tank under license in Leningrad and designated it as T-26 series. Soviet light tank production rapidly took hold, and by the end of 1931 the Soviets had produced 300 light tanks (T-26). Army plans for 1931 called for 12,000 T-26 light tanks based on the Vickers model along with 16,000 T-27 tankettes based on the Mark VI manufactured in Moscow, and a reserve of 2,000 T-26s for wartime. By 1933, USSR had capability to produce 28,000–35,000 tankettes a year.[33]

Just at this juncture when the prospect of Soviet orders receded, Poland stepped forward as Vickers's new biggest East European customer. As noted above, the Poles had been observing Vickers's tank developments for some years. Additionally, as neighbors of the rapidly rearming Soviet Union, Poland showed a keen strategic interest in enhancing its own armored forces. The Poles signed a contract on September 14, 1931, for thirty-eight 6-ton tanks and 103 machine guns worth $595,202 (£176,618). These orders from January to October 1931 accounted for a little more than 20 percent of all military sales by Vickers–Armstrong for the period January–October 1931. By June 1932, the first eight 6-ton tanks on Polish contract were inspected, but delivery was delayed due to time taken in settling with Polish authorities the design of the turrets. A further delay occurred in connection with delivery of these machines owing to trouble with 13mm bullet-proof plate. The Tank Department at Elswick remained well occupied with the Polish contract through the end of the year. During the second quarter of 1933, the Poles placed additional orders worth $397,424 (£77,622) for

---

[31] RG 165, #2281-D-77 (5) J. A. Baer (mil attaché Vienna) to G-2, August 15, 1930; VA, File 158, Vickers–Armstrongs factory Reports Third Quarter 1930; VA, File 160 Vickers–Armstrong Factory Reports for Quarter ended March 31, 1931; VA, Microfilm K612, Russia, July 20, 1931 to Birch; VA, File 164, Quarterly Rept. on Military and Air Armaments, first quarter 1932; RG 165, #2281-D-85 (5) mil attaché Riga to G-2, November 22, 1933; VA, File 165 Vickers–Armstrong factory Reports for Quarter ended June 30, 1932; VA, File 167, Quarterly Rept. on Military and Air Armaments, Fourth Quarter 1932.

[32] VA, File 162, Vickers–Armstrong factory Reports Third Quarter 1931.

[33] VA, File 895, Tanks and Armored Cars built by Vickers 1919–1942; Habeck, 149–150; Gorvan, 10.

twenty-two tank turrets with 47mm guns and nine Vickers-Carden-Loyd Tractors.[34]

Besides purchases from Vickers–Armstrong, the Poles initiated domestic manufacture of the Mk VI tankette designated as the Polish TK, TKS, and TKF models. During 1931, the Polish Army purchased 200 Ford motors for the tankettes and 250 more during 1932. The Poles informed the Ford Co. that they would buy a further 250 motors in 1933. FIAT had a practical monopoly on the manufacture of automobiles in Poland and insisted that the small FIAT motor be tried in this tankette. The Poles complied and tested the FIAT motor as a possible replacement for the Ford. The results proved unsatisfactory as the FIAT motor overheated and did not give service equal to the Ford either in the life of the motor or in speed and reliability. Poland had also purchased a manufacturing license from Vickers–Armstrong for the 6-ton tank, which would receive the Polish designation as the 7TP series.[35]

The success of Vickers's tanks and the proliferation of Vickers's manufacturing licenses heightened competition for the British firm. By 1932, in the Vickers's Board room complaints arose about how the French had succeeded in copying the small Carden-Loyd tank and trailer, and had put one on the foreign market. The Poles, who had a license to manufacture for their own government only, were also asking to be allowed to sell abroad. Specifically, the Poles wanted to enlist Vickers–Armstrong's worldwide organization to help sell their tankette in countries where the Mark VI would not be wanted.[36] By September, the military armaments department reported that "A great deal of copying of our models is taking place. Our Tanks are being copied in America, France and Italy, and our machineguns (Vickers-Berthier and Vickers) by Brno, who are competing with us in Greece and Belgium."[37] In a final indignity, the Soviets were showing their tanks, derived from the Vickers models, and had

[34] VA, Microfilm K611, Poland File, Report on Visit to Poland September 4–18, 1931; VA, File 162, Quarterly Rept. on Military and Air Armaments Sales. Third Quarter 1931; VA, File 165 Vickers–Armstrong factory Reports for Quarter ended June 30, 1932; RG 165, #2281-DD-35 (2) Yeager to G-2, June 22, 1932; VA, File 167, Quarterly Rept. on Military and Air Armaments, Fourth Quarter 1932; VA, File 169, Noel Birch Quarterly Rept on military and Air Armaments, Apr 1–June 30, 1933.

[35] VA, File 895, Tanks and Armored Cars built by Vickers 1919–1942; RG 165, #2281-DD-36 (2) Yeager to G-2, January 5, 1933; RG 165, #2281-DD-35 (1) Emer Yeager (mil attaché Warsaw) to G-2, January 15, 1932; Jońca, vol. 3, 5, 17–18.

[36] VA, File 164, Quarterly Rept. on Military and Air Armaments, first quarter 1932; VA, Microfilm K611, Poland File, Meeting at HQ of State Armaments factories PWV Poland, May 13, 1932.

[37] VA, File 166, Quarterly Rept. on Military and Air Armaments Third Quarter 1932, July 1–September 30.

presented five T-27 Carden-Loyd tankettes and two T-26 6-ton tanks to Turkey.[38]

Gains in aircraft and tank sales were not large enough to offset British losses in naval sales. In the pre-1914 era, Great Britain had typically obtained some 90 percent of foreign orders for warships. By the late 1920s, this position has been entirely reversed, mainly through the success of Italy. As of January 1931, some 30,000 tons of warships were building on foreign account in Italy compared with 5,000 tons in Britain. While the Italian shipbuilder Ansaldo could give twelve years credit on a Turkish order, any British credits for armaments were still expressly excluded from the Export Credits Scheme. Even if the legislation could be amended, the terms of credits necessary to compete with Italy in this field would have been so uneconomical that the British Advisory Committee still would have refused its consent.[39]

The two overriding factors operating in the warship trade for smaller powers were price and credit terms. Price in turn was largely governed by the cost of labor. The more work a firm had the less were its proportionate overhead charges, and that had a great effect on costs. The Italians were making a concerted effort to obtain a monopoly in foreign armament work, and their dramatic gains in that class of work had caused greater enterprise, greater efficiency, and lower costs. There appeared little prospect of British firms being able to compete with the Italians unless something was done to help them. The British Board of Trade rather glumly concluded that "There may be exceptions where a country is anxious to obtain British materiel, either for sentiment or for some particular reason, but the more orders which now go to Italy, the more will go in the future as the foundations of these industries will become stronger with successful performance and greater experience, whilst the relative prestige of our firms and materials will decline... Our material is thought well of, but when it comes to placing orders it nearly always comes back to price and credit terms... Our armament productive capacity has already much decreased compared to what it was in 1914 and it is falling for want of orders."[40]

Italian shipbuilding benefited from Italian Law that provided for the payment of subsidies in respect of merchant ships built in Italian

---

[38] RG 165, #2281-T-13 (1) Cortlandt Parker to G-2, November 9, 1932; David R. Stone, "Soviet Arms Exports in the 1920s," *Journal of Contemporary History*, vol. 48, no. 1 (2012), 62.

[39] BT 56/ 18, Export of Naval Armaments. Summary January 23, 1931.

[40] BT 56/ 18, Memorandum. January 15, 1931.

yards.[41] In addition, the Italians had created an institution with a capital of \$5.26 million (ITL 100 million) subscribed by semigovernmental and political organizations for giving loans to shipbuilders. The Italian government contributed 2.5 percent interest on loans granted by this institution in respect of ships built in Italy, it officially underwrote export credit risks, and the Italian government granted exemption from duty to imported shipbuilding materials. As part of the Fascist system, the Italian government could guarantee shipbuilding yards against strikes. According to Greek naval authorities, the Italian government had provided a direct subsidy of \$243,000 (£50,000) each to builders of two destroyers bought by Greece, and in the case of the contract for the first pair of Turkish destroyers to be built by Ansaldo the Italian government assumed responsibility for 5 percent of the total sum to be paid by the Turkish government, which enabled the firm to borrow from the banks at a reduced rate of interest.[42] Vickers had offered the Turks credit for 60 percent of construction over five years. Italians offered credit for 84 percent of contract over five years.[43]

The loss of business to British firms owed chiefly to their inability to offer sufficiently long credit facilities, and the situation raised the question of the expediency of extending the Export Credits Scheme to include the export of arms, munitions, and war materiel. In the Eastern European market by late 1930, only a single flotilla leader vessel for Yugoslavia was building in Britain. Meanwhile, Italian yards were building two flotilla leaders, one submarine, and one submarine depot ship for Romania, four destroyers, two submarines, and three submarine chasers for Turkey and four coastal motor boats for Greece. Similarly, French yards were constructing one submarine for Greece, along with two destroyers and three submarines for Poland.[44] Noel Birch at Vickers–Armstrong noted in his third quarter report for 1930,

We shall be severely handicapped in the world fight for armament orders until the Government grant an extension of the Export Credit Guarantee Scheme. The Conservatives would not do it because they were afraid of the Labour Party.

---

[41] J. C. Clarke III, "Italo-Soviet Military Cooperation in the 1930s," in D. J. Stoker Jr. and J. A. Grant (eds.), *Girding for Battle: The Arms Trade in a Global Perspective, 1815–1940* (Westport, CT: Praeger, 2003), 184.

[42] BT 56/18, Note by the Secretary of State for Foreign Affairs, December 2, 1930, enclosed in Cabinet. Export of War Materials and Warships; RG 165, #2126–37 (7) Major George Lovell Jr. to G-2, February 13, 1931.

[43] RG 165, #2126–46, Mil attaché London to G-2, March 17, 1931.

[44] BT 56/18, Note by the Secretary of State for Foreign Affairs, December 2, 1930, enclosed in Cabinet. Export of War Materials and Warships.

We are getting more selling help from this Government than we did from the last. I believe now that propaganda and pressure from the banks might do something. The Services are pressing.[45]

Nevertheless, in December 1930 the Foreign Office vehemently opposed such a move as diametrically opposed to the British government's disarmament position. Besides the legal issue of needing an Act of Parliament to extend the export credits law to include armaments, the Foreign Secretary, Arthur Henderson, told the Cabinet that "His Majesty's Government are at present in the forefront of the struggle to secure worldwide limitation and reduction of armaments, and it would be totally inconsistent with their principles and their policy to promote legislation permitting them to extend credit facilities to the export of arms. This aspect of the question is of fundamental importance and must be borne in mind in the consideration of any steps which it may be thought necessary to take with a view to assisting British armament firms to compete in foreign markets."[46]

The political context helps to clarify Henderson's position. The Labour Party returned to government following the general election in May 1929 due in part to the growing strength of the LNU's campaign in opposition to the disarmament policy of the Conservative government. Grassroots popular organizations such as LNU, No More War Movement, Women's International League for Peace and Freedom, and local chapters of the national Peace Council had all pushed for arms limitation or reduction. The new British Prime Minister, Ramsay MacDonald, therefore reappointed Cecil as British representative on the Preparatory Commission for the Disarmament Conference. Cecil was in the process of renegotiating concessions on the incorporation of budgetary limitation and supervision of disarmament that would finally yield agreement on a Draft Disarmament Convention. A week after Henderson's comments above, on December 9, 1930, the Preparatory Commission finally approved a Draft Disarmament Convention by leaving it up to the World Disarmament Conference to resolve the figures for arms reduction and limitation. The Council of the League of Nations ultimately set the date for the World Disarmament Conference for February 2, 1932.[47]

---

[45] VA, File 158, Vickers–Armstrongs Factory Reports Quarterly Rept. Military and Air Armaments Sales Third Quarter 1930.

[46] BT 56/18, Note by the Secretary of State for Foreign Affairs, December 2, 1930, enclosed in Cabinet. Export of War Materials and Warships.

[47] T. R. Davies, *Possibilities of Transnational Activism: The Campaign for Disarmament between the Two World Wars* (Boston: Brill Academic, 2006), 82; C. Lynch, "A Matter of Controversy: The Peace Movement and British Arms Policy in the Interwar Period,"

During the two years leading up to the opening of the Disarmament Conference, Vickers–Armstrong entered a critical phase as the disarmament movement grew. Between December 1930 and February 1932, the disarmament movement proliferated. Over the course of 1930, the Women's Peace Crusade came to represent 2 million voters, and in 1931 peace group memberships peaked with LNU recording 400,000 members.[48] According to Davies, the British disarmament campaign kicked off in earnest on February 9, 1931, when Arthur Henderson addressed a gathering of British activists in London's Queen's Hall arranged by the British branch of the Women's International League. Through the rest of the year, hundreds of provincial disarmament committees were created and over 4,000 disarmament demonstrations took place across the country. In Britain, sixty-five organizations co-operated in the collection of signatures for disarmament petitions, including the Labour and Liberal Parties. As a result, 10,000 British signatures per day were being collected by the end of 1931.[49] Nevertheless, Birch held out hope for Vickers's armaments sales as he remarked to the Vickers–Armstrong Board at the end of the first quarter of 1931 that "There is an improvement in business prospects this quarter, in spite of the world financial crisis and Mr. Henderson's efforts in the direction of disarmament."[50] Birch's optimism was misplaced. In October 1930, work for the Gun Mounting and Submarine departments at the Barrow Work was dropping rapidly, and prospects for new foreign orders looked dim. Foreign competition was fierce and the Czechs at Brno were producing the Vickers machine gun 30 percent cheaper than Vickers itself. As the contract for 75mm Turkish guns neared completion at Barrow the employment both of machines and men was falling off in this section. As the amount of unexecuted work on the order book rapidly decreased, no new orders of any size were in sight, and by the third quarter of 1931 the number of men employed decreased week by week. The Erith Works closed down during the last quarter of 1931 and the company transferred its armaments departments to Crayford.[51] Vickers's number of employed on armaments had dropped from 13,331 in 1930 to 11,747

---

in B. J. C. McKercher (ed.), *Arms Limitation and Disarmament: Restraints on War, 1899–1939* (Westport, CT: Praeger, 1992), 63, 71.

[48] Lynch, "A Matter of Controversy," 63, 71.   [49] Davies, *Possibilities*, 87, 100, 105.

[50] VA, File 160, Quarterly Rept. on Military and Aircraft Armament Sales, for First Quarter 1931.

[51] VA, File 151, Vickers–Armstrongs factory Reports second Quarter 1930; VA, File 159, Quarterly Rept. on Military and Air Armaments Fourth Quarter 1930; VA, File 162, Vickers–Armstrong Factory Reports Third Quarter 1931; VA, File 716, Extent of Works occupied during disarmament period 1928–1934.

by 1931.[52] In terms of military and air armaments for Vickers, "At the moment enquiries would not give one armament firm sufficient work, and we are in competition with ten... We suffer also from our Foreign Office being conscientious."[53]

The British government continued to refuse to provide credit support for armaments, and hoped that other countries would play by its rules rather than facilitating their own armaments businesses. In a Cabinet meeting in January 1931, Secretary of War Amulree raised the question whether the government's policy was really assisting or hindering the policy of general disarmament. Amulree queried whether by neglecting British armaments firms the government might be assisting rather than preventing war. British reluctance had not checked armament production, but instead British firms were losing orders which were being taken by foreign firms. The Foreign Office countered that it sought to persuade foreign countries to adopt the policy of a general prohibition of government subsidies to armament firms, and "It was our policy to persuade foreign countries to adopt British practices in this respect."[54] In an effort to combat the problem of declining British warship exports, the Admiralty hosted a conference with leading shipbuilding firms John Brown, Thornycoft, Vickers–Armstrong, Hawthorne Leslie, and Cammell Laird as well as the Board of Trade in early February 1931. From the Admiralty's point of view, it was extremely important for British firms to try and recover their former position on account of the work which it brought into the country. The question of price was discussed, and although the firms' representatives considered this important, they did not feel that this was the main stumbling block. According to the firms, the real difficulty in regard to these foreign orders was that it had become customary for countries ordering warships abroad to demand long terms of credit for their payments, sometimes as much as ten years, and under present circumstances very few if any British firms could undertake orders on those terms. The firms pointed out that they could not obtain advances from their bankers for building foreign warships, as banks would not regard them as security as they might do in the case of a merchant ship. If the buyer defaulted on a merchant vessel, the ship could be sold to someone else. Warships lacked a comparable, alternative market. Without financial backing, the firms found it impossible to accept

---

[52] D. Edgerton, *Warfare State: Britain, 1920–1970* (Cambridge: Cambridge University Press, 2006), 39.
[53] VA, File 163, Quarterly Rept. on Military and Air Armaments Fourth Quarter 1931.
[54] BT 56/18, Cabinet. Committee on Export of War Material and Warships. January 21, 1931.

long-term payments, and British firms consistently came up against representatives of foreign firms who would go one better than they did in the matter of credit, and so it went on until the order was lost.[55] Vice Admiral Backhouse and Sir Horace Wilson from the Board of Trade followed up the conference by talking with the financial house Baring Brothers to see what could be done. Baring's representative, E. R. Peacock, indicated that "the smaller Powers had been spoiled in the matter of credit payment by the larger Powers seeking for their orders and going to great lengths to obtain them. The consequence was that these bad habits had grown up."[56] When the issue of support for armaments firms came up again in Cabinet Committee at the end of March, the secretary of war, T. Shaw, observed that if the armament firms could receive the necessary financial assistance from the banks, the government would be relieved of all responsibility in the matter.[57]

The Turkish business drove home the vital importance of credit terms for Italian naval exports. In 1932, the Turkish government experienced a severe financial crisis due to the depression of export prices on the world market. As a result, the entire Turkish defense program was in danger of default. Financially strapped, the government had to find the money from abroad to enable it to continue its plans of reconstruction, or modify the plans. On March 1, 1932, the Minister of National Defense met with representatives of the various foreign arms suppliers to try to arrange a postponement of payments until 1936. Among the firms holding contracts were Vickers–Armstrong, Schneider, Škoda, Bofors, Ansaldo, Cantiere Navale, Chantiers ed Saint-Nazaire, Fabrique Nationale, Liege, Gorz, and Erhardt. Faced with an extremely difficult situation, the Turks received unforeseen aid from Mussolini and the Italian government in the form of a $15.33 million (ITL 300 million) loan.[58]

Vickers–Armstrong, exasperated by the aloofness of the British government, decided to lobby the Department of Overseas Trade directly in support of changing the Export Guarantees to include armaments. In particular, Birch wanted the support of Overseas Trade for Vickers's potential customers in the Baltic, especially Finland, Estonia, Latvia, Lithuania, and Denmark, with secondary prospects in Poland, Belgium, and Argentina. Along with urging the extension of the export credit,

[55] BT 56/18, Rept. of a Conference Held at the Admiralty with Representatives of Shipbuilding Firms on February 5, 1931.
[56] BT 56/18, Rept. of a Discussion with Mr. E. R. Peacock on February 9, 1931.
[57] BT 56/18, Cabinet Committee on the Export of War Materials and Warships, March 31, 1931.
[58] · FO 424/276, No. 21, enclosed in Clerk to Simon, February 3, 1932; No. 25, enclosed in Embassy (Angora) to Simon, March 4, 1932; No. 54, Clerk to Simon, June 5, 1932.

Birch also criticized the ineffectiveness of the government's disarmament policy. He complained:

It is questionable whether politicians really understand that discriminating between trade in arms and trade in other goods, makes not the slightest difference when the question of peace or war arises. What we will not supply is quickly supplied by foreign armament firms. There are now ten armament firms and fourteen machine-gun manufacturers in the world. A notable instance of a loss of two millions of trade to England was in the late China War, when England and France agreed not to supply China with arms. Schneider then stepped in, having a controlling influence over Škoda, who supplied the whole of the arms necessary for the war. Italy is particularly active in armament trade, and Spain is now quoting.[59]

As Birch pressed Overseas Trade, H. A. Lawrence, Vickers's chairman, approached the Committee of Imperial Defence to extend the guarantee of export credits to the armaments industry in October 1932. Besides echoing Birch's complaints about losing out to foreign competitors, Lawrence emphasized the importance of Vickers for imperial defense, noting that Vickers–Armstrong supplied vital products to the army, navy, and air force. For Vickers to continue would require the maintenance of large research and experimental establishments. If those facilities were lost, "the forces of the Crown must suffer severely in the event of war."[60]

When the World Disarmament Conference opened in Geneva in February 1932, conditions appeared favorable for resolving the issue. Large peace movements had organized and many of them sent representatives to the Conference. In addition, the international financial crisis of the Great Depression put pressure on governments to reduce military expenditures that appeared unsustainable and to placate domestic political forces.[61] Those same forces adversely affected Vickers. Due to the acute shortage of work, the howitzer shop, submarine extension shop, and shell shop remained closed during the first quarter of 1932, and the shipyard mechanics shop at Barrow had to close during the second quarter.[62] Noel Birch reported that the second quarter of 1932 proved the worst trading quarter ever, and "until disarmament talks

---

[59] VA, File 722, Birch. Notes for the interview with Sir Edward Crowe, Dept. of Overseas Trade, September 7, 1932.

[60] VA, File 722, H. A. Lawrence, Chairman, Vickers Ltd. to Secretary of Committee of Imperial Defence, October 7, 1932.

[61] D. W. Kearn Jr., *Great Power Security Cooperation: Arms Control and the Challenge of Technological Change* (Lanham, MD: Lexington Books, 2015), 92.

[62] VA, File 164, Vickers–Armstrong Factory Reports First Quarter 1932; VA, File 165, Vickers–Armstrong Factory Reports for Quarter ended June 30, 1932.

cease and the financial situation of the world, especially in South America, improves, we cannot expect to do much."[63] Birch noted that the small countries of Finland, Portugal, Lithuania, and perhaps Latvia were the only countries in a position to buy anything, and if the Finnish House of Parliament passed an armament loan, the firm might do business of over $3.28 million (£1 million) in Finland. A British antiaircraft officer had just been appointed to advise Finland on antiaircraft defense. Latvia also wanted a continuous program, but their financial stability appeared questionable.[64] Clearly, Vickers was caught between depression and disarmament.

Contrary to Vickers's hopes in the Baltic, the British government's disarmament policy meant declining to apply diplomatic pressure to help secure a British contract. In November 1932, regarding promises of Finnish armaments orders to Vickers, Overseas Trade considered that given the "overriding importance of the question of general disarmament HMG could not put itself into the position of pressing strongly for the purchase of armaments by Finland at the present time." Overseas Trade refused even to hint at a connection of armaments purchases with the general question of the balance of trade between Finland and Britain, or to link the armaments question in any way with general commercial negotiations with Finland.[65]

In the Vickers–Armstrong Board Room, the effects of the disarmament movement on business drew comment, and shaped product development strategy. Birch worried that a new treaty might adversely affect chances of business in the Baltic States, Finland, and Sweden. He also pointed directly to the negative effect of the Geneva Conference making countries "loath to buy whilst the Disarmament Conference is sitting" and specifically referenced the "unpatriotic endeavors" at home by the League of Nations Union in its cause to do away with the private manufacture of arms.[66] Birch mused that the leading politicians and clerics who sought to eliminate private manufacture of arms were "Quite innocently...playing the part of accessories before the fact to murder."[67] Birch did mention some heartening support from the House of Lords, where Douglas Hogg, the first Lord Hailsham and secretary of war had spoken in defense of the private manufacture of arms on

---

[63] VA, File 165, Noel Birch Quarterly Report of Military and Air Armaments from April 1, 1932, to June 30, 1932.
[64] Ibid.
[65] FO 371/16286, Dept. of Overseas Trade. Memorandum, November 16, 1932.
[66] VA, File 167, Quarterly Rept on Military and Air Armaments, Fourth Quarter 1932.
[67] Ibid.

December 8, 1932.[68] On March 16, 1933, Prime Minister MacDonald presented what would prove to be the last major disarmament plan at Geneva. The proposal came in the form of a complete Draft Convention where Part I provided for French security concerns through supervisory arrangements by a permanent disarmament commission and the maintenance of German arms at existing levels for two years, and Part II included limitations of mobile guns by caliber (4 inches) and tanks by weight (16 tons).[69] In September 1933, Birch reported to the Vickers Board that "The gun market is still undoubtedly slack, but it is likely to improve when the October meeting of the Disarmament Conference comes to an end." With his eye toward Geneva, Birch called for the development of a 105mm long-range gun "in case Disarmament Conference at Geneva decide this is highest caliber to be allowed."[70]

The French case, while moving in parallel with the British disarmament movement, did not have as much strength. In France, as in Britain, popular belief held that the pre-1914 armaments race had been a prime cause of war, but generally pacifism remained a minority movement in 1920s but grew stronger with the Kellogg-Briand pact outlawing war in 1928. By 1930, a pacifist majority existed in France, but it broke into two groups: those who preferred security first then disarmament, and those who supported for general disarmament.[71] The French national disarmament campaign started in 1931 when the chief federation of French trade unions, the Confédération Générale du Travail (CGT) issued a manifesto calling for general disarmament. By February, the Socialist Party, the Radical Party, and the Republican Socialist Party threw their support behind the CGT position. In April, several French Catholic associations, including the Frenchwomen's Catholic League and the Catholic Association of Young Frenchmen, called for disarmament, and in May the chief veterans' organization in France passed a similar resolution. The campaign in France climaxed on December 18, 1931, with a demonstration in Paris by about ten thousand organized by the CGT, the Radical and Socialist Parties, the French League of Nations associations, and the French pacifist groups.[72]

The Great Depression did not immediately put a damper on French armaments firms. In fact, for the period 1930–1934, Hotchkiss, Gnôme and Rhône, and Chantiers et Ateliers de Saint-Nazaire all had balances

---

[68] Ibid.   [69] Davies, *Possibilities*, 140.

[70] VA, File 722, Re-Armament, Noel Birch, Land Service Artillery Models, September 4, 1933.

[71] A. Adamthwaite, *Grandeur and Misery, France's Bid for Power in Europe, 1919–1940* (London: Arnold, 1995), 144, 151, 168.

[72] Davies, *Possibilities*, 102–103.

above their 1929 levels and did not experience sharp declines during the period.[73] Schneider too fared well initially. As of November 1931, the company reported that executed artillery orders continued to support its specialist workshops satisfactorily, and despite the difficulties caused by foreign competition, "This branch of our industry is very lively."[74] In the following fiscal year, Schneider did experience a sharp decline in total orders from F604 million to F445 million and all areas decreased from previous period with the notable exception of artillery and armor which actually increased 28 percent to account for 40 percent of all work. Domestic artillery work predominated with 162 of 205 field guns ordered by France and Polish pieces a distant second at 31 field guns.[75] Despite the persistence of the broader economic crisis, the annual report in November 1932 noted that "the activity of our factory has been able to maintain itself in a satisfactory condition."[76]

Thanks in part to the company's relatively healthy condition, Schneider-Creusot did not seize upon the prospects of Soviet business. In late September 1932, a Soviet representative approached Litzelmann of Schneider about entering into relations with the French firm to acquire 28cm antiaircraft guns and 15cm long guns. With the memories of its assets in tsarist Russia nationalized by the Soviets still fresh, Schneider responded guardedly and with the greatest reserve about entering into relations with the USSR. To avoid getting burned again, Schneider imposed a number of conditions on the Soviets including deposit in a French bank of the sums necessary to cover the furnishing, and the disallowance of Soviet inspectors in Creusot's factories to oversee production. When the Soviets accepted those conditions, Schneider indicated it would only proceed to examine this proposal if the French government granted its approval. The French Foreign Ministry subsequently informed Litzelmann of its approval for Creusot to enter into relations with the USSR for the furnishing of arms, even though generally the French government did not authorize the export of war materiel to Russia.[77] After mulling the proposal over for three months, Creusot rejected the Soviet offers in January 1933 based on political considerations. Schneider told the Foreign Ministry that the firm had declined

---

[73] D. Lefeuvre, "Les lumières de la crise. Les entreprises françaises dans la dépression des années 1930," *Vingtième Siècle. Revue d'histoire*, no. 52, Numéro spécial: Les crises économiques du 20e siècle (1996), 35.

[74] SA, 187AQ029–01, Rapport du Gerant a l'Assemblee, November 28, 1931, 4.

[75] SA, 187AQ029–02, Marche des Industries pendant l'Exercice 1931–1932, 1, 40.

[76] SA, 187AQ029–02, Process-verbal de la Reunion du Conseil de Surveillance, November 14, 1932.

[77] MAE, Europe 1930–1940, URSS 930, Note. September 28, 1932; Matériel de guerre a destination de l'URSS, October 21, 1932.

the Soviets "in order not to be exposed to the criticisms of a portion of certain elements of public opinion in France."[78] Another Soviet inquiry to Schneider at the end of November 1933 about supplying twenty-four 105mm antiaircraft guns with 1,500 shells each met a similar negative result.[79]

Schneider only began to feel the effects of depression and disarmament 1933–1934. Schneider too experienced a downturn in orders and a decrease in profits, though nothing so severe that prevented the company paying dividends every year. The first effect came in the economic realm of currency devaluation. Schneider's Board complained that the depreciation of the Swedish Crown enabled Bofors to engage in "a disquieting price war without excessive sacrifice."[80] Thankfully, large domestic artillery orders propped up artillery sales when foreign sales only accounted for 12.5 percent of new orders acquired and the execution of orders for Romania was completely suspended for nonpayment by 1933.[81] During fiscal year 1933–1934, Schneider's fortunes hit their lowest ebb of the era. The total value for all orders hit a new low of about $22 million (F363 million) and profits also dropped correspondingly. The figure converted into $US looks high because of the overvalued franc. As the artillery business carried a bigger and bigger share of Schneider's work, Schneider's managers voiced growing concerns regarding the difficulties of exports specifically as they related to the Great Depression and disarmament. Pricing took on critical importance as the depreciation of foreign currencies could "impose on Schneider great sacrifice or abandoning the business." More and more foreign governments demanded longer payment terms that "posed financial problems and risks." Whereas in the past the firm had found a solution in Assurance Credits from the French government to fund foreign orders, now "the interdiction of the export of capital obliges recourse to clearing arrangements or other such means." Meanwhile, Schneider's competitors showed no reluctance to offer more solicitous terms for financing, risk and barter "aided by their governments as is the case of Škoda and the exchange of tobacco."[82] For the first time, Schneider complained about the lack of support from the French government. The management believed "they could not count on the active support of the government thanks to the campaign unleashed in France against the

[78] Ibid., Note. Commande soviétique au Creusot, January 4, 1933.
[79] MAE, Europe 1930–1940, URSS 932, MAE to War Min, November 30, 1933.
[80] SA, 187AQ030–01, Marche des Industries pendant l'Exercice 1932–1933, 43.
[81] Ibid., 42.
[82] SA, 187AQ030–02, Marche des Industries pendant l'Exercice, 1933–1934, 46.

Table 5.1 *Schneider's Artillery Business, 1930–1934*

Business Year	Domestic Artillery Sales, $ Millions (Million Francs)	Export Artillery Sales, $ Millions (Millions Francs)	Total Sales (Includes Nonmilitary), $ Millions (Millions Francs)	Profits, $ Millions (Millions Francs)	Artillery as Percentage of All Business
1930–1931	3.13 (79)	4.0 (101)	23.93 (604)	1.03 (26.0)	30.0
1931–1932	5.06 (129)	2.63 (67)	17.46 (445)	0.95 (24.4)	44.0
1932–1933	5.54 (142)	3.94 (101)	15.18 (389)	0.60 (15.3)	65.0
1933–1934	7.22 (118)	6.18 (101)	22.22 (363)	1.27 (20.8)	60.0

Sources: SA, 187AQ029–01, Rapport du Gerant a l'Assemblee, November 28, 1931, 7; SA, 187AQ029–02, Marche des Industries pendant l'Exercice 1931–1932; SA, 187AQ029–02, Process-verbal de la Reunion du Conseil de Surveillance, November 14, 1932; SA, 187AQ030–01, Marche des Industries pendant l'Exercice, 1932–1933; SA, 187AQ030–01, Rapport du Gerant a l'Assemblee, November 30, 1933; SA, 187AQ030–02, Proces-verbal de la Reunion du Conseil de Surveillance, November 5, 1934; SA, 187AQ030–02, Marche des Industries pendant l'Exercice, 1933–1934.

makers of armaments."[83] At long last, Schneider found itself in the same boat as Vickers–Armstrong (Table 5.1).

In the absence of an effective international agreement on disarmament and Germany's withdrawal from the Disarmament Conference in October 1933, the British Committee on the Private Armaments Industry met in early December 1933 to consider what course of action to take regarding the identified handicaps faced by British armaments firms compared to their foreign competitors. The Committee brought together Board of Trade, Secretaries of War, Foreign Affairs, Admiralty, Air, Treasury, and Overseas Trade. The Committee observed that with the exceptions of Britain and possibly Sweden, all other states more or less encouraged the arms trade as a source of revenue or directly assisted the trade for reasons of national defense. Surveying Europe, the capacity for manufacturing arms had generally increased compared to 1914. France, Italy, the Soviet Union, Czechoslovakia, and Poland had each extended its armaments industries. By the same token, Germany, Austria, Hungary, and Bulgaria had clearly indicated plans to overcome the limits imposed on them by the peace treaties. Further unsettling to British policy, "Other minor Powers have equally taken steps to ensure . . . that the maximum industrial effort of the country shall be available in emergency

[83] Ibid., 47.

to manufacture the means of defense. *A race to arms has been taking place... The keenest competition has ensued in the international armament trade* (emphasis added). Fearing or foreseeing future eventualities, and prompted by motives of self-defense, the State has stepped in to encourage and assist its national industry to outbid competitors."[84] While this arms race was occurring, British firms had ceased to perform armaments work, and Vickers–Armstrong had been forced to close departments due to lack of orders. Yet, other countries had not suffered such adverse effects.

The Committee deemed that the time had come to level the field for British firms. The Committee members overwhelmingly endorsed the recommendation to include armaments under the Export Credit Guarantee Scheme. Secondarily, the Committee proposed easing up on licensing restrictions by granting open licenses covering the export of all war materiel to foreign governments recognized by HMG with the exceptions of Germany, Austria, Hungary, and Bulgaria. An open license would solve the problems in the current licensing system, which inhibited manufacturers from clinching an immediate bargain and created liability because licenses could be revoked or modified at any time. The one notable dissent came from the Foreign Office. Since the disarmament negotiations were entering a delicate and critical stage, the Foreign Office suggested deferring the decision on export licensing for a few months in order to see how the disarmament talks concluded. Revealingly, in putting forth its recommendation for inclusion of armaments under the Export Credit Guarantee, the Committee noted that "It will be for the Cabinet to consider whether political objections to such inclusion are so grave as to outweigh the undoubted advantages from the point of view both of defense generally and of the maintenance of the British armament industry."[85]

In the face of strong public support for the disarmament position, the British government well understood the political costs of seeming to support private armaments firms over the greater good of disarmament. When the Cabinet heard the Committee's recommendations in mid-December, Prime Minister MacDonald, voiced his apprehension about the political reaction that would undoubtedly be provoked by the proposed changes. In particular, MacDonald feared that critics of the government would denounce the changes as the first step in a policy of rearmament. The Prime Minister opined that "Our best defense,

---

[84] CAB 27/551, Committee on the Private Armaments Industry, Rept. Walter Runciman, December 8, 1933.
[85] Ibid.

namely, the imperative importance of maintaining our munitions industry and of retaining the services of skilled munitions workers, would be seized upon to support the view that we are beginning another race in armaments, which could only end in war."[86] MacDonald sought some way to blunt the political criticism while still enacting the Cabinet's decision for the proposals. Unable to accomplish that feat, the government did not revise the Export Credit Guarantee to include armaments. The British government's pursuit of disarmament and reduction of the arms trade continued to inform policy into 1934.

Indeed, popular opposition to the private arms trade grew even louder, and pressures mounted from above and below. From above, the Labour Party urged support for measures to control arms traffic coming at Geneva and also called for the prohibition of all private manufacture. From below, grassroots political action led Lord Cecil to include the question of prohibiting the manufacture of armaments by private enterprise on the national Peace Ballot. These pressures did not abate following the adjournment of the Disarmament Conference in June 1934. The US Senate opened the Nye Committee hearings to investigate profiteering, bribery, and shady international collusion among arms private armaments firms and suppliers. Those hearings exposed Vickers,[87] and Vickers–Armstrong felt the heat. In the summer of 1934, Birch reported to the directors "there has lately been an increased outcry against the export of arms."[88] Moreover, the Foreign Office had placed an arms embargo on four countries. Birch related to the board his attempts to impress upon the Foreign Office the futility and detriment of its policies on Vickers's business. Whereas the Foreign Office believed that its embargos only had local effects, Birch tried to explain how tendering for orders in nonembargo countries suffered too because foreign governments worried whether their deliveries would be cut off or not. Furthermore, if an embargo is once placed on export to a country, Vickers could lose trade in that country for years to come. The government naturally goes elsewhere for weapons and it is then tied to its suppliers for renewals, spare parts, ammunition etc. Having tried to no avail to persuade the Foreign Office, Birch wistfully concluded, "How different the conduct of our Foreign Office is from that of the French."[89]

---

[86] CAB 27/551 Cabinet Meeting Minute. December 18, 1933.

[87] D. G. Anderson, "British Rearmament and the 'Merchants of Death': The 1935–36 Royal Commission on the Manufacture of and Trade in Armaments," *Journal of Contemporary History*, vol. 29, no. 1 (1994), 9.

[88] VA, File 173, Sir Noel Birch Quaterly Rept. on Military and Air Armament. Second Quarter from April 1 to June 30, 1934.

[89] Ibid.

Out of fear of stoking the arms race, the British Foreign Office continued to exhibit reluctance to promote the new Turkish naval expansion even though British firms would most likely benefit. Beginning in 1934, Mussolini's allusions to Italian expansion in Africa and Asia triggered an immediate defensive reaction on the part of Turkey and Greece. Out of the heightened fear of Italy, the pattern of Turkish arms imports changed in two ways after 1934. First, and perhaps most obviously, the Turkish government no longer placed any naval orders with Italian firms. In effect the Turks were extricating themselves from any possible reliance on a potentially hostile supplier. Second, Turkey dramatically raised spending allocations for domestic military manufactures and raised taxes to pay for the expansion. Budgetary allocations approved by the National Assembly called for $4.875 million (TL 3.9 million) for domestic military manufactures. While this represented only 6 percent of all military spending within the budget, it was an increase of one-third over the previous year's budget.[90] Unfortunately for Turkey, the country's meager industrial capabilities proved insufficient for the task of naval and air force expansion, and so the Turks contemplated the political consequences of placing orders with the various other potential suppliers. Together, the Turks and Greeks approached the British with plans to double the defensive power of their fleets. However, "Both countries were determined not to be drawn within the orbit of any group of Powers," and so, "both Governments had come to the conclusion that if matter could be arranged they would wish to place orders with Great Britain."[91] Certainly, the British Admiralty clearly recognized the importance of such orders for their industry. The Royal Navy expressed grave concern about the paucity of foreign orders placed in British yards. Deeming a regular inflow of foreign orders as the best means to preserve efficiency in the strategically important British naval industry, Admiralty urged the Foreign Office to support British firms in the Eastern Mediterranean. If Turkey and Greece wanted to pursue naval expansion in spite of British advice to the contrary, "it is very desirable that orders should be placed in Great Britain."[92] Foremost among Foreign Office objections to the Turkish proposal for naval expansion was the fear that any new construction by Greece and Turkey might trigger an Italian expansion which would in turn adversely affect France. In addition, the two

---

[90] US Department of State (USDS), *Records of the Department of State Relating to the Political Relations of Turkey, Greece, and Balkans 1930–39*, Turkish Fears of Italy, June 1, 1934, #767.00/54. For details of the immediate Turkish measures to beef up defenses, see FO 424/279, Nos. 18, 22, 26.

[91] FO 424/279, part XXVIII, no. 44, Consul (Geneva) to Simon, November 22, 1934.

[92] FO 424/279, part XXVIII, No. 63, Simon to Loraine, December 20, 1934.

Table 5.2 *Vickers–Armstrong's Armaments Business, 1930–1933*

Year	Total Armaments Export Contracts, $ Millions (pounds)	Naval Exports, $ Millions (pounds)	Domestic Naval Sales, $ Millions (pounds)	Profits, $ Millions (pounds)[a]
1930	**3.79** (779,388)	**0.325** (66,825)	**4.65** (957,335)	**5.6** (941,971)
1931	**5.55** (1,648,259)	**0.188** (55,795)	**0.108** (32,125)	**3.77** (775,926)
1932	**2.23** (680,854)	**0.123** (37,436)	**2.82** (860,782)	**1.74** (529,038)
1933	**9.44** (1,843,083)	**0.049** (9,507)	**1.40** (274,405)	**2.83** (552,864)

[a] J. D. Scott, *Vickers: A History* (London: Weidenfeld and Nicolson, 1962), 391.
Sources: VA File 533, Armament Contracts and Expenses 1925–1937; VA, File 170, Quarterly Report on Military and Air Armaments. Third Quarter. July 1, 1933, to September 30, 1933; VA, File 160, Rept. on Naval Armament Sales ended March 31, 1931; VA, File 159, Quarterly Rept. Naval Armaments Business Fourth Quarter 1930.

countries would need some kind of financing arrangement. From the British stand point a loan was not possible, and the granting of export credits for the supply of war materiel to a foreign government remained prohibited by statute.[93]

As we have seen, Vickers expressed dismay about the British government's ambivalence regarding the private arms trade and its conflict with the goals of disarmament. Likewise the increasing popular hostility against the armaments business as the "Merchants of Death" provoked disparaging comments in the board room. Yet, the company's bottom line weathered the storm. While Vickers exported less than Škoda did in the period 1930–1933, $21.01 million compared to $30.42 million, the British firm did exceed Schneider's totals of $20.95 million in armaments exports. As Table 5.2 shows, after cratering in 1932, the company rebounded in 1933 led by armaments exports. It seems that Birch was correct when he held that business would pick up again once the Disarmament Conference had ended.

[93] FO 424/279, part XXVIII, No. 47 Loraine to Simon, December 3, 1934; ibid., No. 55, Simon to Consul (Geneva), December 8, 1934; ibid., No. 62, Simon to Loraine, December 20, 1934.

6   Czechs and Balances
Rearmament and the Switch from Peace to War,
1934–1941

The period 1934–1938 saw the end of the remnants of laissez faire in the arms business as supplier governments became increasingly involved. German rearmament triggered corresponding rearmament in Britain and France. In turn, British and French rearmament increased pressure on the armaments firms in those countries to give priority to domestic orders over exports. As the British and French firms found their export sales increasingly hindered or delayed through their home governments' actions, they had to withdraw, leaving the Czechs to dominate the East European markets. Meanwhile, the East European states felt compelled to pursue their own rearmament, and this added to the frenzy of demand for arms purchases, especially for aircraft, tanks, and artillery. Buyer demand was strong, but available suppliers with sufficient financial support were few. The buyer countries maintained a strong desire to acquire large amounts of war equipment, but the Great Depression had aggravated the preexisting problem of lack of hard currency for foreign exchange. The cash-strapped buyer states found themselves severely restricted by the refusal of Britain to grant export credits for armaments, and those conditions opened the way for Germany to gain sales through barter arrangements and clearing agreements that mitigated the need for foreign currency reserves. Beginning in late 1935, the return of German firms, especially Krupp and Rheinmetall, as competitors in the international arms trade added a new dimension to the East European armaments business by initiating intense German-Czech competition in southeastern Europe.

Scholars have argued that while the complementarity of the German industrial economy with Southeastern European agrarian economies enabled the Germans to sell weaponry to the Balkan states in exchange for primary materials on a clearing basis, France and Czechoslovakia lost out because of the incompatibility of the French and Czech economies to absorb the agricultural products of southeastern Europe. Czechoslovakia even refused to pursue this course of action due to staunch domestic agrarian resistance to agricultural imports and Czech industrialists' commitment to free trade principles. French and Czech failure to provide markets for agricultural products thus enabled Germany to penetrate the southeastern European markets. For instance, French financing of Romanian rearmament in February 1936 withered in part thanks to French unwillingness to accept large quantities of Romanian products as payment.[1] In contrast to this argument, we shall see that Škoda managed to hold off the German firms and maintain its markets in southeastern Europe until 1938. Beginning with the German annexation of Austria (Anschluss) in March 1938 and accelerating dramatically after German annexation of the Sudetenland as part of the Munich Conference in September 1938, it was German political dominance not economic compatibility that tipped the scales decisively in the favor of German arms exports.

The second half of the 1930s saw greater restrictions on French arms exports. The Decree of September 3, 1935, subjected French arms exports to more governmental controls by requiring prior authorization from the Ministry of Finance for all war materiel exports and imposing a blanket prohibition on all armaments exports without state approval. French rearmament formally began with a comprehensive Four-Year Plan in September 1936. This rearmament program proved the largest peacetime buildup in French history as acquisitions would rise from $668 million (F14.3 billion) in 1936 to $1.4 billion (F63 billion) by September 1939. The greater participation demanded by the French state meant delays and reduced quantities available for foreign war equipment orders as the completion of French domestic defense contracts took precedence before foreign orders could be filled and delivered. The French could not supply Poland, Yugoslavia, or Romania due to France's defense industries' inability to fill the new orders for their own armed forces. In November 1937, France denied Yugoslavia delivery of twenty tanks. Only in 1938 after the French Army had received all their new light tanks from Renault was that company allowed to take production for East European customers (Poland, Romania, Turkey, Yugoslavia), and it was not until September 1939 that the French government moved energetically to establish a coordinated company to

---

[1] For detailed discussion of the French difficulties, including problems with importing Romanian oil, see N. Jordan, *The Popular Front and Central Europe: The Dilemmas of French Impotence, 1918–1940* (Cambridge: Cambridge University Press, 1992), 108–135; P. N. Hehn, *A Low Dishonest Decade: The Great Powers, Eastern Europe, and the Economic Origins of World War II, 1930–1941* (New York: Continuum, 2002), 262, 268; M. Hauner, "Military Budgets and the Armaments Industry," in M. C. Kaser and E. A. Radice (eds.), *The Economic History of Eastern Europe 1919–1939* (Oxford: Clarendon Press, 1986), 67, 95; Z. Steiner, *The Triumph of the Dark: European International History, 1933–1939* (Oxford: Oxford University Press, 2011), 287.

handle those orders. By then war had already started and it was too late. In effect French rearmament delayed and impeded East European countries' rearmament programs. The war materiel ordered in France by East European buyers in 1935–1936 stayed in France and were requisitioned by the French armed services.[2] Such was the fate of Schneider's contract with Lithuania for seventy 105mm artillery pieces and shells in 1935, and contracts with Romania for forty-five batteries of 105mm field guns plus forty batteries of 47mm guns and shells in November 1936.[3] Indeed, so desperate were the French to increase their own production for rearmament that in late 1938, according to French press, the French Air Ministry had been forced by the low output of French engine factories to buy aircraft engines from Škoda. Škoda made Hispano-Suiza 12 Y engines under license, and the Czech firm would start providing twenty-five engines per month to France.[4] Socialist Léon Blum's Popular Front government passed the Law of August 11, 1936, permitting the total or partial expropriation of establishments that made or traded armaments. The nationalization decree on March 13, 1937, removed Schneider from the business. By September 27, the French government had taken over armaments production at Le Creusot. Schneider appealed to the Conseil d'État, but lost.[5] Back in 1935, Schneider's directors had reported to the shareholders' meeting that the armaments share of the business had reached 58.6 percent (up from 26 percent in 1929) and "the part of artillery and armor is more and more important."[6] By 1939, Schneider's total orders reached record levels with artillery representing 55 percent and naval construction another 18 percent, but significantly only 0.1 percent of artillery and munitions orders were derived from abroad.[7] In this way, the French rearmament program pushed away East European business opportunities.

---

[2] Steiner, *Dark*, 275, 394; M. Thomas, "To Arm an Ally: French Arms Sales to Romania, 1926–1940," *The Journal of Strategic Studies*, vol. 19, no. 2 (1996), 234–236, 253; R. Frankenstein, "Intervention etatique et rearmement en France 1935–1939," *Revue économique*, vol. 31, no. 4, *Histoire économique: La France de l'entre-deux-guerres* (1980), 743–781; M. Thomas, *Britain, France and Appeasement: Anglo-French Relations in the Popular Front Era* (Oxford: Berg, 1996), 186; J. J. Clarke, "The Nationalization of War Industries in France, 1936–1937: A Case Study," *The Journal of Modern History*, vol. 49, no. 3 (1977), 414–416.

[3] SA, 0064Z0764–02, contract with Lithuania, September 20, 1935; SA, 01F0495, contract with Romania, April 28, 1936; 01F0596–02, contract with Romania, November 6, 1936.

[4] AIR 5/1179, AA no. 1011/865/1, October 31, 1938.

[5] SA, 187AQ031–02, Rapport du Conseil de Surveillance process-verbal, November 12, 1936; Segal, 310–311.

[6] SA, 187AQ031–01, Marche des Industries pendant l'exercise 1934–1935.

[7] SA, 187AQ033–02, Marche des industries, 1938–1939, 4–5.

In Britain, Vickers–Armstrong rapidly recovered work and workers thanks largely to domestic rearmament. By June 1934, the firm already held naval contracts worth $18.08 million (£3,652,497), of which foreign orders only accounted for 13 percent. Moreover, the bulk of foreign orders, roughly 80 percent, came from an Estonian order for two submarines. By September, the number of men employed at Elswick rose above 4,500 for the first time since 1929. Prospects improved even more the next year. By December 1935, the number of workers at Elswick hit its highest mark since the merger in 1928 (7,000 workers), and all departments in the works were very fully occupied.[8] Despite the heavy domestic sales, Birch worried about abandoning the foreign business for short-term gains over three to four years. When rearmament ended the firm would have to confront the expanded Royal Arsenal as a competitor, and his experience following the war had convinced him that the government would cut off Vickers before reducing the personnel of government factories. Birch also lamented the loss of potential foreign orders due to financial difficulties. On those grounds negotiations for orders with Bulgaria, Bolivia and Turkey had terminated, and the enquiries from those countries involved substantial monies ranging from $1.23 million to $7.40 million (£250,000–1.5 million).[9] Birch mused in March 1936 that

when this rush is over we shall find ourselves, the Arsenal and Beardmore and perhaps others, competing for work that would not keep a cat, and our foreign trade gone! It has been said that it is disloyal to the country to take foreign work now even when asked to by the government. The reverse is really the case. No sane Englishman thinks we are going to war within three years and no patriot could possibly wish for an industrial system of mobilization which goes to pieces in three years because the men cannot be kept at the bench.[10]

By January 1938, Vickers–Armstrong found itself getting behind in most of its armament products because of the difficulty of man-power. Employment rose from 46,928 in July 1936 to 63,768 in October 1937 as according to Vickers's managing director, Commander Charles Craven, "the re-armament program was superimposed on an industry which was more prosperous than it had been since the War."[11]

---

[8] VA, File 175, Half-yearly Report on Naval Armament Business from July 1, 1934, to December 31, 1934; VA, File 174, Vickers–Armstrong Works Reports to Directors, Third Quarter 1934; VA, File 179 Vickers–Armstrong Works Reports to Directors, Fourth Quarter 1935.
[9] VA, File 179, Half-yearly Report on Military and Air Armaments, second half 1935.
[10] VA, File 722, Birch to Neilson, March 14, 1936.
[11] Ibid., Re-Armament, C. W. Craven to Sir Thomas Inskip, January 19, 1938.

For Birch and Vickers, the priority of British contracts had crowded out potential foreign sales, and once those buyers turned elsewhere, they might be lost for good. Excepting 1931, the year of the financial crisis, Vickers's foreign business had been gradually and steadily increasing over the period 1930–1936. Birch believed that "but for the pressure of Government orders, and in spite of Germany having entered the foreign market, our business this year would have increased and probably gone on increasing."[12] Retaining a few of the best customers, i.e., those who did not require credit, remained the only course of action. Foreign governments already complained about the prospects of long delivery. The firm had given up on business with Bulgaria (except for a few tanks) Greece, and China because the financial conditions were not acceptable, but whether these could have been altered or not, these countries had rejected Vickers's terms of delivery as unacceptable. Domestic government sales had inhibited the design of new tanks for foreign sales as the War Office have taken up the whole of the time of Vickers's staff. In June 1936, the War Office did make a concession to Vickers by freeing the two-man turret tank for foreign sales as long as the tank varied from the War Office pattern.[13] However, just a month later the War Office disallowed Vickers from taking the tank orders until the program for the British Army had been completed. At the current rate of progress, it seemed to the company that they would not finish the army program until 1941 or 1942, and "It would be a monstrous thing if we were to be kept out of foreign business for this lengthy period."[14] For 1937, the firm's domestic orders for military and air armaments totaled $26.35 million (£5,270,716) compared to foreign sales of $3.82 million (£763,457). Naval sales showed an even more glaring difference in domestic and foreign business with domestic accounting for $53.72 million (£10,743,955) versus only $1.01 million (£202,523) for exports.[15]

For Vickers, the Spitfire aircraft presented yet another instance where British domestic rearmament forestalled foreign purchases. During the first quarter of 1937, the firm's delivery of 310 Spitfires for the RAF was three months behind schedule. Over 1938 Vickers busied itself with another RAF order for 200 Spitfires worth $5.6 million (£1.2 million) while fending off foreign enquiries. In January 1938, the Turks wanted

[12] VA, File 181, Half-yearly Rept on Military and Air Armaments. From January 1, 1936, to June 30, 1936.
[13] Ibid.
[14] VA, File 722, The Foreign Sales Situation – Land Armament, July 28, 1936.
[15] VA, File 185, Vickers–Armstrongs Ltd. Works Reports to Directors Quarter Ended June 30, 1937; VA, File 187 Vickers–Armstrong Works. Reports to Directors, fourth quarter 1937, Half-yearly report on Military and Air Armaments July–December 1937.

to order fifty Spitfires from Vickers, but as this plane type was not on the open list, and in light of production situation, Vickers had no Spitfires available for export before the end of 1939.[16] The Yugoslavs wanted to make trial flights in the Spitfire, and General Simovich, Chief of the Yugoslav Air Force, spoke of the efforts being made by the French, the Germans, and the Italians to capture the Yugoslav market for aircraft, and he indicated that unless permission were forthcoming for the trial flights in the Spitfire machine within a month or two, the Yugoslav government might be forced by the time factor to turn to other suppliers. The delay in production of the Spitfire caused serious embarrassment all around as well as being the crux of the matter as regards Yugoslavia. The Air Ministry raised no objection to the release of drawings of the Spitfire to Turkey and Yugoslavia, but the ministry raised strong objections to Vickers diverting, at present, technical staff to instruct licensees. The Air Ministry gave permission for drawings of the airframe only, not the engines.[17] Romania's desire to buy ten Spitfires also remained unfulfilled. The RAF ordered a further 183 Spitfires during the first quarter of 1939 for $3.33 million ($848,000), and to meet demand Vickers was already running overtime and night-shifts. Estonia and Greece each ordered twelve Spitfires, but deliveries were suspended at the outbreak of war.[18]

The British and French governments did not confine their restrictions on arms sales only to the small states of Eastern Europe. The Soviet Union also ran afoul of the Western governments' priority for domestic rearmament over arms exports. In 1936, the Soviets had made requests to Britain for technical aid agreements covering naval construction. The Royal Navy rejected the Soviet proposal due to the shortage of skilled technical staff for its own rearmament requirements. Admiralty informed the Soviet naval attaché that similar requests had been refused to the Greeks and Portuguese on the same grounds. The Soviets then approached the Yarrow Shipbuilding Co. about building a forty-knot destroyer and supplying of technical assistance in Russia. Although the Admiralty would allow the destroyer to be built, it would not permit any of Yarrow's staff to go to the Soviet Union as their services were needed at home. In 1937, the Soviets appealed jointly to Vickers and the

[16] VA, File 722, Supermarine during the rearmament period; FO 371/21927, Fethi Okyar (Turkish Ambassador London) to FO, January 21, 1938; FO 371/21927, Air Min to FO, May 9, 1938.
[17] FO 371/22478, Campbell to Eden, February 3, 1938; Enclosure Strange (mil attaché) to Campbell, January 28, 1938; Ingram to Campbell, February 17, 1938; VA, File 352, Spitfires Turkey, Barnes to Supermarine Aviation Works, December 13, 1938.
[18] VA, File 722, Supermarine during the rearmament period.

French firm Chantiers de la Loire for battleship armament and armor to no avail. The British government even declined a Soviet order for diesel engines when the Soviets had accepted an expected twenty-one month delay in delivery because the order would interfere with British rearmament orders.[19] Although the Soviets had successfully placed aircraft and engine orders with Renault and Hispano-Suiza, the French Defense Ministry suspended delivery citing the necessity of French rearmament. In exasperation, the Soviets expressed amazement that the execution of these contracts passed to France should have encountered such difficulties both on the part of the firms concerned and by the French administration, when the Soviet Union had not encountered such difficulties with the execution of arms orders from Italy.[20]

As the French retreated from exports, the Czechs stepped up even more. In 1935, Czechoslovakia became the world's largest exporter of armaments led by ČZB and Škoda. Foreign purchases absorbed two-thirds of ČZB's rifle and machine gun output. Out of the 120,000 light machine guns produced by 1938, ČZB exported 90,000. Although China occupied the position of single biggest customer by purchasing 30,000 light machine guns, Eastern European states figured prominently on the client list too. The most important arms deal discussed during the 1930s between Yugoslavia and Czechoslovakia was the large order for light machine guns. Originally the contract for 10,000 weapons called for payment with Yugoslav state bonds under Czechoslovak government guarantee. Only then would Czech firms agree to sell to Yugoslavia a package worth $28.0 million (CZK 700 million) against sales of tobacco and raw materials such as copper, zinc, and lead. However, the Belgian firm FN threatened to ruin the Czech sale by underbidding ČZB's price by half. Because the Czechoslovak Army was pushing so strongly for standardization of equipment throughout the Little Entente, the Czechoslovak Ministry of Defense involved itself directly and offered to subsidize ČZB from its own funds in order to lower the price of Czech weapons. As a result, in 1935–1936 ČZB upped the number to 15,000 machine guns of which 10,000 would cost Yugoslavia absolutely nothing. Such price slashing beat the Belgians, but it cost the Czech Ministry of Defense a $1.36 million (CZK 34 million) payout to ČZB. Romania and Yugoslavia together accounted for over 37 percent of ČZB's

[19] BT 11/706, Seal to Laurence Collier, December 23, 1936, encl: minute by Controller meeting with Soviet Naval attaché; BT 11/706, R. G. H. Hemderson to F. L. Yapp (Vickers), June 1, 1937: Yapp to Reginald Henderson, May 31, 1937: J. H. Peck to P. S. Falla, April 23, 1937.

[20] MAE, Europe 1930–1940, URSS 931 Jean Payart (Moscow) to George Bonnet (MAE), December 12, 1938.

exports, importing roughly 17,000 light machine guns each. Remaining customers in the region included Turkey 9,805 (1935–1939), Lithuania 3,138 (1928–1937), and Bulgaria 3,000 in 1938. Among the 12,094 heavy machine guns manufactured by ČZB, two-thirds (8,286) went to Romania starting in 1936. ČZB also exported 500 million small arms cartridges of which Romania acquired 50 percent and China 30 percent. In total, the value of ČZB's exports reached $20.3 million (CZK 580 million) in 1937 and over $24.3 million (CZK 700 million) in 1938, of which Yugoslav and Romanian sales yielded $17.24 million (CZK 496.6 million) 1937–1938. Driven by these foreign sales, ČZB's workforce expanded from 6,000 employees in 1934 to 12,000 by 1938.[21] Just as the armaments business had led Škoda's precipitous drop in 1931 it also caused the steep rebound in 1934. During 1930–1931, Škoda's armaments sector declined 46 percent, but during 1933–1934 it rose 224 percent. While Schneider turned into an essentially domestic supplier for the French government, Škoda exported 55.2 percent of its entire armaments production 1936–1938. Moreover, the share of armaments production in Škoda's output continued to increase over the years growing from 51–52 percent in 1936 to 61 percent in 1937 and culminating at 69 percent in 1938.[22]

The key to Škoda's success in this period lay in solving the financing problem that perennially had bedeviled armaments sales negotiations. The customers of Eastern Europe did not hold significant hard currency reserves to pay for their orders outright, and they generally suffered from lack of creditworthiness to merit favorable borrowing terms. The French government previously had provided major funding for arms purchases through guaranteed loans and credits, but the Great Depression had weakened French financial strength with negative consequences for potential East European buyers. Buyer states did have raw materials and agricultural products to offer in trade, but barter deals that filled warehouses with tobacco or wheat seemingly offered little promise for private armament company profits and a healthy corporate bottom line. The buyer states of southeastern Europe had lacked money even in the good times, but with the Great Depression they experienced extreme penury. Unable to pay in hard currency, the states tried to make other

---

[21] Hauner, 61, 66, 73, 76; RG 165, #2331-II-23 (2) Military attache Albert Gilmer to G-2, May 11, 1934; #2331-II-23 (7) Miliatry Attaché Lowell Riley to G-2, September 6, 1938.

[22] P. H. Segal, *The French State and French Private Investment in Czechoslovakia, 1918–1938* (New York: Garland, 1987), 310–311; RG 165, #2331-II-13 (7) Mil Attache J. S. Winslow to G-2, February 16, 1937; Hauner, 60; V. Karlický, *Svět Okřídleného Šípu Koncern Škoda Plzeň 1918–1945* (Plzeň: Škoda a.s. 1999), 227.

arrangements. For example, Greece held out prospects to Vickers for 450 machine guns in 1932, but payment was bound up with the question of barter. In 1934, Breguet managed to sell aircraft worth $3 million (RL 300 million) to Romania only by forgoing payment in francs. Instead, for the first time the Romanian state paid for large orders abroad in its own national currency. Seemingly the only way to conduct international business would be through some kind of clearing basis. Most agricultural countries turned to protective measures, and southeastern European countries mostly had agricultural products to barter. In 1934, under a recent barter and credit agreement between the Romanian and Czechoslovakian governments, Romania sold 50,000 tons of wheat to Czechoslovakia with proceeds placed to the credit of Škoda on the amortization of sums due on the new or modified contract with Škoda. This arrangement served Romanian interest very well since Bucharest had terrible difficulties finding real money to pay for the needed munitions. At first Škoda was willing to accept only some raw materials it could use in production such as tin, copper, or steel alloying elements. Later the firm accepted other products such as tobacco and cotton.[23]

Škoda found a way out of the pitfall by creating its own export trading company. Facing the necessity of having to dispose of large amounts of local currencies received as payment for armament deliveries, the company found itself obliged to start exporting goods and raw materials from these countries, where they had funds available, in order to exchange these goods on the world markets again in gold currencies. To cope with the work involved it was found necessary to form a separate company and that was the origin of Omnipol, established in 1935.[24] In November 1935, Škoda negotiated with the Czechoslovak and Romanian governments to have Omnipol collect Romanian exports to the amount of the Czechoslovak credit for purchases of Škoda armaments. In this way, Škoda profited from the arms sales to Romania and from reexporting Romanian materials through its unique export company.[25] From very modest beginnings, Omnipol developed into the largest compensation and clearing company in Europe, if not the world, with a turnover of many millions pounds sterling annually. Omnipol functioned as a selling organization for Škoda for steel and machine works, railway works,

---

[23] VA, File 165, Noel Birch Quarterly Report of Military and Air Armaments from April 1, 1932, to June 30, 1932; FO 371/18451, Richard Humphrey (Commercial Sec Bucharest) to Dept. of Oversees Trade, FO, July 4, 1934; RG 165 Entry 77 Romania 6505, #2724-V-60, F. L. Whitley to G-2, 1934; Karlický, 150.

[24] Karlický, 202.

[25] A. Teichova, *An Economic Background to Munich: International Business and Czechoslovakia 1918–1938* (Cambridge: Cambridge University Press, 1974), 206, n. 3.

automobiles, and trucks. Through Omnipol, Škoda increased its exports from $1.15 million (CZK 30 million) in 1933 to $34.97 million (CZK 1 billion) in 1937. This figure was reached while dealing exclusively in peace articles (not armaments) such as fitting out sugar factories, breweries, rolling stock, textile-cigarette-cigar factories, shipbuilding, motorcars, trucks, boilers, and electric motors.[26]

Meanwhile, Germany reentered the arms export field in a substantial way. Prior to November 1935, Germany had been legally shut out of armaments exports to the region. On July 9, 1935, Hitler considered the ban on German arms exports no longer in force. On August 16, 1935, the umbrella organization of German industry (Reichsgruppe Industrie) and the Economics Ministry agreed to establish a cartel for exports of war materiel, Ausfuhrgemeinschaft für Kriegsgerät (AGK). AGK officially commenced operations on October 30, 1935, one week before the German government legalized arms exports on November 6, 1935. Hermann Göring assumed direct control of AGK on December 5, 1936, and wanted all export of war materiel settled in hard currency or raw materials essential to arms production. The AGK functioned as a self-governing body of the German armaments industry to further the business of German arms exports.[27] Even before the legal change, Göring had worked to promote German war materiel abroad during his trips to Hungary and Yugoslavia in May-June 1935 by proposing those governments exchange their raw materials for German war materiel. In fact, Hungary ordered in Germany 50 heavy tanks, 50 light tanks, 100 fighters, 100 bombers, 150 large artillery pieces, and 1,000 machine guns in September 1935 with the order to be executed in three years with payment in five years through delivery of livestock and grain. Around the same time, the German government made a very important offer of war materiel to Yugoslavia valued at 10 million dinars. Employing the commercial methods which it had adopted recently in Central Europe and notably in its relations with Yugoslavia, the Reich offered to the government in Belgrade to regulate this order uniquely by means of compensation where Germany would agree to purchase all agricultural products and livestock that Yugoslavia could export to the limit of the indicated sum. In November 1935, the two countries signed the German-Yugoslav Clearing Agreement establishing the exchange of Yugoslav

---

[26] T 160/874, Memorandum. Barter Trade. Dr. Richard Schüller, April 11, 1939.
[27] C. Leitz, "Arms as Levers: 'Matériel' and Raw Materials in Germany's Trade with Romania in the 1930s," *The International History Review*, vol. 19, no. 2 (1997), 313; M. Pelt, *Tobacco, Arms and Politics: Greece and Germany from World Crisis to World War, 1929–41* (Copenhagen: University of Copenhagen Press, 1998), 89, 151.

agricultural products for German motorized material.[28] Already by the
end of 1935, the Germans had exported aircraft and components valued at $4.17 million (RM 10.3 million) compared to British exports
of $7.17 million (£1.4 million) in 1933, $9.4 million (£1.9 million) in
1934, and $12.81 million (£2.6 million) in 1935. British officials wor-
ried that the Germans would capture an increasing share of the world
armaments trade by selling at prices below cost for immediate delivery
from stocks already held by the German armed forces with the intent
to apply the resultant credits to the purchase of strategic raw materials.
With British industry fully occupied for several years in producing armaments to the order of the British government, the Germans would "clear
the international field for the Reich."[29]

Among German armaments firms, Krupp and Rheinmetall dominated
the business activities of the AGK,[30] and these two firms strove might-
ily to win portions of the markets in Southeast Europe. Consequently,
that region witnessed intense competition between Škoda and Krupp.
In 1935, the Škoda director's report warned that "especially in recent
times German industry, supported extraordinarily effectively by its government, is getting ready for a fierce struggle for which we must mobilize
all our strength," and in particular Krupp headed the list of competitors
causing Škoda much concern.[31] Škoda had good cause to worry about
Krupp. The German behemoth had been the biggest armaments firm in
the world prior to the Great War, and now it had thrown off the shackles
of Versailles and prepared to reclaim its former dominant position. The
size of the Krupp enterprise gave the Czechs pause. Škoda employed
about 36,000 people compared to Krupp's 82,000 during the period
1936–1937. With regard to artillery production, Krupp would eventually report orders for 1,847 pieces of artillery and 560,050 shells for the
period January 1, 1936 – June 30, 1939.[32]

As had been the case with the French government and Schneider, the
Nazi government and German armaments firms did not have identical
goals or interests in their pursuit of arms exports to Eastern Europe. For
the Nazi state, the arms trade with the region should serve as a tool to
acquire hard currency and secure strategic raw materials and foodstuffs
for the benefit of a self-sufficient German war economy. Therefore, even

---

[28] Leitz, "Arms Exports," 139; MAE, Europe 1930–1940, Hongrie. 103 François-Pancet
to MAE, September 20, 1935; MAE, Europe 1930–1940, Yougoslavie. 149–150,
Dampierre (Belgrade) to Laval, September 26, 1935; Dampierre to MAE, November
26, 1935.
[29] CAB 48/4, CID. German Aircraft Industry. March 9, 1936.
[30] Leitz, "Arms Exports," 148.   [31] Quoted in Teichova, 214.
[32] Karlický, 226; R. J. Overy, *War and Economy in the Third Reich* (Oxford: Clarendon
Press, 1994), 138; Leitz, "Arms Exports," 149.

though the Nazi government pushed its own rearmament at breakneck speed, Göring and other officials aggressively supported the export of German war materiel in exchange for those critical strategic resources such as Romanian oil, Yugoslav copper, Turkish chrome, and wheat from various southeastern European countries. For economic strategic reasons, the Nazi regime exhibited a greater permissiveness toward the export of war materiel to the region than the British or French states. While Britain and France imposed tighter restrictions on arms exports starting in 1935, Germany loosened up its restrictions to include exporting arms even to potentially hostile countries.[33] Ideally, Göring wanted a hard currency quota of 15 percent of all payments for war materiel, but in reality the arms trade failed to generate much in the way of hard currency reserves. For example, in 1936 Germany collected only 4 percent of hard currency on payments from Turkey and only 11 percent from Hungarian sales. Meanwhile, Bulgaria made no payments with foreign currency at all. In fact, by mid 1938 German exports to the entirety of southeastern Europe brought in a measly 1.5 percent of total foreign currency received by the Nazi state.[34] The German clearing accounts chronically ran deficits with many of the countries of the region, and Germany could only reduce those deficits through the supply of war materiel. In late 1936, the AGK observed that "Bulgaria, Turkey, Hungary and above all Greece used their clearing balances to pay for a proportion of German war material deliveries . . . and the value of German war material supplies, e.g., to Greece, had already been eaten or smoked."[35] In contrast to the state's short-term strategic goals of securing raw materials and hard currency, the German firms considered arms exports as part of a broad, long-term trade policy to acquire new markets and increase market share in existing markets. For example, Krupp's commitment to arms exports formed part of a strategy for the long-term profitability of the firm. Krupp had the same fears as Vickers about being left high and dry after domestic rearmament ended. Nazi rearmament proved very profitable at the moment, but it could not maintain an upward trajectory indefinitely. When the domestic demand cooled, Krupp would be left with massively expanded capacity and no buyers. Arms exports in the present would help secure those markets and customers for Krupp in the future, when foreign markets would be vital for the firm's survival.[36]

---

[33] G. Ránki, *Economy and Foreign Policy, the Struggle of the Great Powers for Hegemony in the Danube Valley, 1919–1939* (Boulder, CO: East European Monographs, 1983), 146; Leitz, "Arms Exports," 153; Hehn, 4, 15, 36, 278.
[34] Leitz, 142.   [35] Quoted in Leitz, "Arms Exports," 143.
[36] Pelt, 152; Leitz, "Arms Exports," 153; H. James, *Krupp: A History of a Legendary German Firm* (Princeton, NJ: Princeton University Press, 2012), 184–185.

Between 1935 and 1937, German exporters made gains not only in the countries that had been allied with Germany in the Great War, but also with former Entente countries such as Greece, Yugoslavia, and Romania. In the analysis of AGK in late 1936, German firms had beaten the French for sales even in pro-French countries based on "the political weakness of France during the past year, trust in the quality of German materiel, and, last but not least, the effect of clearing agreements between Germany and these countries which had led to such lively commercial relations."[37] A key element in German success was German willingness to accept payment in the form of raw materials. Although China was the single biggest German customer, the role of southeastern Europe as a market for German armaments exports grew. In 1936, total German armaments exports amounted to $20.0 million (RM 49,225, 508). The biggest Eastern European customers for German producers were Hungary $2.42 million (RM 5.95 million), Bulgaria $2.02 million (RM 4.96 million), the Soviet Union $1.40 million (RM 3.45 million), and Turkey $0.93 million (RM 2.29 million). Among smaller customers Yugoslavia purchased $232,520 (RM 572,000) worth of armaments followed by Greece $208,130 (RM 512,000), and Finland $91,463 (RM 225,000). Poland and Austria each purchased roughly $63,414 (RM 156,000) worth of German war materiel. Among German exports, the single largest category was rifle ammunition $5.12 million (RM 12.6 million), followed by artillery shells $2.5 million (RM 6.16 million), artillery pieces $2.45 million (RM 6.03 million), aircraft $1.63 million (RM 4.0 million), and rifles $0.89 million (RM 2.2 million).[38] By the end of 1937 Hungary accounted for 15 percent, Turkey 8.3 percent, Greece 7.6 percent, and Bulgaria 7 percent of German armaments contracts, and by 1938 the Balkan states' share of German arms exports had climbed to 40 percent.[39]

A host of potential East European customers pleaded for British and French war supplies and suppliers with little or no success. In frustration, these countries turned to Germany. Generally, German firms found their biggest customers among their former wartime allies, Hungary, Bulgaria, and Turkey, but German gains in these markets could not be assumed. Bulgaria showed great keenness to order antiaircraft guns from Vickers and mountain artillery from Schneider.[40] In August 1935, Vickers's agent in Bulgaria reported a Bulgarian Military Mission

---

[37] Quoted in Leitz, "Arms as Levers," 313.
[38] GFM 33/2843, Reichsgruppe Industrie Die Geschäftsführung to AA, February 10, 1937; Reichsgruppe Industrie to AA, January 13, 1937.
[39] Leitz, "Arms Exports," 146.
[40] FO 371/20371, Bentinck (Sofia) to FO, January 20, 1936.

wished to visit England for a demonstration of the firm's 75mm anti-aircraft and 105mm guns. On Vickers's end, the real difficulty involved how the Bulgarian government could pay in sterling in the event of their placing orders for any of this equipment. Reportedly, a firm in Sofia was prepared to take the contract from the Bulgarian government in Bulgarian currency and open a sterling credit in London to pay Vickers for the supplies. As Yapp wrote to Birch, "We are quite unable to understand how these people could arrange a sterling credit in London. Until clear how they can pay, we are not inviting Mission."[41] Vickers showed great reluctance to complete the deal for fear of Bulgarian inability to pay, even though the terms would be in pounds sterling. Schneider, Rheinmetall, Madsen, Škoda, and Krupp were all contending for the orders. The Bulgarian government decided in September to order 48 artillery pieces and 24,000 shells from Schneider. However, the French government, in consultation with the Yugoslav and Czechoslovak governments, nixed the order on the grounds that supplying Bulgaria would violate article 81 of the Neuilly Treaty, which prohibited Bulgaria from importing armaments.[42] Ultimately, Krupp gained the contract for twenty large caliber antiaircraft guns (88mm) along with smaller antiaircraft guns, forty mountain guns, and ammunition in the amount of $15.36 million (BGN 1.2 billion). Krupp was willing to accept payment in the form of Bulgarian State bonds valid for five years. Whereas Vickers gave the impression of being distinctly lukewarm, Krupp eagerly competed for the orders and sent six people to Sofia for the purpose. Moreover, they offered better credit terms than Vickers had considered.[43] Inside Vickers, Birch explained that the Bulgarian order for twenty 75mm antiaircraft guns valued at $912,050 (£185,000) had been placed with Krupp because the German firm had accepted Bulgaria's financial conditions "which were not satisfactory to us."[44]

Having secured its antiaircraft guns and artillery from Germany, Bulgaria was still in the market for British tanks and aircraft. After two months of negotiations, the Bulgarians were slated to sign the contract with Vickers for eight medium tanks, but the War Office forbid Vickers to accept the order since it would delay the British rearmament program.[45] As the Bulgarian War Minister, General Lukov told the British

---

[41] VA, File 722, Yapp to Birch, August 26, 1935.
[42] *Documents Diplomatiques Français, 1932–1939* (DDF) 1er série, Tome XIII (Paris: Imprimerie Nationale, 1984), doc. no. 200, 289–290.
[43] FO 371/20371, Bentinck to Eden, April 16, 1936.
[44] VA, File 181, Half-yearly Rept. on Military and Air Armaments. From January 1, 1936, to June 30, 1936.
[45] FO 371/20371, Howard (Sofia) to FO, July 23, 1936.

ambassador, Bulgaria "was not going to become a second Abyssinia." Vickers was their preferred supplier, but if the British did not supply, Bulgaria would look to Germany. The Bulgarian president noted, "It is always so easy to place orders in Germany. No payment was made. Bulgaria was already sending some 60 percent of her exports to Germany and, by purchases made in that country, she was able to reduce her balance in Reichmarks . . . The Poles were going to receive tobacco and other Bulgarian produce in payment for the aeroplanes which they will supply. The French, too, were making some favorable arrangements."[46] According to Lukov, British methods were dilatory, French methods were somewhat better. German methods were excellent as Germany was ready to supply goods on the nail. Nevertheless, Bulgaria did eventually buy sixty small Vickers tanks and eight medium Vickers tanks in early 1938.[47]

Bulgarian aircraft rearmament began in 1935 with requests for technical assistance and orders placed in Czechoslovakia. Such a move by Bulgaria incensed Yugoslavia, and together Yugoslavia and France pressured Prague to submit the twelve planes to the Yugoslav government for review. Yugoslavia raised concerns that the Bulgarian acquisitions violated the Treaty of Neuilly and showed that Bulgaria was following the German repudiation of Versailles. Joint Yugoslav-French disapproval forced the Czechs to abandon the Bulgarian delivery, but the next year Bulgaria proceeded to buy new combat aircraft from Germany and Poland. In 1936, Bulgaria ordered six German day bombers (Siemens-Halske), twelve Dornier bombers, six Heinkel pursuit planes, and twenty Polish pursuit planes from PZL. The delivery of the Dornier bombers in February 1937 marked Bulgaria's resolve to scrap the Neuilly Treaty and modernize its aviation forces. It also indicated that Bulgaria now looked to Germany as the supplier for most of its rearmament requirements.[48]

In Yugoslavia, Škoda held a quasi-monopoly of military supplies, notably artillery, and Schneider had ceded the Yugoslav market for war materiel to the Czech firm. Škoda also possessed considerable connections to supporters within the Yugoslav government and Yugoslav armed services. For example, General Joksimovoitch, the Yugoslav Military Technical Inspector, determined war orders. He formerly served as the Director of Artillery 1923–1931, and it was under his tenure that

---

[46] Ibid., Bentinck to Eden, May 29, 1936.

[47] RG 165, #2281-V-36 Williamson to G-2, February 25, 1938.

[48] MAE, Europe 1930–1940 Yougoslavie. 149–150, Naggiar to MAE, March 20, 1935; RG 165, #2677-17 (3) Mil attaché Royden Williams (Istanbul) to G-2, September 5, 1936; FO 371/20371, Ross (military attaché) to Bentinck, May 27, 1936; RG 165, #2677-19 (2) Royden Williamson (mil att Istanbul) to G-2, February 19, 1937.

all big orders were passed to the Czechs. Joksimovoitch had a reputation of opposing the acquisition of French materiel and actively championing buying from the Czechs in a bid for armaments unification. He once branded a general officer as a "heretic" for proposing the order of Brandt and Hotchkiss materiel. However, by April 1935, Yugoslavia and the Czechs talked about liquidation of payments of past orders because Yugoslavia had fallen behind about $29 million (CZK 700 million) from the Škoda artillery order of 1928. The arrears were now to be paid by tobacco produced in Yugoslavia for the Czechs. The terms of the tobacco arrangement involved Yugoslav deliveries over the next twenty-five years between 3,000 tons and 4,500 tons annually. For new orders, Yugoslavia was talking with Škoda for antiaircraft guns worth $20.83 million (CZK 500 million) payable in twelve years, delivery by October 1937 and with ČZB for 10,000 automatic rifles made in Czechoslovakia and 1,000 made in Kragujevaç through Czech personnel for $8.33 million (CZK 200 million) payable over even years at 5 percent interest to be completed in 1939. In September 1935, Litzelmann of Schneider informed the French Foreign Ministry that Yugoslavia sought to order $19.8 million (F300 million) of war materiel in Czechoslovakia. The whole order would be passed to Škoda, considering that they had the right to the entirety of future orders without retrocession to Creusot. Schneider effectively had abandoned Yugoslav orders to Škoda in return for a free hand in Poland. The Yugoslav and Czechoslovak governments also discussed orders worth $29.17 million (CZK 700 million) over twenty-five years at 6 percent interest to include ten to fifteen batteries of 155mm artillery and tractors, ten-fifteen batteries of 105mm long guns, 200 37mm pieces, and six batteries of 75mm field guns. Because Yugoslavia lacked the necessary credit to pay Škoda, the Czech government would accept payment through compensation in grain.[49]

Yugoslav rearmament suffered repeated rebuffs from Britain. In December 1936, the Yugoslav government desired to obtain from Britain arms and equipment in the amount of $4.91 million (£1 million). The British War Office prepared to provide the Yugoslavs with the names of British firms, but contracts had to be made solely between the Yugoslavs and the private firms to avoid any appearance that the British government in any way served as an agent in the matter. Because Yugoslavia had no foreign currency reserves with which to pay for British war materiel,

---

[49] MAE, Europe 1930–1940, Yougslavie. 148, Naggiar to MAE, January 17, 1934; Note de renseignements General Joksimovitch. September 3, 1934; Yougoslavie. 149–150, Note de Reseignements. Belgrade, April 1, 1935; Note. September 5, 1935; Emile Naggiar (Prague) to MAE, October 1, 1935; Note de Renseignements. September 24, 1935.

Belgrade suggested that Yugoslavia could supply the British government directly with certain raw materials, such as iron ore, bauxite, and copper. The British government could then pay the contractors the comparable value. The British Export Credits Guarantee Department rejected the Yugoslav proposal for a clearing arrangement out of hand on the grounds that they were "bound to consider cases entirely on their commercial and financial merits without regard to political considerations of any kind," and that the legal prohibitions against granting any guarantees in respect to sales of munitions of war prevented British approval.[50] Out of political considerations, Anthony Eden urged Neville Chamberlain to approve arms sales to Yugoslavia. Eden asked "whether the Treasury can think of any (emphasis in original) financial expedient which would enable us to demonstrate in a practical manner our friendship for and support of Yugoslavia, and thus maintain our influence in Belgrade against the powers of attraction exercised by Italy and Germany . . . the political issue at stake is of such great importance that this is a case where we would be justified in making above all a specific effort to supply Yugoslavia with some at least of the materials which she wants to buy in this country."[51] In a creative move to get around British restrictions on financing arms sales, the Yugoslav ambassador in London unsuccessfully proposed to Eden that the equipment purchased could remain technically the property of the British government, but it could be stored in Yugoslavia in case of emergency. Through the spring and summer of 1937, other Yugoslav attempts to purchase British equipment also foundered. The British government rejected Belgrade's request to buy three 2-gun batteries of coast defense artillery in the UK because of the adverse effect it would have on British domestic orders. Likewise, a Yugoslav request for aircraft and aircraft engines could not go forward due to British requirements of rearmament, although in this instance the Foreign Office did approve release of one machine of Blenheim type on the understanding that the Yugoslav government enter into negotiations with Bristol Aeroplane Co. for purchase of a license to construct those machines in Yugoslavia.[52]

In terms of airpower, Yugoslavia ended up turning to domestic production of foreign models. The Yugoslav Air Force had been equipped mostly with French and Czech combat aircraft produced domestically

---

[50] BT 11/695, Yugoslav Army Credit. Minute Sheet, February 25, 1937.
[51] Ibid., Eden to Neville Chamberlain, March 13, 1937.
[52] Ibid., Eden to Campbell, December 2, 1936; S. H. Phillips to FO, June 8, 1937; ADM Ross to Milanovitch, May 21, 1937.

under license since the early 1930s.[53] As part of rearmament and modernization starting from 1935, Yugoslav air authorities informed Škoda that they had rejected the Avia fighter in preference for thirty-two British Hawker Hurricane fighters to be built in Yugoslavia under license for $1.25 million (55 million dinars). For bombers, the Yugoslav Air Force considered Potez, Farman, and Glenn Martin before narrowing the field to just Breguet and Dornier. Ultimately, the Yugoslavs opted for the German Dornier DO-17 bomber because they could use their clearing account to pay the $1.44 million (RM 3.55 million) for it. General Marich, Yugoslav Minister of War complained to British military attaché Major Strange in February 1937 about the deplorable Yugoslav position where every single country was working overtime on rearmament but Yugoslavia found itself unable to keep pace on account of a temporary inability to find the large capital sums required. In his budget speech to the financial committee of the parliament, Marich said he was creating domestic war industries as fast as he could, so as to be independent in the first place of Czechoslovakia which was too vulnerable to attack, yet both time and money were required before Yugoslavia could be self-supporting. In a countermove against the Germans, Britain did deliver two Bristol Blenheim bombers to Yugoslavia at the end of 1937.[54]

Romania launched its ten-year rearmament program on April 27, 1935, in response to Hungarian Army modernization and rearmament. Romanian rearmament remained closely tied to the armaments industry of its ally Czechoslovakia, from which Romania received 70 percent of its imported weapons. Romania acquired 248 Škoda 100mm light howitzers in the mid 1930s and secured an additional 180 150mm medium howitzers from 1936 to 1939. In 1936, Romania ordered 126 Škoda medium tanks Mk LT 35, and additionally purchased thirty-five small 4-ton tanks from the ČKD works of Prague 1936–1937. In January 1937, a Czech government armament loan to Romania allowed for supplies up to $17,482 (CZK 500,000) with Škoda for motorization of the Romanian Army. As of late 1937, Škoda had received the great bulk of Romanian armament orders placed abroad because the firm seemed the logical choice in view of the political, economic, and financial ties that bound

[53] Hauner, 93.
[54] MAE, Europe 1930–1940, Yougoslavie. 151, Dampierre to MAE, June 3, 1935; Dampierre to MAE, June 6, 1935; Dampierre to MAE, June 8, 1935; MAE, Europe 1930–1940, Yougoslavie. vol. 149–150, Min Air to MAE, February 12, 1936; Captured German War Documents, GFM 33/2843, Reichsgruppe Industrie to Foreign Ministry, February 6, 1937, frame E512841; BT 11/695, Major Strange to Campbell (Belgrade), February 22, 1937; AIR 5/1179 F. Beaumont (air attaché Prague) to Air Ministry, December 13, 1937.

Romania and Czechoslovakia. Thanks to Omnipol deliveries could be easily made with payments in oil likewise easily delivered. The uniformity of armament would facilitate the combined employment of the two armies. By then, though, Škoda was deluged with orders from many sources, notably from Czechoslovakia itself which conducted its own rearming, mechanizing, motorizing, and fortifying frontiers at a prodigious rate. Thus, Škoda began lapsing far behind on deliveries. Consequently, though Romania appeared as a favored customer, Bucharest did not get everything it wanted as quickly as it wanted from Škoda.[55]

Besides the Czechs, Romania participated in a clearing agreement with Germany, and Romania routinely ran an account surplus due to large German import of Romanian oil. The growing importance of Romanian oil in the trade with Germany, increasing from 49 to 60 percent of Romania's exports to Germany from 1935 to 1936, generated a serious trade imbalance to Romania's credit amounting to $20.33 million (RM 50 million) during 1937. Unable to spend that money anywhere but Germany, the Romanians sought German help to rebuild their arms and aircraft industry. Using clearing credit, the Romanian Air Ministry completed a contract for twelve Focke-Wulf FW-58 aircraft in February 1937, and took delivery of the planes between April and June that same year. Despite Romanian hype, the Germans found arms exports to Romania during 1936–1937 below their expectations. True, contracts with Romania as a share of the AGK's total sales rose from 3.2 to 5.5 percent, but their value rose by only $1.06 million (RM 2.602 million). Six submarines composed the bulk of German arms sales to Romania, providing $14.22 million (RM 35 million) in sales, followed by $2.4 million (RM 6 million) for two torpedo boats, and lastly $0.61 million (RM 1.5 million) for the Fokker-Wulf planes. Using their German petroleum credits, Romania employed German technicians to build a shipyard at Galatz under the auspices of the Resita Company. Romania planned to build two of the submarines and torpedo boats there.[56]

In 1936, Greek rearmament began in earnest as a response to the Italian attack on Ethiopia in October 1935. The person most directly responsible for Greek rearmament was General John Metaxas. Almost

[55] M. Axworthy (with C. Scafeş and C. Craciunoiu), *Third Axis Fourth Ally: Romanian Armed Forces in the European War, 1941–1945* (London: Arms and Armour Press, 1995), 27–29; Hauner, 63; AIR 5/1179, AA no. 10/37 Romanian Armament Order for Škoda Works, February 11, 1937; RG 165 Entry 77 Romania 6505, #2724-V-53 (2) military attaché Belgrade to G-2, November 6, 1937.

[56] Leitz, "Arms as Levers," 317, 319; GFM 33/2843, Reichsgruppe Industrie to Foreign Ministry, February 6, 1937, frame E512847; RG 165, #2723-17 E. Villaret to G-2, November 6, 1937.

immediately upon assuming the position of War Minister and Vice President of Council of Ministers on March 5, 1936, Metaxas indicated that he would place as many orders as possible with Germany. Metaxas delivered on his pledge to the Germans. In all, Greece bought $17.32 million (RM 42.6 million) worth of war equipment from Germany 1936–1941. German sales amounted to the equivalent of 65 percent of the total Greek expenditure on military equipment for the period, as compared to just 6 percent for the French. Through 1935 Schneider-Creusot had exercised a monopoly in Greece. Rheinmetall now posed the greatest challenge to Schneider. Rheinmetall's single biggest customer was Hungary, where the company did business worth $7.22 million (RM 17.76 million) in 1936, followed by Bulgaria with $4.54 million (RM 11.18 million) of munitions orders. Beyond these former wartime partners, Rheinmetall branched out into Greece as its third biggest buyer $4.31 million (RM 10.6 million).[57] Significantly, the Schneider–Škoda Artillery Agreement had allotted Greece to Schneider, so Rheinmetall's gain meant Schneider's loss. As Mogens Pelt has shown, Greece would serve as the test model for the expansion of the German arms trade into the Southeastern European markets of former wartime enemies. Although Greece conducted its trade with France and Germany through clearing accounts, Rheinmetall benefited from the much larger scale of German-Greek trade. Over the period 1935–1937, the value of Greek exports to France averaged only $2.28 million (GRD 228 million). annually. With such meager French demand for Greek products, Greece could not hope to sell enough to France to pay for its rearmament. On the other hand, Greece had run up a credit of $13 million (RM 32 million) on its clearing account with Germany and used that means to purchase $9.55 million (RM 23.5 million) in German armaments in 1936 and another $6.7 million (RM 16.5 million) in 1937. Undergirded by the larger volume of German imports from Greece, Rheinmetall secured its base in Greece and ejected Schneider. By the second half of 1937, Rheinmetall credited its newly established stronghold in Greece to internal political developments in the country including the end of the pro-French Republic with the restoration of Monarchy in 1935 and establishment of Metaxas dictatorship on August 4, 1936.[58]

Rheinmetall's success aside, the Germans did not achieve dominance in the Greek arms market across the board. For example, the Germans did not make significant inroads in the machine gun market. The Greek

---

[57] Pelt, 145–146, 72; GFM 33/2843, Reichsgruppe Industrie to Foreign Ministry, February 6, 1937, frames E512839–E512847.
[58] Pelt, 125, 143, 152, 158, 160.

Army had purchased predominantly French equipment previously, and possessed 6,000 light machine guns and 1,752 heavy machine guns manufactured by Hotchkiss. Under rearmament Greece bought 600 new Hotchkiss 7.92mm guns for $320,000 (DRG 32 million) and 300 German machine guns. In terms of machine guns, Hotchkiss continued to hold sway in the Greek Army. In the teeth of intense French opposition, Greek expenditures for air force machine guns totaled $982,000 (GRD 98.2 million) out of which Czech suppliers sold $560,000 (GRD 56 million) and Vickers $102,000 (GRD 10.2 million). For its new fleet units, the Greek Navy purchased four destroyers from the British firm Thorneycroft in July 1936 for $7.5 million (GRD 750 million) each and two light destroyers from Yarrow of Glasgow.[59] Revealingly, the Greeks did purchase the armament for the destroyers from German yards as "an expedient made necessary by the large block of foreign marks credit which Greece has in Germany."[60]

Payment and price issues dominated Greek decisions for aviation purchases. The Greek Air Force had approached Britain and Germany for an immediate purchase of fifty modern combat aircraft in 1936. Lacking the foreign currency required to buy in Britain, the Greeks hoped to purchase thirty planes in Germany through tobacco sales with the German clearing account. Even with a clearing account credit, German prices were still too high due to the desperate Greek economic situation. Ultimately, the Greeks used their tobacco sales with Poland to purchase thirty-six cheaper PZL Polish aircraft for $1.7 million (GRD 170.2 million).[61] Dornier, Bristol, PZL, Gnôme-Rhône, Potez, and Hispano-Suiza all jostled for Greek favor to supply bombers over the course of 1937. Initially, Greek authorities selected the Bristol Blenheim over the Dornier Do-17 based on the superior combat qualities of the British aircraft, and Greece placed an order for thirty-six Blenheims. By the end of the year, though, the Greeks reduced the number of Blenheims to eleven and instead bought twenty-four Potez aircraft because the French price was 40 percent less expensive and the French extended terms of payment over four years. Thus, out of $3.38 million (GRD 338.2 million) allocated for air force rearmament in 1937, the French contract claimed the lion's share with $2.06 million (GRD

---

[59] Pelt, 68–71, 74; VA, File 722, Rearmament Period. Foreign Sales, Sir Frederick Yapp's files, Group Captain A. C. Winter (RAF) to Birch, January 21, 1935; RG 165, #2674–28, Military attaché Belgrade to G-2, November 3, 1936; #2674–49 (1) Whitley to G-2, January 18, 1937.

[60] RG 165, #2674–40 (5) F. L. Whitley, mil attaché to G-2, July 3, 1936.

[61] AIR 40/1404, Medhurst to Boyle, July 19, 1936; Air attaché Rome to Air Intelligence, Air Ministry, London, July 11, 1936; Com Sec Athens to Air Ministry, October 22, 1936; Pelt, 73.

206 million). The Greeks did purchase twelve Dornier Do-22 aircraft for $279,000 (GRD 27.9 million).[62] In 1938, the Greek King George II expressed to Packer, the British naval attaché, "his concern at the weakness of his Air Force and said that here was another field in which we could help Greece, but that we did not seem inclined to give our assistance in provision of aircraft on a basis of easy payments... When Germany wished to show her feeling for Bulgaria she made her a present of 12 aeroplanes and we would not even let Greece have aeroplanes on extended payment."[63] Greece had wanted to buy twelve Blenheims, and had been willing to accept Bristol Company's terms to pay one-third at contract signing, another third after acceptance of aircraft in London, and the final third after arrival in Greece for a total price of $980,700 (£210,000) at 5 percent interest. The Blenheim deal then fell through because the Greek terms were unacceptable to British banking houses since the National Bank of Greece required $326,900 (£70,000) in overdraft credit. Due to the increased price, the Greek National Defense Council reviewed the Blenheim order, and the Greek Air Minister recommended purchasing the French Potez aircraft instead because they were cheaper than the Blenheims. The Greeks then approached France for a credit of $14 million. The French government had agreed in principle, but was determined not to have any intergovernmental obligation since the Metaxas regime in Greece could not offer a guarantee of parliament in principle. Credits would therefore be based on purely commercial basis and operated under an agreement between the Banque de Paris et des Pays-bas and an ad hoc Greek commercial syndicate. French industry would supply the armaments to the value of $7 million immediately, and the whole amount would be repaid through sales of Greek produce over fifteen years.[64]

As part of its rearmament program in 1935, Turkey initially approached France and Britain. The French proved to be unreliable suppliers as their own rearmament program expanded. In 1935, the Turkish government had placed an order for thirty-six airplanes with Dewoitine and negotiated an order of $13.2 million (F200 million) for torpedoes with the firm of Normand and another with Schneider-Renault for

---

[62] AIR 40/1404, Medhurst to Air Ministry, November 17, 1937; Pelt, 74, 153–154.

[63] ADM 116/3949, H.cA. Packer, naval attaché Athens to Director Naval Intelligence, October 12, 1938.

[64] FO 371/22356, Bristol Aeroplane to National Bank of Greece, January 4, 1938; Waterlow to FO, January 21, 1938; Major Boyle to Ross, February 4, 1938; Arliotti to Rush (Westminster Bank), February 9, 1938, enclosed in Waterlow to FO, February 16, 1938; FO 371/22357, Hopkinson (Athens) to FO, May 7, 1938; Hopkinson to FO, May 12, 1938; AIR 40/1404 Aircraft for Greek Government, March 4, 1938; ADM 116/3949, Waterlow (Athens) to FO, December 29, 1938.

artillery, planes, radio equipment, and submarines worth $26.4 million (F400 million).[65] In April 1935, the French government requisitioned the thirty-six Turkish planes for its own air force. This was particularly galling for the Turks because twelve of the planes were ready and were supposed to be delivered in Turkey on April 15. The Turkish ambassador, Shükrü Kaya, accused the French of exaggerating the German threat, to which the French Ambassador retorted that the Turks were exaggerating the Italian threat. As the Turkish ambassador protested, "For us, these 36 planes are the total of our aerial defense; for you this is a mere trifle, above all the 12 finished planes."[66] The Turks responded rather bitterly to the French action. The Turkish Minister of Foreign Affairs informed the French Ambassador in Ankara that political relations between the two countries had been adversely affected by the French requisition. Furthermore, he noted that the Turkish government might refrain from ordering materials of war from France because this incident had opened the Turks' eyes to the risk of their orders being requisitioned by the French government despite all the previous assurances to the contrary. Due to the unreliability of the French, the Turkish government was considering directing its orders "towards countries which are not so exposed to the requisition: Holland, Switzerland, and above all the United States."[67]

Meanwhile, the Turks continued in their efforts to entice Britain with possible arms orders by revealing the extent of their new naval construction program, which included one large and two to three small cruisers. The Turks informed the British that they wished to place the contracts for larger ships in either Britain or France. This latest Turkish communication seemed obviously calculated to induce the British to relent and provide the financing if they really wanted the contracts. When the British did not respond favorably, the Turks moved to increase the stakes. In March, the Turkish government allocated $38 million for new naval construction and bases, and entered into negotiations with two German firms for contracts to modernize the old arsenal at Kasimpaşa. Then in May, the Turks let it be known that they were conducting negotiations for naval orders with Spain for as much as $16.76 million. By spring 1936 in light of the international situation, Turkey had decided on a program of rearmament that could not wait for a domestic industry to be created to carry it out, but which largely relied on foreign purchase. The Turks opened negotiations with the British for $3.68 million (£0.75 million) worth of airplanes in March. Specifically, the Turks were looking to

---

[65] DDF, 1er série, Tome X (Paris: Imprimerie Nationale, 1981), doc. no. 241, 390–391.
[66] Ibid., 390.   [67] DDF, Tome XI, no. 24, Kammerer to Laval, June 5, 1935, 28–29.

acquire fifty fighters and thirty bombers. For bombers, neither Odeons nor Bristols could be had except for cash, and neither firm could satisfy Turkish demands for swift delivery. The Martin Company insisted that all payments and all tests occur in the USA.[68] The Turkish ambassador, Aras, hinted to Eden that the Italians were most eager to offer aircraft as a means to win back Turkey diplomatically. Nevertheless, the Turks would much prefer to place their orders in Britain. Eden reported the "Aras had, however, laid stress in his opening remarks on the fact that the French Government had on occasion themselves financed armaments transactions with Turkey, and as His Excellency clearly hoped that His Majesty's Government would follow a similar policy, I was obliged to tell him that this was not possible for His Majesty's Government."[69] Aras's explanations notwithstanding, in the above remarks one can easily discern the Turks' endeavors to apply pressure on Britain to consent to the financial arrangements and to accept the Turkish orders. Given the discord in Franco-Turkish relations arising from the requisition of Turkish aircraft and the continuing fear of Italy, Turkish innuendoes about turning to either one of those two countries for military material hardly appeared credible. The British reaction indicated that London was not swayed by the Turkish hints. Indeed, the Turks were unable to complete any orders in Britain during 1936 even though such orders would probably represent just the first round of orders emanating from Turkey and would very likely be followed by further contracts that would ensure the employment of British labor and materials for a number of years.[70] Owing to the failure to come to an agreement regarding the financing of the air contracts, Turkey had decided to place certain orders in Poland. In August 1936, the Turks ordered sixty PZL aircraft from Poland priced at $38,750 (T£46,500) apiece. To ease Turkish payments the Poles required no hard currency. Instead Turkey paid half in Turkish currency and half in goods with the whole order to be completed by January 5, 1937. The Poles would build forty aircraft in Poland and twenty in Turkey at the Kayseri plant.[71]

The British could be as unaccommodating to the Turkish government as the French when it came to giving priority to domestic rearmament to the detriment of foreign sales. After two months of negotiations,

---

[68] FO 424/279, part XXIX, no. 11, Consul (Geneva) to Simon, January 21, 1935; no. 41, Loraine to Simon, March 8, 1935; no. 51, Grahame to Simon, May 3, 1935; CAB 48/4 CID. Turkey. Request for British Cooperation in Developing National Industry. March 6, 1936; RG 165, #2094–53 (3) Williamson to G-2, August 4, 1936.
[69] FO 424/280, part XXXI, no. 9, Eden to Loraine, January 30, 1936.
[70] FO 424/280, part XXXII, no. 93, enclosure in Col. Woods to Eden, December 2, 1936.
[71] RG 165, #2094–64 (2) Royden Williamson (Istanbul) to G-2, August 1, 1936.

Turkey gave an order for eight tanks to Vickers, and the contract was to be signed in July 1936. However, the British War Office forbade Vickers to accept the order as it would delay the British program of rearmament. The following year the Turks enquired to Vickers–Armstrong concerning 15" coast defense guns. The British Admiralty deemed it unacceptable for Vickers–Armstrong to accept the Turkish work as the Turkish business would have far reaching negative effects on the British building program, and so the Admiralty instructed Vickers to decline this work.[72] The firm found itself in the strange position of purposefully not seeking trade abroad. As Birch noted in his end of year report for 1936, unless the political situation changed, the firm's foreign trade faced imminent decline, and Germany in particular would take full advantage of the situation. Vickers had had to turn down enquiries for artillery from Denmark, Finland, Greece, Holland, Iraq, Paraguay, Romania, Siam, and Turkey. Even without encouraging them to buy, Vickers had to turn down business to the amount of $5.28 million (£1,076,350).[73]

Encountering difficulties with Britain and France over financing and deliveries, the Turkish government made overtures to Germany. During a meeting with the German Ambassador in Ankara in April, Shükrü Kaya remarked that, "Turkey did not in any way look askance at the reestablishment of a standing German Army but even welcomed it, both for reasons of general policy and because the Turkish army hoped for a favorable opportunity to improve its own equipment by drawing on the German industry."[74] Late in 1935, a group of German naval experts met with Turkish representatives to advise the Turks on naval rearmament, and negotiations commenced with Krupp for artillery and other armaments. According to the British military attaché, part of the German contract called for forty-eight Krupp 75mm mountain guns, and the Germans quoted prices were far below that of other competitors as a sacrificial measure to obtain the order. In June 1936, after more than six months of negotiations, Krupp had secured its first major contract with Turkey.[75] According to Karl Pfirsch, deputy director at Krupp, the

---

[72] FO 371/20371, Howard (Sofia) to FO, July 23, 1936; ADM 116/4195, S. H. Phillips to Air Ministry and Board of Trade, December 2, 1937.

[73] VA, File 183, Half-yearly Rept on Military and Air Armaments, July–December 1936.

[74] *Documents on German Foreign Policy 1918–1945* (DGFP), Series C, vol. IV (Washington, DC: US Government Printing Office, 1962), no. 43, Ambassador in Turkey to Foreign Ministry, April 21, 1935, 74.

[75] DGFP, no. 144, Ambassador in Turkey to Foreign Ministry, June 8, 1935, 284; no. 449, Ambassador in Turkey to Foreign Ministry, December 6, 1935, 889–891; FO 424/279, part XXX, no. 25, Enclosure in Major Sampson to Loraine, November 15, 1935; IWM, KA, File 47B, Pfirsch (Ankara) to Krupp, April 29, 1936; Meeting with Turkish War

Turkish contract had restored "the previously predominant position of the Krupp company which it had enjoyed before the war."[76] Pfirsch's comments were not hyperbole. German orders in Turkey were impressive. Krupp's orders amounted to over $13 million (RM 32 million) for 185 artillery pieces of various calibers and sixteen antiaircraft guns. For its part, Rheinmetall's Turkish orders accounted for an additional $3.14 million (RM 7.72 million). The Turks also bought one 8,000-ton submarine tender from the Germans owing to Germany's clearing arrangements, which allowed the Turks no other choice but to spend from their account in Germany. At the same time, Turkey ordered from Germany thirty older Gotha planes and bought the plans to construct this plane at Kayseri.[77]

Škoda fought back against the German advances, winning Turkish contracts of its own 1936–1938. The Turks placed three tractor orders between April and December 1936 for a combined 335 tractors based on the clearing arrangement. Škoda also managed to pick up an order for twenty batteries of 150mm heavy artillery pieces (80 guns) complete with tractors. By the end of 1937, Škoda had delivered fourteen batteries along with 246 out of the total 615 tractors contracted. The Germans took notice. The AGK reported for the calendar year 1937 that Škoda was again the strongest competitor for field and heavy artillery and complained the Czech firm had been seeking a monopoly position in the Balkan lands with all means. In early 1938, the Turks ordered seventy-five armored cars from Škoda. In part, Škoda had been able to stand up to the German challenge due to the terms of the clearing arrangement. Thanks to the devaluation of the Czech Crown, the terms of trade had shifted sharply in favor of the Turks, making the Czech goods cheaper.[78] Conversely, the Germans lost out in Turkey on $16.26 million (RM 40 million) worth of orders due to the German government's pursuit of hard currency earnings through arms exports. When the Germans pushed Turkey to pay 6 percent of the total price in

Ministry, April 29, 1936; Meeting with Turkish War Ministry, May 2, 1936; Telegram Pfirsch to Krupp, May 4, 1936.
[76] Leitz, "Arms Exports," 145.
[77] GFM 33/2843, Reichsgruppe Industrie to Foreign Ministry, February 6, 1937, frames E512842, E512847; RG 165, #2126–52 (2) Williamson to G-2, August 5, 1936; #2094–53 (4) Williamson to G-2, September 16, 1936.
[78] RG 165, #2281-T-14 (1) J. A. Crone to G-2, April 14, 1936; #2281-T-14 (2) Royden Williamson to G-2, July 7, 1936; #2281-T-14 (3) Royden Williamson to G-2, December 12, 1936; WO 106/1594D, Turkey Military Attaché's Report, 1937, Lt. Col. Ross, December 21, 1937; IWM, KA, 141, Reichsgruppe Industrie AGK, Jahrbericht 1937; RG 165, #2281-T-14 (4) Williamson to G-2, February 26, 1938; RG 165, #2281-T-14 (3) Royden Williamson to G-2, December 12, 1936.

hard currency at Göring's insistence, the Turks turned back to Škoda for financial reasons.[79]

As the international tension between Germany and Britain grew, the Turkish government became more successful in procuring war materiel from both. For example, in August 1937 Turkey managed to purchase twelve Blenheim aircraft in Britain and sign a contract with Krupp for the construction of four submarines. In September, the Turks approached Germany for more war orders especially middle caliber artillery pieces from Krupp. By the end of the year, British and German firms were contending for a Turkish program which consisted of ten submarines, four destroyers, twelve aircraft, and nine heavy guns for the Dardanelles. Regarding these orders, Krupp's representative in Ankara was offering a 20 percent reduction on any British prices, but the Turks hoped to obtain these armaments in the UK if it were financially possible. However, Turkish leaders did not want to be caught between two rival blocs, therefore Turkey needed to find an additional supplier along with Germany and Britain. Because of past difficulties with France and Italy, neither of those two could serve this function. The US, then, became the logical choice. In a meeting with the US Ambassador in Ankara in 1937, the Turkish Foreign Minister expressed the Turkish desire to stay clear of the two conflicting groups in Europe, and expounded on the importance of adequate arms to maintain that policy. As the American Ambassador reported, the purpose of Dr. Aras's visit was to ascertain the status of the purchase from the US of forty Vultee aircraft. The contract had specified that the planes be delivered in July 1937, but the delivery had been delayed for some reason. These American planes represented about one-third of the replacement complement within the first Turkish aviation program. It was essential that it be properly equipped. The Turkish concerns about their aviation program were well-founded. In 1933, Turkey had 310 planes, but only 150 of them could actually be considered first line aircraft. By 1937, only 131 planes were first line, so as part of the modernization of their air forces, Turkey bought forty fighters from Poland, twenty Martin bombers in the US, ten Heinkel bombers from Germany, and two Bristol bombers from Britain.[80]

[79] Pelt, 152; Leitz, "Arms Exports," 142.

[80] FO 424/281, part XXXIV, no. 17, Loraine to Halifax, August 18, 1937; ibid., no. 23, Loraine to Eden, August 20, 1937; *Akten zur Deutschen Auswärtigen Politik 1918–1945 (AzDAP)*, Série D, Band V (Baden-Baden, Germany: Imprimerie Nationale, 1953), no. 538, Mackensen memo, September 23, 1937, 598; ADM 116/4195, Loraine to Eden, December 18, 1937; USDS, #767.00/74, Robert F. Kelley to Secretary of State, November 15, 1937; FO 424/278, No. 18, Graham to Vansittart, March 19, 1933; ibid., no. 22, Simon to Morgan, March 23, 1933; Selim Deringil, *Turkish Foreign Policy*

Superficially, Turkish purchases during 1937 seem to demonstrate a policy aimed at avoiding the British and German blocs. Although it is true that Britain and Germany both received war orders, the trend in Turkish purchases was clearly toward placing orders outside those two. Thus, the US and Poland received most of the aircraft purchases. Actually, the real reason for the relatively small proportion of British war materiel among the Turkish procurements was the perennial difficulty of financing the sales. With delivery to Turkey of twelve Blenheims ordered in 1937, the Turks wanted to order twelve more. Major Abell of Bristol Aircraft Co. considered that Turkish terms for the twelve Blenheims unacceptable to the company since they meant that the company would be locking up about £300,000 for two and a half years. Unable to get credit or guarantee from the British government, Bristol's only course was to tell the Turks they could not take the order except on the same terms as previous twelve, i.e., one-third payment on conclusion of the contract and balance on the acceptance of planes at the company's air hangar. Major Abell wished to let the Foreign Office know Bristol's position and to assure them that the company was most anxious to accept the order and had done their utmost to reach some satisfactory arrangement. The company realized that the order was important from a political view. At the same time, it appealed to them financially because the Turks had also expressed the wish to construct the aircraft and engines under license in Turkey so that this order might lead to something important. However, despite its good will, the company found the Turkish terms unacceptable on economic grounds.[81]

Ultimately, the German annexation of Austria in March 1938 convinced the British that it was time to override the Trade Facilities Act of 1921 and open up credit to Turkey for war orders.[82] Turkey presented a special case even before the Anschluss. The Foreign Office realized the difficulties of placing Turkish orders, but nevertheless urged upon political grounds, that the wishes of the Turkish General Staff "should be considered in the most sympathetic spirit possible" because "Turkey is one of the few countries upon whose cooperation HMG may be able to count with reasonable certainty in the event of a general deterioration in the international situation and it is important that HMG should take such steps as are within their power to facilitate the placing of

---

during the Second World War: An Active Neutrality (Cambridge: Cambridge University Press, 1989), 33.
[81] FO 261/1, Air Ministry to FO, January 21, 1938; FO 261/1, R. J. Bowker to Major Boyle, Air Ministry, February 8, 1938.
[82] DDF, 2e Série, Tome IX (Paris: Imprimerie Nationale, 1974), no. 509, Corbin to Bonnet, June 2, 1938, 1008.

armament orders in this country by the Turkish Government."[83] Such facilitation necessarily would include granting permission to shipbuilders and other firms to undertake such orders and making it possible for the Turkish government to pay for such orders.[84] As Percy Loraine, the British Ambassador in Turkey reported in February 1938, Turkey wanted to build in British yards, and he urged London to respond positively to Turkish requests or risk serious negative political repercussions. Loraine advocated unchaining British financial resources, the one tangible advantage Britain had over Germany, in order to generate employment at home and build up a friendly Turkish Navy in the Eastern Mediterranean, a region of supreme strategic importance to Britain. He concluded, "There is so much to gain by letting the Turks have British ships; there is so little to lose – a relatively inconsiderable sum of money, barely the cost of one day's way's."[85] In late April, Yapp from Vickers informed the Admiralty that his firm could offer the Turks 10 percent down on $14 million (£3 million), but Vickers wanted a guarantee from the British government for payment in the event of Turkish default. Lord Halifax recommended a special Act of Parliament as the best method to arrange Turkish funding. In May, Britain and Turkey signed an Armaments Credit Agreement whereby Turkey received a credit of $28 million (£6 million).[86]

The Turkish Foreign Minister was most appreciative of the British aid, but at the same time the Turks avoided any notion of an alliance with Britain. Moreover, the Turks had no intention of renouncing Germany as a supplier. Turkey placed an order on June 21, 1938, with Rheinmetall to erect a gun factory capable of monthly production of four 75mm field or mountain guns, four 75mm antiaircraft guns, four 105mm field or mountain guns or howitzers, and two 150mm guns. The factory was to be completed in about two years and paid for with Treasury Bonds at 6 percent over ten years. In July 1938, the new Turkish Foreign Minister, Menemencioglu, met with Ribbentrop to discuss German-Turkish relations. Menemencioglu made it clear that the Turks considered themselves neutral, and he enquired about the possibility of

[83] ADM 116/4195, Lacy Baggallay to Admiralty, January 4, 1938.   [84] Ibid.
[85] ADM 116/4195, Loraine to Cadogan (FO), February 23, 1938.
[86] ADM 116/4195, G. M. to FO, April 23, 1938; ADM 116/4195, Halifax Memorandum by Secretary of State for Foreign Affairs Turkish Armaments Credits, April 30, 1938; "Agreement between His Majesty's Government in the United Kingdom and the Government of the Turkish Republic regarding an Armaments Credit for Turkey: London, May 27, 1938," *House of Commons 1938–9* vol. 28, Accounts and Papers (13), Treaty Series No. 49. Additional information can be found in S. R. Jordan, *Report on Economic and Commercial Conditions in Turkey* (London: His Majesty's Stationery Office, 1939), 32.

further orders of German war materiel to make Turkey independent of England. By September, 1938, the Germans offered a credit of their own worth $60.73 million (RM 150 million) which included war orders.[87] At last, the Turks got the bidding war they were seeking. In fact, Turkey was eager to place orders in Britain. Now that the British had untied the purse strings, the Turks had the possibility of acquiring even greater amounts of materiel. When the Turks expressed an interest in perhaps doubling the size of their orders for warships and planes, Loraine emphasized to London that "Such things they must get from England and not from Germany."[88] Thanks to the British Armaments Credit, Turkey was able to order the twelve Blenheims and applied for another six. Additionally, the Turks entered into discussions with Vickers about constructing Spitfire aircraft under license.[89] After seventeen years, the British government finally entered the armaments business.

The German ascendance over the arms business in southeastern Europe came in 1938, and it derived from German political dominance and territorial expansion at the expense of Austria and Czechoslovakia. Through 1937 Škoda had fended off the German challenge and retained predominance in the southeastern European markets. AGK had anticipated significant armaments sales to southeastern Europe, especially Yugoslavia and Romania, but by mid 1937 Škoda had confounded the Germans and secured the orders for the Romanian Army and the Yugoslav Army. By German estimates, Romania bought at least RM 60 million worth of arms from ČZB and Škoda. In its analysis of German failure in Yugoslavia and Romania, AGK pointed to internal political resistance in those countries against German efforts to penetrate the arms market, as well as the effectiveness of Škoda's offensive. Disappointingly for Germany, AGK's trade with the region had only brought in $1.61 million (RM 4 million) of hard currency in 1937. German arms exports to southeastern Europe failed as a method to gain foreign currency and raw materials for the German rearmament program. Nor did Germany achieve Göring's goal of dominating the Balkans through the armaments business. The Germans had a high dose of pessimism about their economic prospects in the region at the end of 1937. The situation changed dramatically when the German annexation of Austria in

---

[87] *New York Times*, July 21, 1938, cited in Monica Curtis (ed.), *Documents on International Affairs 1938*, vol. 1 (London: Oxford University Press, 1942), 299; FO 371/21931, Loraine to Halifax, July 16, 1938; *AzDAP*. Série D, Band V, Ribbentrop memo, July 7, 1938, no. 548, 615; ibid., Wiehl to Berlin, September 15, 1938, no. 552, 620.

[88] FO 424/282, part XXXVI, no. 29, Loraine to Halifax, October 27, 1938.

[89] FO 261/1, Bowker FO Minute, April 30, 1938.

March 1938 dealt a major blow to Škoda by exposing the physical vul-
nerability of Czechoslovakia. Göring understood that the Anschluss had
opened the door for German economic control in southeastern Europe.
Likewise, AGK noticed that the absorption of Austria had created great
doubts among the countries of southeastern Europe about reliance
on Škoda for their armaments to the benefit of German armaments
firms.[90]

In response to German moves, buyer countries urgently tried to accel-
erate the pace of deliveries from Škoda as Czechoslovak rearmament
suddenly added to demand pressures. The Czechoslovak Army ordered
150 LT-38 tanks from the ČZB's Prague plant in July 1938 along with
300 new medium tanks, whereas Škoda mainly exported its tanks.[91]
When the American military attaché Lowell Riley visited Škoda's Plzeň
factory in late July 1938, he observed that the plant was now working three shifts, and most of the armament being constructed was for
Romania and Yugoslavia, and "a considerable amount of the work being
done was not for Czechoslovakia, but for the Little Entente . . . about
100 light tanks for either Romania or Yugoslavia."[92] The Turkish General Staff had become concerned about the possible failure of Czech
firms to deliver the orders placed there, and accordingly requested that
the firms speed up delivery. The firms consented to do all they could
with the consequence that by December almost all outstanding orders
in Czechoslovakia had been delivered except for heavy guns. Czechoslovakia's own defenses suffered as one-third to one-half of the country's
armaments production was exported, and the government did not forbid
arms exports until September 3, 1938. In April 1938, the Czechoslovak
Air Force frantically sought to buy fast bombers from Britain, France,
or Holland. Unable to obtain them from any of those countries, the
Czechs turned to the Soviet Union where they could buy twenty SB-
1 bombers straight away and also obtain the license to build them. After
taking delivery of the Soviet bombers, the Czechs bought another forty
in May.[93] On the eve of the Munich Crisis, the Czech military attaché
in Rome approached the Italians to purchase Italian aircraft against cash
payment for immediate delivery, to the value of half a billion francs. He
was told that the Italian government would like the hard cash, but "the

---

[90] Leitz, "Arms as Levers," 321–322; Pelt, 90–91, 197.   [91] Hauner, 85.

[92] RG 165, #2331-II-13 (9) Lowell Riley to G-2, July 27, 1938.

[93] WO 106/1594D, Military Attaché's Annual Report on the Turkish Army for 1938, Ross,
December 16, 1938; Hauner, 61, no. 20; FO 371/21581, MacDonald (Air Attache
Prague) to Minister (Prague), April 25, 1938; FO 371/21581, Speaight to Newton,
August 4, 1938.

political situation would not permit such a transaction without unfortunate reactions elsewhere,"[94] i.e., Germany.

The Munich Conference of September 1938 and the resulting German annexation of the Sudetenland dealt a double blow to Czechoslovakia. Munich severely compromised Czechoslovakia's physical defenses and put the writing on the wall for the imminent German mastery of Czech defense enterprises. Contemporaries had discerned the immense potential value of Czech war industries to the German war machine even before Munich. After visiting Škoda in June 1938, the journalist Frank Hanighen of the *New York Post* wrote, "Škoda is the brightest jewel in the well-studded prize which Hitler wanted to take on May 21st."[95] Although ČZB's monthly tank production capacity of 20 light and 20 medium tanks fell well below Germany's 130 tanks per month, 80 percent of German armor was inferior to Czech models.[96] After Munich, the assessment by American military intelligence of a German acquisition of Škoda warned that "the accomplishment of this transaction will prove of immense military importance to Germany and Europe and give Germany a dominating influence in the world armament business... German control of Škoda will mean the military equivalent to Germany of many divisions and make her without rival in the world in the armament field."[97]

To unload as much as possible and to deny the Germans, the Czechoslovak government along with Czech firms engaged in a kind of fire sale of armaments. In December, the Czechs sold much of weapons removed from the Sudetenland fortifications to Romania for $15 million. The inventory included 600 Škoda antitank guns (47mm) and 600 ČZB machine guns (7.92mm). The Czechoslovak General Staff supplied the British air attaché with a list of items of potential interest including Škoda antiaircraft guns and military aircraft available for purchase. Škoda itself offered to sell manufactured weapons to Britain including antiaircraft guns, tanks, medium guns, and ammunition which had been prepared for the Czechoslovak government prior to Munich but now had become surplus.[98] The Director of the Czech aircraft company Voboril

---

[94] AIR 5/1179, Medhurst (air attaché Rome), September 3, 1938.
[95] RG 165, #2331-II-13(8) Military Attache Lowell Riley to G-2, June 18, 1938.
[96] Hauner, 85.
[97] RG 165, File #2655-B-395 (2) G-2 Report Annexation of Sudeten lands. November 3, 1938, 23.
[98] RG 165, Entry 77, Romanian 9505, Mil attaché Belgrade Lt. Col. E. Villaret to G-2, March 6, 1939; AIR 5/1179, A. H. H. MacDonald (Prague) to Air Intelligence, December 17, 1938; FO 371/21581, FO Minute. October 31, 1938; Note by Morton. Possible Offer for sale by the Czech government of surplus armament stores, October 22, 1938.

inquired if Britain had any interest in his products. There was likelihood that Germany might place an order with his company, "and as they are only equipped for a limited output it would be a case of supplying either one or the other. Mr. Cerny openly expressed his preference for supplying Great Britain rather than 'the other country.'"[99] R. V. Stolle, manager of ČKD, discussed the purchase by the British government of his company's trainer aircraft. Motivated by the prospect of major financial loss from the stockpile of pre-Munich arms, the Schneider group proposed to the French government that Škoda's war materiel be transferred to Balkan countries, with the British and French governments guaranteeing payment. After the Munich Crisis, the Germans even gave the French first refusal to buy all the arms at their disposal. Not wanting to provide Germany with hard currency, the French delayed giving any official reply, and so the Czechs sold arms to Germany. A similar pattern happened with aircraft. The Germans wanted one of the Soviet designed bombers to test. The Czechs offered aircraft to the French for immediate delivery, but again received no French reply.[100]

Schneider's days of ownership in Škoda were now clearly numbered. In early December, Yves Rochette, the former president of Škoda and one of Schneider's representatives, retired and returned to France. To quell rumors of French abandonment, Škoda issued a statement denying reports published recently in the foreign press that part of its share capital held by Schneider-Creusot was taken over by French government when French armament industry was nationalized. Škoda also denied rumors that the French government was in the process of liquidating its participation in Škoda as it intended to discontinue its economic relations with Czechoslovakia (the French government owned no stake in Škoda). In late December, the German government notified the Czechoslovak government and Škoda of its intention to obtain Škoda's arms deliveries and also its demand for the integration of Škoda into the organization of German armaments manufacturing. The Czechoslovak government then conveyed to UEIF that either Škoda would begin making arms for Germany, or the French group should surrender its interests in Škoda to a group designated by the Czechs. UEIF came to terms with Prague on December 23, 1938. The Czech group paid UEIF $30 per share ($9.2 million) for its 315,000 shares with ČZB (the Czechoslovak government) acquiring the largest portion with 210,000

[99] AIR 5/1179, Slade (air attaché Prague) to Air Ministry, January 10, 1939.
[100] AIR 5/1179, Slade to Air Ministry, December 23, 1938; Segal, 315; AIR 5/1179, Macdonald to H.M. Charge d'Affaires, Prague, February 24, 1939.

shares.[101] According to the CFO of Škoda, Vaclav Skrivanek, "Since the Munich Agreement, French capital interests had exhibited an inclination to liquidate their financial participations in Central Europe and that the willingness of Schneider et Cie to surrender their Škoda holdings at a reasonable figure proved too attractive to resist."[102] The transfer of French shares to the Czech group was completed on January 31, 1939.[103]

Thus, by the end of 1938, two seeming constants of the interwar armaments business in Eastern Europe had drawn to a close. Schneider no longer owned any part of Škoda, and the British government no longer abstained from offering credit guarantees for armaments exports. As rearmament gathered speed across the region, the tenor of the armaments dynamic changed as well. The arms trade underwent a transformation from its business mode into the first stages of economic warfare. German arms exports would be the springboard to bind the strategic raw materials and foodstuffs of southeastern Europe to the German war economy. By taking direct aim at Czechoslovakia, the Germans prepared to gain control of the Czech firms at their source rather than having to best them for markets in southeastern Europe.

Bounced Czechs and Forged Alliances, 1939–1941

Removing the French business interests from Škoda served as the first step in Nazi Germany's efforts to take over the armaments business in Eastern Europe. As long as a semblance of an independent Czechoslovakia continued to exist, German methods conformed to regular business norms. The French had exited through a legitimate and relatively profitable stock buyout. In mid-February 1939, a German commission arrived in Prague to purchase Czech made military aircraft, and the German air attaché held two cocktail parties to which he invited representatives of all Czech aircraft firms. At the same time, the Germans bought eighteen 305mm, seventeen 210mm, and six 240mm heavy guns from Škoda to be delivered by the end of March.[104] Yet, the Czechs had palpable fears that German control of the Czech armament industry was

---

[101] RG 165, #2331-II-13(11) Military attaché Major Lowell M. Riley to G-2, December 7, 1938; MAE 1930–1940, Europe 1930–1940, Tchecoslovaquie 167, Lacroix (Prague) December 24, 1938 tel.; Segal, 316; Hauner, 80.

[102] RG 165, #2331-II-13 (12) Mil attaché Riley to G-2, January 6, 1939.

[103] Segal, 316.

[104] AIR 5/1179, AA no. 23/39, February 14, 1939; AIR 5/1179, AA no. 29/39, February 17, 1939.

coming with ČZB and Škoda at the top of the list. Talk among private firms expected the Germans to take 60 percent ownership.[105] The blow fell on March 15, 1939, when Germany occupied Bohemia and Moravia. The extension of the German Protectorate to Bohemia disquieted Škoda's bondholders as the French decided to suspend quotation of Škoda bonds.[106] As the new political authority, the Nazi government staked its claim to the armaments assets of the country. In 1939, Secretary of State Hans Kehrl of the Reich Economic Ministry and Karl Rasche, director of Dresdner Bank, acting as trustees of the German government, pressured the Czechs to sell 43.3 percent of ČZB shares and 8.6 percent of Škoda shares. The Reich government paid CZK 42.65 million (RM 6.6 million) for Škoda and $7.86 million (RM 19.58) for ČZB, and then transferred the shares to the Reichswerke Hermann Göring. Although the Göring Works exercised effective control of Škoda through political power, formal majority ownership did not come until early 1940 through the pooling of German-held shares.[107] Since the Czechoslovak government had held the majorities of Škoda and of Brno shares, the Nazis had no difficulty in taking them over at once after the occupation of Prague. Yet even in the middle of 1939 their boards of directors still showed a majority of Czech names and no direct representation of the Göring works, although Karl Rasche of the Dresdner Bank-Berlin also served as a director of the Göring-dominated Sudetenlandische Bergbau AG.[108] The director general of Škoda was Adolf Vambersky, a Škoda employee raised to the directorship on March 10, 1938, as the successor to Vilém Hromadko, when the latter had succeeded Loevenstein as company president. The Nazis pushed Hromadko to resign as president after Wilhelm Voss took over the directorship on April 30, 1941. Voss, an officer in the SS, had joined the Göring Works in 1938 as administrative director.[109] Significantly, Göring rejected Krupp's expressed interest in acquiring Škoda and instead kept it for himself as part of the state-owned Reichswerke Hermann Göring steel complex.[110]

---

[105] AIR 5/1179, AA no. 40/39, February 28, 1939.

[106] SG, Box 5898 V. I. Lenin á Pilsen Dossier Études Emprunts 6% Škoda April 19, 1939.

[107] German Economic Department of the Allied Control Office: Central Office for Germany and Austria (GED), 43/0/34, *German Industrial Complexes. The Hermann Göring Complex*, June 1946, 17; Overy, *War and Economy*, 147, 151–155; R. J. Overy, *Goering: The "Iron Man"* (London: Routledge and Kegan Paul, 1984), 113–115; Karlický, 649–650.

[108] K. Lachmann, "The Hermann Göring Works," *Social Research*, vol. 8, no. 1 (1941), 33.

[109] GED, 28, 56, 64; Karlický, 600–601.   [110] Overy, *War and Economy*, 139.

Hermann Göring himself took an active part in the armaments business. In July 1937, Göring, as the leader of the Four-Year Plan, had overseen the formation of the Reichswerke AG für Erzbergbau und Eisenhütten Hermann Göring, a state-owned corporation for coal and steel production capitalized at $2.02 million (RM 5 million) with eight out of the nine board members having no connection to private industry. As its capital increased to $162.6 million (RM 400 million) in 1938, making it the third largest German stock company after I. G. Farben (RM 720 million) and Vereinigte Stahlwerke (RM 460 million), the Göring Works proved a major challenger to private industry.[111] With the backing of the Nazi government, the Göring trust took control of Rheinmetall-Borsig through the acquisition of 53 percent of the firm's shares in July 1938. Consequently, the Göring Works became an armaments firm and a powerful competitor of Krupp.[112] Göring sold arms to the Spanish Republicans for personal profit during the Spanish Civil War. His shipments included 19,000 rifles, 101 machine guns, and 28 million cartridges. Through his interests in Rheinmetall, Göring had dealings with the Greek arms trader Prodromos Bodosakis-Athanasiades, the owner of the Greek Powder and Cartridge Factory (Poudreries et Cartoucheries Helleniques). Bodosakis sold weapons to both sides in the Spanish Civil War by acting as an intermediary between Rheinmetall and the Greek government. Bodosakis conveyed orders for weapons to Rheinmetall while the Greek government provided end-user certificates stating that the equipment was destined for the Greek Army. After Rheinmetall delivered the wares to Greece, Bodosakis would transship them to Spain. In 1938, Bodosakis's company was ordering shipments from Rheinmetall worth up to $16.26 million (RM 40 million) each, and in the process generating personal profits for Göring and members of the Greek government.[113] In March 1938, the Field-Marshal had broached the subject of arms sales with a British art dealer who happened to be a family friend. As related to British officials, the art dealer was lunching with the Görings in Berlin when Göring lamented the difficulties he was encountering in acquiring foreign exchange necessary for the simultaneous development of German rearmament and the Four-Year

---

[111] Lachmann, 27, 29.
[112] Lachmann, 35; Leitz, "Arms Exports," 139 n. 32; Rheinmetall's annual reports in IWM, FD689/46; GED, 7.
[113] A. Beevor, *The Battle for Spain: The Spanish Civil War 1936–1939* (New York: Penguin Books, 2006), 152, 330; M. Pelt, "Germany and the Greek Armaments Industry: Policy Goals and Business Opportunities," in J. Lund (ed.), *Working for the New Order: European Business under German Domination, 1939–1945* (Copenhagen: University Press of Southern Denmark, 2006), 141–156.

Plan. He then astounded the art dealer with an invitation to find a purchaser for German armaments anywhere in the world, preferably in the UK, South Africa, or Egypt. Göring offered the art dealer a handsome commission in spite of protestations that his knowledge of such matters was "confined to the essential difference between a hand grenade and a Hobbema." Göring provided the art dealer with a list of items available for sale, and, "Great emphasis was laid on the necessity for a prospective purchaser dealing only with the Field-Marshal and on the fact that the prices quoted are subject to all sorts of negotiations." The informant indicated to British authorities his belief that Göring was pursuing a private deal by which he and the German Treasury might profit.[114]

With Škoda in its hands thanks to the quintessential hostile takeover, Germany could now exercise tremendous leverage over that firm's former customers in southeastern Europe, especially Romania and Yugoslavia, as these countries lost their most important armaments supplier. To secure Romanian oil for Germany, Rheinmetall had concluded an arms contract with Romania worth $3.1 million (RM 7.71 million) for 174 3.7cm antiaircraft guns and licensed domestic Romanian production in July 1938. Rheinmetall's business accounted for 85 percent of AGK's contracts with Romania for war materiel. On March 23, 1939, Germany concluded a trade agreement with Romania establishing oil for armaments, and early in 1939 Yugoslavia negotiated with Krupp an armaments contract worth $40.16 million (RM 100 million) paid with payment over ten years guaranteed by the Reich government. Belgrade wanted to purchase an additional $40 million (RM 100 million) worth of war planes, but the needs of German rearmament led the Wehrmacht to limit the sale of war materiel to foreign states. In June 1939, a secret German-Yugoslav protocol established a ten-year credit for strategic metals copper, zinc, and chrome. The German arms trade with Yugoslavia and Romania expanded dramatically from 1938 to 1939. For Romania, German arms imports rose from $3.9 million (RM 9.6 million) to $43.3 million (RM 107.9 million), while Yugoslavia witnessed a similarly large boost from $4.7 million (RM 11.6 million) to $29 million (RM 72.7 million).[115]

Neither Britain nor France could match Germany's unique capacity to manufacture and deliver armaments quickly thanks to German absorption of Czech war industries. The occupation of Czechoslovakia

---

[114] FO 371/21581, Richardson (CID) to Cadogan, November 9, 1938, Enclosure: Morton to Nicholls, March 15, 1938.

[115] Leitz, "Arms as Levers," 320, 322; R. Schönfeld, "Deutsche Rohstoffsicherungspolitik in Jugoslawien 1934–1944," *Vierteljahrshefte für Zeitgeschichte*, vol. 24. Jahrg., 3. H. (1976), 218, 222; Pelt, *Tobacco*, 198–199.

had netted Germany 1,582 airplanes, 469 tanks, 500 antiaircraft guns, 1,966 antitank guns, 2,175 pieces of field artillery, 1,090,000 rifles, 57,000 machine guns, and 114,000 revolvers thereby providing enough equipment to equip thirty divisions or approximately 50 percent of the German Army, and Germany now accounted for 15 percent of the global industrial production, second only to the US.[116] Still, Britain had substantial financial resources. British policy makers had not considered Czechoslovakia in particular, or Eastern Europe generally in calculations of the military balance in Europe, and therefore the military value of preserving Czechoslovakia had not factored into British calculations about Munich. Only after Munich, in October 1938, did an interdepartmental committee on economic aid to Central and Eastern Europe recommend special means to increase British trade with the area. The idea of encouraging Romania and Yugoslavia to resist German economic expansion through British credits and markets drew fire from Treasury, BOT, and some in the Foreign Office who wanted economic policy to be divorced from political or strategic considerations. Over those objections Halifax endorsed the plan for a limited, total amount of £10 million for credits to all the countries of the region. As Talbot Imlay observed, the question had shifted from whether to help Eastern Europe, to which countries should be helped.[117] To wage strategic competition with Germany, Britain passed a New Export Credit Act to extend $46.7 million (£10 million) to a number of countries to buy British armaments. For example Greece became eligible for $9.34 million (£2 million) and Romania $4.67 million (£1 million).[118] To help sort out the demands from foreign states to purchase war materiel from British firms, by early 1939 the British government had developed a prioritized list of countries requesting armaments. The first group with highest priority included countries from southeastern Europe such as Turkey, Greece, Romania, and Yugoslavia. Bulgaria was placed in the second category along with countries of northeastern Europe, such as Finland, Estonia, Latvia, and Lithuania. The British government put Poland in the third, lowest category. Latvia had ordered 200 machine guns from Vickers for $149,440 (£32,000) and wanted to

---

[116] H. Volkmann, "The Nationalist Socialist Economy in Preparation for War," in Militärgeschichtliches Forschungsamt (ed.), *Germany and the Second World War. Vol. I: The Build-up of German Aggression*, trans. P. S. Falla, D. S. McMurry, and E. Osers (Oxford: Oxford University Press, 1990), 334; Glyn Stone, "The British Government and the Sale of Arms to the Lesser European Powers, 1936–39," *Diplomacy & Statecraft*, vol. 14, no. 2 (2003), 261; Hehn, 38; Steiner, *Dark*, 729.

[117] T. C. Imlay, *Facing the Second World War: Strategy, Politics, and Economics in Britain and France 1938–1940* (Oxford: Oxford University Press, 2003), 79, 94.

[118] Stone, "Lesser Powers," 246.

buy 100 105mm howitzers in late January. Vickers would be unable to start delivery for two years as an order for antiaircraft mountings for the War Office took precedence, and the Latvian order was deemed a hindrance. In the end, the Latvians gave up and dropped the issue at the start of April. In February, the Turks expressed their desire to buy fifteen Spitfires in Britain and assemble an additional forty-five in Turkey from materials purchased in Britain. The exigencies of Britain's rearmament meant that the War Office could not satisfy foreign demands without interfering with Britain's own program. Romania had requested 450 aircraft and Poland 250, but as of April the Committee of Imperial Defence estimated that only 124 aircraft in total could be supplied to foreign countries by the end of 1939.[119]

The Bulgarian Minister requested Britain devote some portion of £10 million Export Credit Guarantee Act to Bulgaria. In anticipation, Bulgaria already had contacted Vickers regarding two submarines, but discussions had not yet reached the point of financial disclosure. The Yugoslav government also exhibited interest in the purchase of war materiel in Britain, twenty batteries antiaircraft guns, based on prospects of financing from the export credit. A Bulgarian Mission visited Bristol Aeroplane and claimed that $9.34 million (£2 million) out of the special credits would be available to them, of which half could be spent on aircraft. Bulgarian aircraft requests in Britain included sixty Westland Lysanders, thirty Hawker Hurricanes, twelve Spitfires, one hundred Rolls-Royce Merlin engines, and ninety Bristol Pegasus engines. Unfortunately for the Bulgarians, the British government declined to grant their request for any credits on March 2, 1939. Having been rebuffed by Britain, in May the Bulgarian War Ministry authorized expenditures of $57.7 million (4.5 billion leva): $19 million in Germany, in Bulgaria $6.4 million, in Italy $2.56 million, and in France $2.56 million. Some $12 million worth from Germany had already been purchased.[120]

Under these highly restrictive circumstances, the allowance for Vickers to sign a contract for twelve Spitfire fighters with Greece for $443,068

---

[119] FO 371/23988, Committee of Imperial Defence. Order of Priority of Countries Requiring Armaments from UK, February 23, 1939; FO 371/23605, Orde (Riga) to Halifax, January 24, 1939; Latvian Minister to Collier, January 26, 1939; Vale to Orde, April 1, 1939; VA, File 352, Spitfires Turkey, Turkish Embassy (London) to Vickers–Armstrong, February 2, 1939; FO 371/23989, Committee of Imperial Defence. Minute. April 20, 1939.

[120] FO 371/23722, Ingram to Coote, January 19, 1939; FO minute. Ross. Bulgarian Request for share of £10 million Credit, February 9, 1939; FO minute. Ross. Purchases of aircraft by Bulgarian Government, February 11, 1939; Major Vassilev to Major Boyle, February 20, 1939; Rendel to Halifax, May 8, 1939.

(£112,740) indicated the strategic importance of Greece for British policy. In Greece, Metaxas had changed his assessment of Greek prospects in a coming military conflict. Up to this point, Metaxas had been preparing Greece for a Balkan war in which the Greek Army would be the key. With tensions heating up between Germany on one hand and Britain and France on the other, Metaxas turned his attention to the role of Greece in a Mediterranean war. Consequently, at the start of 1939, the air force and navy rose to the fore as the chief concerns. Metaxas confirmed to the British Ambassador Sydney Waterlow that the Greek government now wanted warships rather than guns for coastal defense. Furthermore, he wanted Britain to supply that naval and air material and France to supply the Greek Army. After long negotiations, the Greeks confirmed an order for twelve Bristol Blenheims on March 20.[121] Despite the expression of a pro-British purchase orientation by Metaxas, Greek purchases of German aircraft did not cease. In April, Colonel Gazis, Chief of the Greek Air Ministry, informed the British air attaché that Greece had signed with the German firm Henschel for sixteen army cooperation craft. Gazis explained the purchase on the grounds that the German company had offered such easy terms of payment that the Greeks could not miss the opportunity to get sixteen planes with a small cash payment and terms over five years. With the savings from the cheaper German planes, Gazis wanted to buy better British aircraft. He specified Blenheims (twenty-four for $1.65 million) and Spitfires (twelve for $510,900). At roughly the same time, twelve Dornier floatplanes arrived from Germany after many months of delay.[122]

Holding a place in the highest priority category did not guarantee Greek access to British armaments. Vickers–Armstrong wanted to tender for antiaircraft guns in Greece, but the British Admiralty insisted that such an order could not be permitted to interfere with Admiralty deliveries up to and including 1941. In similar fashion, in May 1939 Cammell Laird received a Greek enquiry for the construction of two submarines. The British firm consulted with the British Admiralty to learn whether they could freely bid for these vessels. A key part of any such bid would include reliance on Admiralty for supervision and the supply of materials usually supplied by the Admiralty for conducting the

---

[121] VA, File 356, Greece Spitfire, March 11, 1939; ADM 116/3949, ADM to Dept. of Naval Intelligence, January 12, 1939; Waterlow to Halifax, January 25, 1939; Medhurst (air attaché), Ross (mil attaché), Packer (naval attaché) to Waterlow, January 24, 1939; FO 371/23769, Waterlow to FO, March 20, 1939; AIR 40/1404, Waterlow (Athens) to FO, March 20, 1939.

[122] AIR 40/1404, Medhurst (air attaché Athens) to Air Ministry, April 27, 1939; Air attaché Athens to Air Ministry, April 20, 1939.

trials with Royal Navy officers. Cammell Laird would not be prepared to construct these ships unless the Admiralty provided that assistance, however, the Royal Navy could not spare the resources from its own program. Consequently, the British firm did not tender for the submarines, and in fact the Greeks never did acquire submarines in the period. In June, the Greeks fared better with British purchases. The British government approved a Greek order for 1,760 antitank guns and ammunition with 150 to be delivered in September and the rest in February 1940, and also an order for fourteen tanks to be delivered in May 1940. The Greeks also managed to secure another contract for twelve Blenheims at $1.12 million (£285,000).[123]

During 1939, the Germans and the British employed the arms trade to leverage Eastern European countries. The potential flow of arms could be opened or closed as an overt instrument of punishment or reward. With the fear of Italy once again uppermost in their minds, the Turks sought support from Britain and France in the form of a formal Mutual Assistance Pact. Having learned of the impending pact with Britain and France, the Germans moved to preempt the arrangements by putting direct pressure on Turkish armaments supplies. German Ambassador Weizsäcker reported that, "I have repeatedly and emphatically told them that even the slightest deviation from this course would be regarded by us as a defection to the opposite camp and as a breach of Turkey's solemn assurance to us, a breach which could not fail to have dire consequences not only for political but naturally also for economic and other relations between Germany and Turkey."[124] In order to make this threat credible, Hitler and Göring decided to withhold from Turkey the delivery of six 24cm guns.[125] After Turkey did sign the pact with Britain and France on May 12, 1939, the Germans pulled the plug on arms deliveries. As a result, on May 25, 1939, all Turkish military missions in Germany for purposes of buying or inspecting armaments were sent packing and they were informed that no further work would be done on orders destined for Turkey. The Turkish Mission assigned to the Germania ship building yards, which had completed one submarine for Turkey and was building others, was informed that there was no reason to return to work the next day. Germany would not deliver the remaining submarines under construction for Turkey. The commissions assigned to the establishments

---

[123] AIR 40/1404, Ingram to FO, May 9, 1939; Palairet to FO, June 30, 1939; FO 371/23769, Palairet to FO, June 26, 1939; ADM 116/3949, Johnson (Cammell Laird Co.) to Admiralty, May 2, 1939; Coxwell (ADM) to Cammell Laird, May 9, 1939.

[124] DGFP, Series D, vol. VI, no. 226, Weiszäcker to Foreign Ministry, April 18, 1939, 277.

[125] Ibid., no. 321, Weiszäcker to State Secretary, May 3, 1939, 416.

of Krupp, Heinkel, and Messerschmidt received similar messages. By June, a German industrial credit to Turkey for $15.7 million for the construction of armament factories was also in jeopardy.[126] Then on July 25, 1939, Göring decreed a general reduction of the German arms trade with the Balkans, and few days later through AGK he ordered that the arms trade with Greece was to be handled in a dilatory fashion.[127]

As the Germans attempted to strong arm, the Turks out of their alignment with Britain and France by withholding arms exports, the British increased the potential rewards. The Foreign Office informed the Turkish government on June 29, 1939, that Britain was preparing to grant credit facilities for $23.58 million (£6 million) conditional on Turkey signing a Treaty of Alliance. The Admiralty would provide $13.56 million (£3.45 million), the War Office $3.14 million (£800,000), and the Air Ministry $6.88 million (£1.75 million) contingent on the Export Guarantee Bill passing in Parliament. By July 31, under the Anglo-Turkish Armaments Credit Agreement, the British had approved contracts in the amount of $813,439 (£206,982) for eighteen Blenheim airplanes and parts, naval orders worth $23.19 million (£5,899,680) for two destroyers (Denny), two destroyers (Vickers) and armaments for four destroyers, four submarines, and two minelayers. For land armaments, artillery contracts worth $2.7 million (£689,200) for 15" and 13.5" guns also gained approval.[128]

In light of worsening German-Polish relations, the British government reassessed Poland's importance in June 1939. Poland was spending the equivalent of $14.15 million (£3.6 million) per month on military readiness with one-third for mobilization of personnel and two-thirds for munitions production as part of its ongoing war of nerves with Germany. To help pay for its preparations, Poland submitted financial request to Britain for munitions ($70.74 million), industrial credits ($25.55 million), and a cash loan of $94.3 million (£24 million). The Poles regarded British support as critically important in order to dispel the German notion that Poland's determination was bound to collapse owing to the country's financial difficulties. At the urging of the Foreign Office, therefore, Poland was promoted to the very top of the list based on the conviction that without British and French assistance, Poland's will to resist

---

[126] USDS, #767.00/87, enclosure no. 4, MacMurray to Secretary of State, August 4, 1939; ADM 116/4196, Committee of Imperial Defense. Allied Demands sub-Committee. Export Credits for Turkey and Poland, June 28, 1939, 4.

[127] Pelt, "Tobacco," 243.

[128] ADM 116/4196, Minute Sheet, Credit to Turkey for Purchase of Armaments, June 29, 1939; Treasury. Anglo-Turkish Armaments Credit Agreement, July 31, 1939; Annex I. Contracts already formally approved.

Germany would collapse. Although the British Treasury nixed the cash loan, negotiations proceeded apace for British armaments, especially aircraft. The British government agreed to provide Poland with 100 Fairey bombers and fourteen to fifteen Hawker Hurricanes directly out of government stocks rather than from the private firms. The Fairy Battles were supplied as ready on hand and the British Air Ministry offered for immediate delivery 100 of these first line airplanes to Poland. This was the first major attempt of the British government to dispose of some equipment to other nations. The Poles never received the British consignment of fourteen Hurricanes, one Spitfire, 600 tons of bombs, and 112 Browning machine guns because the war started before they could be delivered. Instead, Britain redirected these items to Turkey, whence as of October 15, 1939, Turkey had received from Britain twenty-six Fairey Battles, fourteen Hurricanes, and the one Spitfire.[129]

The direct involvement of the Air Ministry in the Polish business foreshadowed a more hands on approach to the arms trade by the British government. The War Office and Air Ministry informed Vickers–Armstrong at the start of August that in the existing special circumstances, the British government would conduct sales of armament and aircraft to certain countries directly, and that negotiations between such foreign governments and private firms would be discontinued. When Sir Charles Craven of Vickers complained to the government about this turn of events, he was informed that the War Office and Air Ministry appeared to have misunderstood their instructions. The government policy did not intend to eliminate any role for the private firms. Rather, foreign customers would address their initial enquiries for armaments, aircraft, warlike stores, and, indeed, everything appertaining to the supply of their armed forces, to the particular government department concerned. It would then be for that government department to decide whether to undertake supply in response to the particular enquiry, or advise the customer to make a direct approach to commercial undertakings. This new policy was meant to handle the ever-increasing demands of the rearmament program.[130]

Meanwhile, the Germans employed arms deliveries to entice the Soviets into an economic arrangement to trade arms for oil and foodstuffs

---

[129] Stone, "Lesser Powers," 247, 264; ADM 116/4196, Committee of Imperial Defense. Allied Demands sub-Committee. Export Credits for Turkey and Poland, June 28, 1939, 6, 8; RG 165, Entry 77, Poland 9510 Aviation Exports and Imports, #40245, Rept. Military attaché London, July 10, 1939; Rept. Military attaché London, June 14, 1939; RG 165, #2094–75 (3) Kluss to G-2, November 1, 1939.

[130] VA, File 532, Lord Chatfield to Commander Sir Charles W. Craven of Vickers, August 8, 1939: C. W. Craven to Lord Chatfield, August 1, 1939.

as a means to improve diplomatic relations with Stalin. In February 1938, Soviet–German economic negotiations had proceeded based on German need for raw materials and foreign exchange to sustain rearmament. On December 22, 1938, the Germans had proposed a new trade credit worth $80.32 million (RM 200 million) in exchange for Soviet raw materials valued at $60.24 million (RM 150 million) a year. Even though the Germans considered Soviet raw materials essential for rearmament, Soviet exports to Germany actually had decreased from $20 million (RM 50 million) in 1938 to $2.4 million (RM 6 million) in the first quarter of 1939. The trade negotiations recommenced at the end of February 1939, but Soviet demands for a larger credit brought the negotiations to a halt in March.[131] At the same time, the German takeover of Czechoslovakia disrupted Soviet dealings with Škoda as German authorities froze the Soviet armaments contracts which had been agreed upon in April and June of 1938. In April 1939, Aleksei Merekalov, the Soviet ambassador in Berlin, delivered a formal protest to Weizsäcker about the German hindrance of the delivery of Škoda contracts and the prevention of the Soviet engineering commission from even entering the Škoda plant. The Soviets wanted to buy the plans and the right to manufacture a wide range of Škoda arms, especially antiaircraft artillery of all calibers, and a large corps of draftsmen was busy making up the plans. The April meeting served as the prelude to broader discussions as the Germans used the issue of Soviet-Czech trade relations as the departure point for an improvement in German-Soviet political and economic relations. On May 5, 1939, the Germans informed the Soviets that their Škoda contracts would be honored.[132] Once Škoda resumed its activity for the USSR, a representative of Škoda served as charge d'affaires to the Soviet government for arms, motors, and airplanes. In June, the Soviet commission obtained authorization from Berlin to resume purchases from Škoda. Voss, Rasche, and Hromadko of Škoda went on mission to Russia, and the German Reich sent a Škoda envoy to Moscow to offer the Soviets arms, aircraft engines, and other military items. Škoda concluded

---

[131] Steiner, *Dark*, 892; M. G. Hitchens, "Germany, Russia, and the Balkans: Prelude to the Nazi-Soviet Non-Aggression Act April–August 1919," unpublished dissertation, University of Colorado at Boulder, 1979, 549, 554, 557.

[132] *Ministerstvo Inostrannykh Del SSSR, God krizisa 1938–1939, tom 1, 29 sentiabria 1938 g. – 31 maia 1939 g. dokumenty i materialy* (Moskva: Izdatel'stvo Politicheskoi Literatury, 1990), 360, 389, 457; R. J. Sontag and J. S. Beddie (eds.), *Nazi-Soviet Relations 1939–1941, Documents from the Archives of the German Foreign Office* (Washington, DC: Department of State, 1948), 1–2; RG 165, #2331-II-13 (5) Lowell Riley to G-2, April 5, 1939; Hitchens, 558, 562, 569; Steiner, *Dark*, 882–883, 889; G. Roberts, *The Soviet Union and the Origins of the Second World War: Russo-German Relations and the Road to War, 1933–1941* (New York: St. Martin's Press, 1995), 69, 73.

a contract with the USSR in the amount of $8.62 million (CZK 250 million) payable in two years including howitzers of medium caliber and 150mm. The USSR also purchased the right to make 350mm guns in the Soviet Union.[133]

The armaments trade helped pave the road to the Nazi-Soviet Non-Aggression Pact. By mid-July, the Soviets showed willingness to sign an economic treaty with Germany, and the Germans hoped to entice the Soviets into a political agreement. However, given the past hostility in Nazi-Soviet relations, Stalin sought a way to test German goodwill. To that end and before any economic treaty had been signed, in July the Soviet government placed large orders in Germany valued at $3.65 million for heavy machinery, including lathes for antiaircraft guns, gun-boring machines, turbines, and machine tools. Although the economic aspects of cheaper prices and more favorable terms of delivery were ostensibly the reasons for these large orders being directed to Germany, political considerations played a role in this trade as well. Before Germany and the Soviet Union could achieve a working relationship and more friendly political relations, the Kremlin demanded some tangible evidence that Hitler intended to live up to future commitments with regard to German-Soviet relations. Only then could Stalin seriously entertain any German gestures of friendship. The delivery of German machinery for the manufacture of armaments to the USSR carried great political as well as economic importance.[134] With the successful placement of this order, the Germans passed the Soviet test. The two governments signed the Trade Agreement on August 19. The German-Soviet Trade Agreement granted the Soviets a merchandise credit of $80 million (RM 200 million) to purchase from Germany industrial products, machine tools, and armaments in exchange for $72.3 million (RM 180 million) worth of Soviet raw materials, especially oil, grain, and lumber. As Dr. Karl Schnurre, a chief German trade negotiator noted, "Apart from the economic import of the treaty, its significance lies in the fact that the negotiations also served to renew political contacts with Russia and that the credit agreement was considered by both sides as the first decisive step in the reshaping of political relations."[135] The Nazi-Soviet Non-Aggression Pact followed just days later on August

---

[133] GED, 56; MAE 1930–1940, Europe 1930–1940, Tchecoslovaquie. 167, Naggiar, June 23, 1939; 39 Giovani (Prague), June 29, 1939; MAE 1930–1940, URSS, 931, MAE to President du Conseil, August 18, 1939.

[134] RG 165, Entry 77, USSR File 6510, July 18, 1939. Summary of Comments on Telegram no. 383 from Embassy at Moscow.

[135] Sontag and Beddie, 85.

23, 1939, thereby enabling the German invasion of Poland and the start of the Second World War in Europe.

With Britain and France now at war with Germany following the German invasion of Poland on September 1, 1939, both sides cancelled some arms sales. The Reich Economic Ministry issued a decree on September 2, 1939, calling for the continuation of arms exports to most European countries including the Soviet Union and all Southeastern European states, but excluding Greece and Turkey.[136] The list of war materials denied to Turkey by Germany consisted of the following: ten 24cm guns, twelve 21cm guns, nineteen 15cm guns, sixty-eight aircraft (fighters and bombers), one submarine, and sixty 7.5cm antiaircraft guns.[137] In late April, the Turks had placed aircraft orders with the Germans for sixty Messerschmidts, eight Heinkels, and six Dornier flying boats. In early October, Germany cancelled the Turkish Messerschmidt order, and by October 15 the Germans had cancelled all remaining German war orders for Turkey.[138] Britain and France helped greatly in mitigating the consequences of German wrath on Turkey. In late September, the Allies increased the total export credit for armaments to Turkey to $98.25 million (£25 million) of which France would give $15.72 million to offset the lost German industrial credit. Moreover, the Treaty with Britain and France included a very secret suspension clause, making a declaration of war by Turkey dependent on armament supply by the French and Britain.[139] In early October, ten Bristol Blenheims had arrived to Turkey from Britain, and the Turks had on order fifty Curtiss-Wright trainers, fifteen Hurricanes, thirty Supermarine Spitfires, thirty Blackburn Skuas; twenty-five British trainers, twenty-five French Henriot trainers, and thirty French Morane-Saulnier fighters.[140] Nevertheless, British authorities too cancelled a number of foreign sales during the fall of 1939. In September, the British government suspended delivery of twelve Spitfires to Estonia ordered in 1938.[141] The next month the Foreign Office conveyed instructions to "procrastinate our supply of war material to Latvia," in the wake of Soviet incursions in the Baltic States because "the Estonian collapse has altered the whole position and that

---

136 Leitz, "Arms Exports," 152.
137 FO 424/283, part XXXVIII, no. 134, Knatchbull-Hugessen to Halifax, December 4, 1939.
138 RG 165, #2094–75 (1) Kluss to G-2, April 26, 1939; #2094–75 (2) Kluss to G-2, October 9, 1939; #2094–75 (3) Kluss to G-2, November 1, 1939.
139 ADM 116/4198, Porter to Kenzie, September 26, 1939.
140 RG 165, #2094–75 (3) Kluss to G-2, November 1, 1939; #2094–75 (2) Kluss to G-2, October 9, 1939.
141 FO 371/23605, Capt. Bateman (Air Ministry) to Collier, September 13, 1939.

Latvia is now probably past praying for."[142] The Air Ministry at this time secretly ordered the cancellation of the Greek contract with the Bristol for twelve Blenheims.[143]

The use of Czech industrial assets, in particular Škoda and ČZB, contributed significantly to the German armaments business. According to AGK arms export statistics formerly Czech firms provided approximately 30 percent of all German armaments contracts in 1939 and the first half of 1940 (29.4 percent and 31.5 percent respectively).[144] Between September 1, 1939 and May 31, 1940, Bulgaria received from Germany 253 aircraft, of which 215 were produced by formerly Czech firms. Czech-built planes for Bulgaria included thirty-two Škoda bombers (SB-71), seventy-three Avia fighters (BH-534), twenty-eight Avia trainers, and sixty-two Smolik reconnaissance planes (S-328).[145] German-Yugoslav trade led in October 1939 to another protocol by which Yugoslavia would exchange raw materials for armaments deliveries from Messerschmidt and Škoda on a train for train basis. Under the terms of the German-Yugoslav secret protocol of October 5, 1939, Yugoslavia promised to increase deliveries of copper, lead, and foodstuffs while Germany agreed to provide 100 fighters, thirteen trainer planes, seven Škoda flak batteries (7.5cm), twenty Škoda flak guns, and 420 Škoda guns artillery pieces (3.7cm).[146] Germany's arms exports to Romania only increased following the German invasion of Poland. In the period August 25–December 30, 1939, Romania received $17.03 million (RM 42.4 million) worth of German war materiel, and new contracts worth roughly $40 million (RM 100 million) were signed by December 28, 1939, with delivery expected during 1940.[147] In early December 1939, Škoda concluded a contract with the Soviets to furnish $12 million (RM 30 million) of war materiel in exchange for Russian raw materials. The Germans eagerly awaited the conclusion of this accord as the reserves of Škoda's and Brno's raw materials had been exhausted until the end of the year.[148]

The Germans took over all Czech tank production, but allowed sale of Czech tanks with license rights to Bulgaria, Hungary, Romania, and Sweden. The Germans also incorporated most of the Czech armor into three new German Panzer divisions after the Polish campaign.

[142] Ibid., Lascelles to Major Tuckey, October 4, 1939.
[143] AIR 40/1404, October 17, 1939, Most Secret.   [144] Leitz, "Arms Exports," 151.
[145] FO 371/23723, Brodie to Rendel, October 9, 1939; RG 165, #2677–22 (1) Mil attaché Sofia to G-2, November 3, 1939; #2677–19 (5) Mil Att Belgrade to G-2, June 6, 1940.
[146] Schönfeld, 222; Hehn, 113.   [147] Leitz, "Arms Exports," 151.
[148] MAE, Europe 1930–1940, URSS, 931, Tel. Ankara to MAE, December 3, 1939.

By the time of the French campaign in May 1940, Czech-built tanks accounted for one-third of the entire German tank force.[149] Following the fall of France, Germany ordered 600 light tanks from ČKD, and the Yugoslav Army purchased 700 Praga trucks and 150 Škoda trucks by early 1941.[150]

The aggrandizement of the Reichswerke Hermann Göring reached unprecedented scale in the period 1940–1941. A branch of Škoda under the name Hermann Göring was established in Bucharest in May 1940. Albert Göring, Hermann's brother, served as director of this metallurgical firm and also oversaw Škoda's business with the Romanian Army. By midsummer of 1940 Albert Göring and Guido Schmidt, manager of the Austrian Göring works, held seats on the board of the Resita Works as representatives of the shares formerly owned by ČZB. By now Resita was the largest iron and steel works of Romania accounting for 80 percent of the country's steel. Additionally, Albert Göring represented the majority interest and sat on the board in another Rumanian armament factory, the Copsa-Mica and Cugir metallurgical works. The second largest steel and armaments works in Romania, the Malaxa concern, suffered the same fate as Resita. Malaxa himself was put on trial for having charged undue profits. Then, the Romanian government issued a decree ordering the confiscation without indemnity of 50 percent of the shares held by Malaxa and the expropriation of the rest of his shares and bonds at a fixed price. Finally, the Reichswerke Hermann Göring claimed 50 percent of all its shares and took over management of the whole Malaxa concern. In this way, the Göring Works expropriated Malaxa and controlled the entire Romanian steel industry in 1941.[151] In an even more stunning move, the Reichswerke Hermann Göring took charge of Schneider-Creusot. Following the fall of France, the Germans imposed their supervision over the management of the Schneider concern on June 28, 1940. Specifically, Göring placed the Schneider plants under the management of Rheinmetall-Borsig. With Rheinmetall's oversight Schneider produced a turnover of $11.6 million (RM 29 million) in 1942 and $9.72 million (24.3 million) in 1943. In Czechoslovakia Albert Göring became general director the Škoda Works, which employed 38,000 men in the middle of 1941. All told, by mid 1941 the Reichswerke Hermann Göring controlled a sprawling

---

[149] Hauner, 86.
[150] RG 165, #2281-II-20 (2), Mil attaché Berlin to G-2, August 23, 1940; #2281-V-21 (6), mil attaché Belgrade to G-2, February 13, 1941.
[151] Lachmann, "Göring Works," 34–35; K. Lachmann, "More on the Hermann Göring Works," *Social Research*, vol. 9, no. 3 (1942), 396–397; GED, 23.

industrial and armaments empire consisting of hundreds of companies and a labor force of 600,000.[152]

The ascendance of the Göring Trust between 1937 and 1941 to the position of supreme armaments enterprise in Europe marks the end of the story of the interwar armaments business in Eastern Europe. In 1938, Hermann Göring had remarked that he wanted to make his Works "the greatest industrial enterprise in the world,"[153] and by 1941 that goal seemed within reach. Superficially, the pattern of Göring's expansion resembled the business strategy followed by Schneider, namely, acquire control of the majority shares in Škoda and then use the Czech enterprise as the springboard to dominate the markets of southeastern Europe. In a few short years, his Reichswerke had broken apart the Schneider–Škoda alliance that had dominated the armaments business in Eastern Europe 1919–1938, and then absorbed each of the partners in turn under the auspices of its management. Along the way, the Reichswerke took over the Romanian armaments sector for good measure.

However, the nature of the Reichswerke as a Nazi state enterprise led to key differences that distinguished the business behavior of the Göring Works from that of Schneider and Škoda in the preceding years. First, the triumph of the Reichswerke owed everything to the imperialist expansion of the Nazi state and its takeover of Czechoslovakia. We need to remember that the Czechs had competed successfully against the Germans and still dominated the markets in southeastern Europe through 1938. Second, Göring's motivation for command of southeastern Europe markets had less to do with the usual corporate desire for profits and market share and everything to do with the strategic interests of the Nazi war machine to secure raw materials and foodstuffs considered vital to the German war economy. Third, without German military successes 1939–1941, the Reichswerke could not have gained hegemony in Eastern Europe.[154] The defeat of France and the retreat of Britain from the continent enabled the German takeover of Schneider. Taking these differences into account, the rise of the Reichswerke ushered in a qualitatively new era in the armaments business in Eastern Europe. As the preferred *modus*, the Göring Works absorbed the spoils of territorial conquest by seizing the management and ownership of well-integrated enterprises intact rather than creating new production capacity.[155] As

---

[152] A. Radtke-Delacor, "Produire pour le Reich. Les commandes Allemandes àl'industrie Française (1940–1944)," *Vingtième Siècle. Revue d'histoire*, vol. 70 (2001), 102–104; Lachmann, "More on Göring Works," 397; GED, 1, 45.

[153] Quoted in Lachmann, "Göring Works," 27.

[154] Overy, *War and Economy*, 144–145, 159–174.

[155] Lachmann, "The Hermann Göring Works," 38.

Harald Wixforth and Dieter Ziegler have shown, the expansion of the Reichswerke owed much to blackmail and theft, and served as a prototype for other state and Nazi Party controlled enterprises. The Reichswerke also provided a model for the brutalization of business practices in occupied Europe.[156]

[156] H. Wixforth and D. Ziegler, "Die Expansion der Reichswerke 'Hermann Göring' in Europa," *Jahrbuch für Wirtschaftsgeschichte/Economic History Yearbook*, vol. 49, no. 1 (2008), 257–278.

7   Conclusion

More than any other factors, the Schneider–Škoda alliance and the British refusal under the Trade Facilities Act to provide credit guarantees for anything having to do with armaments shaped the contours of the interwar armaments business. The interactions of these two factors brought about French and Czech dominance in the Eastern European arms market through the majority of the period. Even though Schneider owned the majority shares in Škoda, the Czech firm actively changed from the junior partner into an equal partner with Schneider by the end of the twenties, and during the thirties Škoda far exceeded Schneider as the prime armaments exporter to Eastern Europe. Indeed, the rise of Škoda stands as one of the most important novelties in the interwar era compared to the pre-1914 armaments business, and the company's centrality in the interwar period merits much more scholarly attention than it has received to date. Shifting the analysis from the macro-economic level of national economies to the micro-economic level of the armaments firms reveals that the idea that economic incompatibility doomed southeastern Europe to German hegemony is in need of revision. Škoda fought the Germans to a standstill in arm sales to Eastern Europe up to Munich.

For its part, the Trade Facilities Act functioned as a tool for disarmament by default in the hands of the British Treasury and more importantly Overseas Trade. Motivated more by purely financial considerations than political ones, Treasury consistently took a hands-off position on credit guarantees for foreign arms sales. If private financing could be arranged, Treasury would not raise objections to the arms sales per se. However, since private financing was rarely sufficient for Eastern European customers, Treasury's policy effectively eliminated many British sales by passive resistance. Overseas Trade, on the other hand, more actively supported disarmament on principle even over the objections of the War Office, Admiralty, and the Air Ministry.

A survey of the many armaments deals negotiated and signed in Eastern Europe does not generally confirm the popular, conventional

220

critique of the "Merchants of Death." When Vickers's leadership was hauled into court to testify before the Royal Commission on the Manufacture of and Trade in Armaments, the managing director, Commander Charles Craven, and the director of foreign contracts, F. Yapp, acknowledged that some "palm greasing" had occurred in their foreign armaments business, but that such bribes never induced a country to seek arms. Yapp insisted that "orders are placed without any solicitation."[1] That proposition generally held true. Bribery and corruption abounded, but the initiative to buy arms came from the Eastern European states. Similarly, the argument that the armament salesmen actively pushed the small countries to buy arms that they could not afford by taking loans from foreign banks does not reflect the process most accurately. In many instances, the buyer countries wanted to buy and borrow more than the suppliers and banks deemed appropriate. Even the French found Polish and Romanian credit demands too much at times based on their poor creditworthiness. The one glaring exception to these generalities was Seletzki, who did manufacture a war scare and pay massive bribes not simply to get orders for Škoda, but to gin up demand to an unprecedented scale. Also, Schneider and Škoda did collude in market-sharing arrangements for artillery, but the firms had engaged in serious competition as well.

Even though a comprehensive disarmament agreement never materialized, the disarmament process had real effects on the armaments business. The public hostility generated against the "Merchants of Death" from pacifists, League of Nations supporters, government investigations, and those in favor of disarmament had consequences for the armaments firms themselves. Inside the board rooms the armaments managers not only lamented the negative press and popular disapproval leveled at their firms, but they actually moderated their behavior and eschewed some business ventures to avoid anticipated public outcry until the disarmament din died down and was replaced by rearmament.

The armaments business in Eastern Europe also sheds light on the role of alliances. Three types of alliances received attention in this study: state–state (traditional diplomatic alliances), company–company (corporate alliances), and state–company (joint ventures). Considering corporate alliances as akin to traditional state alliances, John Conybeare and Dong-Hun Kim have argued that, "As in the case of states, corporate alliances may be offensive or defensive or pledges of neutrality

---

[1] Quoted in D. G. Anderson, "British Rearmament and the 'Merchants of Death': The 1935–36 Royal Commission on the Manufacture of and Trade in Armaments," *Journal of Contemporary History*, vol. 29, no. 1 (1994), 19–20.

with respect to, for example, expanding or protecting or staying out of markets . . . Alliances, irrespective of whether the players are states or non-state actors, involve coordinating actions in ways that are agreed on in advance."[2] They also note that state–state and corporate alliances fail at about the same rate (25–30 percent), and the biggest internal threat to a corporate alliance comes from mutual presence in the same market.[3] Joint ventures between a host Eastern European state and a foreign private armaments company offered a means for the states to acquire know-how and develop indigenous arms production capabilities. However, historically most joint ventures fail because "cooperating with competitors is risky business" as competition between joint venture partners outside of the agreement undermines the chances of survival.[4]

Certainly the arms trade failed to create bonds of loyalty or obedience between buyer countries and their suppliers, and formal alliances did not guarantee smooth business relations. There was much rivalry within the Franco-Czech alliance as competitor suppliers, and even between Schneider and Škoda though the French firm nominally owned Škoda. The Czech ambition to be the sole suppliers of war materiel to the countries of the Little Entente conflicted with the French government's strategic considerations that since Romania and Yugoslavia could not make their own war materiel those countries should equip with French materiel to assure reprovisioning in time of war. Alliances did not guarantee arms sales, even during the period of Franco-Soviet Collective Security (1935–1938), as Schneider still refused to treat with Soviet orders out of lingering resentment over the Soviet nationalization of its business interests in tsarist Russia and Schneider's anticommunism. Meanwhile, at the French Foreign Ministry some interpreted Russian efforts to buy arms from France as an attempt "to compromise us."[5]

Over the whole interwar period, the Czechs had the fullest integration of arms business and diplomacy through the alliances with Romania and Yugoslavia as part of Czech strategy to serve as the "Arsenal of the Little Entente." Yet the Romanians exerted reverse influence on the Czechs by getting Prague to foot the bill for Romanian purchases and pressuring Škoda to renegotiate its prices on artillery contracts through the political maneuvers of the Škoda scandal 1930–1933.

[2] J. Conybeare and D. Kim, "Democracy, Institutionalization, and Corporate Alliances," *The Journal of Conflict Resolution*, vol. 54, no. 5 (2010), 719.
[3] Ibid., 722, 736.
[4] S. H. Park and M. V. Russo, "When Competition Eclipses Cooperation: An Event History Analysis of Joint Venture Failure," *Management Science*, vol. 42, no. 6 (1996), 875–890, quote 887.
[5] R. J. Young, *In Command of France: French Foreign Policy and Military Planning, 1933–1940* (Cambridge, MA: Harvard University Press, 1978), 146.

Could arms sales from Britain and/or France have swung Romania, Hungary, and Bulgaria into an anti-German coalition or activated the Little Entente as anti-German military alliance up to 1938? Martin Thomas has argued that Romanian and Yugoslav disappointment with lack of French armaments supply proved crucial to the dismissal of a proposed military alliance with France, but nonetheless the Little Entente was insufficient as a vehicle for the strategic containment of Germany's eastward expansion.[6] Putting aside the question of whether France and Britain should have sacrificed some of their own rearmament to supply Eastern European countries, the negative case of British and French efforts to woo Turkey into the war makes it seem unlikely that arms sales alone could have achieved such results. In the context of real political commitment to the region, however, arms sales might have served as an important manifestation of potential Allied support. Hypothetically, the time for such moves would have been in defense of Czechoslovakia before Munich.

As Joseph Maiolo has shown, this quest for military-industrial self-sufficiency was the universal military-political lesson of 1914–1918 and the compelling keep up or give up logic that drove the arms race forward during the interwar era. Economic war planning and arms rivalry shaped the thinking of all the Major Powers, and contributed to the outbreak and expansion of the Second World War.[7] The processes of arms racing that Maiolo has shown for the Major Powers applied equally to the East European states. Not just the Soviet Union, but also Romania, Czechoslovakia, Poland, Greece, Yugoslavia, Turkey, and Bulgaria eagerly sought the development of a domestic military industry. Joint ventures served as the most common vehicle for domestication of war industries. Usually the host government partnered with a foreign private company to establish a production facility in country, train native workers, and provide licensing and technical agreements to complete the technology transfer. Overall, these various efforts did not yield substantial results, and most of the countries remained dependent on foreign suppliers. However, Czechoslovakia did achieve self-sufficiency. In terms of aviation, Poland too, transformed into a serious competitor as an exporter of military aircraft in its own right during the period. In terms of joint ventures, most attempts to establish domestic production through foreign joint ventures failed, especially in the military aircraft business. In cases where production was successfully domesticated,

[6] M. Thomas, *Britain, France and Appeasement: Anglo-French Relations in the Popular Front Era* (Oxford: Berg, 1996), 185, 232.
[7] J. Maiolo, *Cry Havoc: How the Arms Race Drove the World to War, 1931–1941* (New York: Basic Books, 2010), 1–5.

the newly established state enterprises quickly turned into competitors for export sales against their former foreign private partners. In this regard, in spite of having a socialist system, the Soviet experience with the armaments business conformed to the Eastern European pattern of relying on joint ventures and technical licenses. The Soviets differed from their Balkan counterparts in that the USSR proved a more reliable and responsible customer in terms of paying on time and in full.

The Second World War began in Eastern Europe. The Czech Annexation crisis of 1938 laid the tripwire and the German invasion of Poland in September 1939 set off the explosion. Given Hitler's desire for war, such a conflict very likely would have occurred in any case. What is less well understood, however, is the role that the armaments business in Eastern Europe during the 1920s and 1930s played in shaping the way that conflict actually developed from its outbreak up to the German invasion of the Soviet Union in June 1941. The effects of the forces of disarmament, depression, and rearmament on the armaments business in Eastern Europe had made Czech defense industries, especially the firm Škoda, the biggest arms exporters in Europe and the most important arms suppliers to other Eastern European countries. The German absorption of the Czech armaments industry bolstered Germany's own rearmament, and German manipulation of Czech war industry also helped facilitate the Nazi-Soviet Non-Aggression Pact, thereby directly contributing to the start of the war in Europe.

Index